Lautréamont's
Maldoror

TRANSLATED BY ALEXIS LYKIARD

THOMAS Y. CROWELL COMPANY
New York   •   Established 1834

Apollo Edition 1973

First published in the United States of America in 1972

Translation, preface, notes, and bibliography
copyright © 1970 by Alexis Lykiard

Printed in the United States of America

L. C. Card 72-82600
ISBN 0-8152-0343-8

Contents

Translator's Preface

No manuscript of *Les Chants de Maldoror* exists: it has been lost as irretrievably as its author's own bones.

The three earliest complete editions (Lacroix, Verboeckhoven: Brussels 1869; E. Wittman: Paris and Brussels 1874; and L. Genonceaux: Paris 1890) supply the text generally accepted by twentieth-century editors.

Chant Premier was published separately and anonymously by Balitout, Questroy et Cie., Paris, in August 1868, and subsequently reprinted at Bordeaux in Evariste Carrance's anthology *Parfums de l'Ame* (January 1869). Lautréamont revised this section for the Lacroix, Verboeckhoven first edition, making mostly insignificant changes, of which the principal was the deletion of various specific references to one Georges Dazet, a former schoolmate who would be a dedicatee of the later *Poésies*.

I prefer Lautréamont's final revised version—the flawless impersonal pearl rather than the rough-edged oyster. So do most editors, although the earlier version is occasionally reprinted, notably in Soupault's 1958 edition. [*See* Bibliography.]

Censorship problems and wary publishers were responsible for the book's not being sold in France during Lautréamont's lifetime; copies of the early editions are extremely rare. Until almost half a century later, when Cendrars and the Surrealists Breton and Soupault hailed Lautréamont as a forefather who with Baudelaire and Rimbaud was part of an unholy Trinity of genius, this exciting and revolutionary classic remained truly an 'underground' work, little discussed and less read.

Lautréamont's dazzling style with its wild pyrotechnics welded poetry and parody into a coherent and beautiful structure, full of sensitivity as well as strength. I hope this new translation of *Les Chants de Maldoror*—the first complete annotated edition to be generally available in the UK (and, ironically, on the centenary of Lautréamont-Ducasse's death)—may persuade readers to try the Count in French. For faced with strange puns and punctuation; with curious syntactical constructions which weave unexpected opposites into daring new patterns; with grim humour continually dissolving ecstatic lyrical flights in a cloud of ambiguous and teasing commas, a translator can only approximate. Nevertheless, both the previous English translations of *Les Chants de Maldoror* in 1924 and 1943 (*see* Bibliography) were incomplete and woefully inaccurate.

I do not wish to seem churlish towards my predecessors, but my main aim is the restoration of a previously mutilated and misrepresented text. I believe that the lack of recognition in this country for one of France's great writers is unfortunate, and I hope this translation will help to redress the balance on its author's behalf.

The translation is dedicated to Ali Dilber.

ALEXIS LYKIARD

I

May it please Heaven that the reader, emboldened, and become momentarily as fierce as what he reads, find without loss of bearings a wild and sudden way across the desolate swamps of these sombre, poison-filled pages. For unless he bring to his reading a rigorous logic and mental application at least tough enough to balance his distrust, the deadly issues of this book will lap up his soul as water does sugar.

It would not be good for everyone to read the pages which follow; only the few may relish this bitter fruit without danger. So, timid soul, before further penetration of such uncharted steppes, retrace your steps, do not advance. Hear my words well: retrace your steps, do not advance, resemble the eyes of a son who respectfully looks away when faced with an august maternal gaze; or, rather, a horizon chevron of chilly cranes which in winter with much meditation fly powerfully through the silence, full sail, toward a specific spot on the skyline, whence springs a strange strong wind—sudden herald of the storm. The oldest crane, forming by herself the spearhead's tip, sees this, and shakes her head like a rational person, causing her beak to click, uneasy (as I would be in her place), while her old neck, denuded of feathers and contemporaneous with three generations of cranes, cranes in peevish waves which give warning of the ever-approaching tempest. Calmly, after surveying all sides several times with her experienced eyes, cautiously, the leader (for it's she who has the privilege of displaying her tail-plumage to her less intelligent companions), with the vigilant cry of a doleful sentry, to repel the common enemy, deftly swerves the apex of the geometric figure (perhaps a triangle, but impossible to see the third side traced in space by these curious birds of passage), now port, now starboard, like a clever captain; and manoeuvring with wings apparently no larger than a sparrow's, she takes then, being no booby, another—safer and more philosophic—course.

Perhaps, reader, you would have me invoke hatred at the opening of this work! How do you know you won't sniff it up, paddling in innumerable pleasures, as much of it as you wish, with your wide, thin, haughty nostrils, your belly uppermost like a shark in the dark fine air, as if you understood the importance of this action no less than the importance of your legitimate appetite, slow and majestic, for the ruby flux? I assure you that the latter will delight those twin hideous holes in your unspeakable snout, O monster, if first you set yourself to inhale three thousand times the accursed awareness of The Eternal! Your nostrils, vastly dilated with sublime content, with static ecstasy, will ask nothing better of space—now become embalmed as if in perfumes and incense—for they shall be sated with a perfect happiness, like angels living in the magnificence and peace of the pleasant heavens.

I shall set down in a few lines how upright Maldoror was during his early years, when he lived happy. There: done.

He later perceived he was born wicked: strange mischance! For a great many years he concealed his character as best he could; but in the end, because this effort was not natural to him, each day the blood would rush to his head until, unable any longer to bear such a life, he hurled himself resolutely into a career of evil . . . sweet atmosphere! Who could guess whenever he hugged a rosycheeked young child, that he was longing to hack off those cheeks with a razor and would have done so often had not the idea of Justice and her long cortège of punishments restrained him on every occasion. No liar, he confessed the truth, admitting he was cruel. Mankind, did you hear? He dares repeat it with this quivering quill! A force, then, stronger than the will. . . . Curse it! Would a stone want to elude the law of gravity? Impossible. Impossible for evil to form alliance with good. As I was saying above.

There are some who write seeking the commendation of their fellows by means of noble sentiments which their imaginations invent or they possibly may possess. But *I* set my genius to portray the pleasures of cruelty! These are no fickle, artificial delights, they began with man and with him they will die. Cannot genius be cruelty's ally in the secret resolutions of Providence? Or, if cruel, can't one possess genius? My words will provide the proof: all you need do is listen to them, if you like. . . .

Excuse me: I seemed to feel my hair stand on end, but it's nothing, for with my hand I easily manage to restore it to rest.

He who sings here does not claim any novelty in his cavatinas. On the contrary, he congratulates himself that the elevated and evil thoughts of his hero are in every man.

Throughout my life I have seen, without one exception, narrow-shouldered men performing innumerable idiotic acts, brutalising their fellows, and corrupting souls by every means. The motive for their actions they call *Glory*. Seeing these exhibitions I've longed to laugh, with the rest, but that strange imitation was impossible. Taking a penknife with a sharp-edged blade, I slit the flesh at the points joining the lips. For an instant I believed my aim was achieved. I saw in a mirror the mouth ruined at my own will! An error! Besides, the blood gushing freely from the two wounds prevented my distinguishing whether this really was the grin of others. But after some moments of comparison I saw quite clearly that my smile did not resemble that of humans: the fact is, I was not laughing.

I have seen men, hideous men with terrible eyes sunk deep in their sockets, outmatch the hardness of rock, the rigidity of cast steel, the shark's cruelty, the insolence of youth, the insane fury of criminals, the hypocrite's treachery, the most extraordinary play-actors, priests' strength of character, and the most secretive, coldest creatures of heaven and earth. I have seen moralists weary of laying bare their hearts and bringing down on themselves the implacable wrath from on high. I have seen them all together—the most powerful fist levelled at heaven like that of a child already wilful towards its mother—probably stimulated by some denizen of hell, their eyes brimful of remorse and yet smarting with hatred, in glacial silence, not daring to spill out the unfruitful and mighty meditations harboured in their hearts, meditations so crammed with injustice and horror, enough to sadden the God of mercy with compassion. Or I've seen them at every moment of the day from the start of infancy to the end of dotage, while disgorging incredible curses, insensate curses against all that breathes, against themselves and Providence, prostitute women and children and thus dishonour those parts of the body con-secrated to modesty. Then the seas swell their waters, swallow ships in their abysses; earth tremors and hurricanes topple houses; plagues and divers epidemics decimate praying families. Yet men are unaware of all this. I have seen them also blushing and blench-ing with shame at their behaviour on earth—but rarely. Tempests, sisters of cyclones; bluish firmament whose beauty I do not admit; hypocrite sea, image of my heart; earth with mysterious womb; inhabitants of the spheres; the whole universe; God who grandly created it, you I invoke: Show me one honest man! . . . May your grace multiply my natural strength tenfold, for at the sight of such a monster I might die of astonishment. One dies at less.

———

One should let one's fingernails grow for a fortnight. Oh! how sweet to snatch brutally from his bed a boy who has as yet nothing

upon his upper lip, and, with eyes open wide, to feign to stroke
his forehead softly, brushing back his beautiful locks! And all of
a sudden, just when he least expects it, to sink your long nails
into his tender breast, but not so that he dies, for if he died you
would miss the sight of his subsequent sufferings. Then you drink
his blood, sucking the wounds, and during this time, which should
last an eternity, the child weeps. Nothing is as good as his blood,
still warm, and extracted in the manner mentioned—except it be
his tears, bitter as salt. O Man, have you ever tasted your blood
when you've inadvertently cut a finger? Good, isn't it, for it has
no taste. Besides, don't you recall how one day in your dismal
reflections you raised a hand, palm cupped, to your sickly face
moistened by the tears falling from your eyes? And then how the
hand inevitably found its way to the mouth, and the mouth
drained the tears in long draughts from this cup which faltered
like the teeth of a schoolboy who glances sidelong at his born
oppressor? How good they are: they taste of vinegar. The tears,
one might say, of her who loves most of all; but the child's please
the palate more. The latter, not yet knowing evil, does not deceive,
while the most loving of women will, sooner or later, betray. . . .
This I surmise by analogy though I do not know what friendship
and love are (it's unlikely that I shall ever accept them, and not, at
any rate, from the human race). Feed then, since your blood and
tears do not disgust you, feed confidently upon the adolescent's
tears and blood. Blindfold his eyes while you rip his quivering
flesh, and having listened for long hours to his sublime screams
akin to the piercing death-rattles forced from the throats of the
mortally injured in a battle, rush off like an avalanche, race back
from the nextdoor room, and pretend to be coming to his aid.
You'll untie his hands with their swollen nerves and veins, restore
sight to his distraught eyes as you resume sucking his tears, his
blood. Then how real repentance is! The divine spark within us,
which so rarely appears, manifests itself—too late! How the heart

overflows at being able to console the innocent whom one has harmed!

"Child, you who have just suffered cruel pains: who could have perpetrated upon you a crime I do not know how to name! Unfortunate youth, how you must suffer! And even if your mother knew this she would be no nearer death (so abhorrent to the guilty) than I am now. Alas, what is good and what is evil? Are they both one single thing with which we furiously attest our impotence and passion to attain the infinite by even the maddest means? Or are they two different things? Yes . . . they had sooner be one and the same . . . for if not, what will become of me on Judgment Day? Forgive me, child: he who confronts your noble and holy countenance—he it is who broke your bones and tore the flesh that hangs from various parts of your body. Was it my sick mind's delirium? Was it a hidden instinct distinct from reason, like that of an eagle tearing at its prey, that drove me to commit this crime? And yet I suffered as much as my victim! Forgive me, child. I want us—once freed from this fleeting life— to be entwined throughout eternity, to form one being only, my mouth gummed to yours. Even in this way my punishment will not be complete, for you will rend me incessantly with both teeth and nails. I shall deck my body with scented garlands for this expiatory holocaust, and together we shall suffer, you through tearing me, I through being torn . . . my mouth gummed to yours. O blond, soft-eyed child, will you now do what I counsel you? I want you to do it despite yourself, and you will gladden my conscience."

This said, you will simultaneously wrong a human being and have that same human being love you: the greatest happiness one can conceive. Later, you could place him in hospital, since the cripple couldn't earn a living. They'll call you a good man: laurel wreaths and gold medals shall hide your bare feet, and be strewn over the great tomb with its ancient slab.

O You whose name I do not wish to inscribe upon this page

consecrated to the sanctity of crime: I know your forgiveness was as immense as the universe. But *I* exist still!

———————

I have made a pact with prostitution so as to sow chaos among families. I remember the night preceding this dangerous liaison. Before me I saw a tomb. I heard a glowworm huge as a house say to me: "I shall enlighten you. Read the inscription. This supreme command comes not from me."

A vast blood-red light—at the sight of which my jaws chattered and my arms fell limp—spread throughout the air to the horizon. Feeling I would fall, I leaned against a ruined wall, and read: "Here lies a youth who died of consumption. You know why. Do not pray for him."

Many men would not, perhaps, have had as much courage as I. Meanwhile a beautiful woman, naked, came and lay down at my feet.

I (sad-faced, to her): "You may rise." I held out to her that hand with which the fratricide slits his sister's throat.

The glowworm (to me): "You, take a stone and kill her."

"Why?" I asked him.

He (to me): "Beware, you are the weaker, for I am the stronger. This woman's name is *Prostitution*."

Tears in my eyes, rage in my heart, I felt an unknown strength born within me. I grasped a great rock, and after many attempts raised it, with difficulty, chest-high. My arms got it on to one shoulder. I clambered to the top of a mountain, and from there I crushed the glowworm. Its head sank underground to the depth of a man; the boulder rebounded as high as six churches and toppled back, into a lake whose waters subsided a moment, swirling, hollowing out an immense inverted cone. Calm returned to the surface. The sanguine glow shone no more.

"Alas!" screamed the beautiful nude: "Alas, what have you done?"

I (to her): "I prefer you to him because I pity the unfortunate. No fault of yours if eternal justice created you."

She (to me): "One day men will do me justice. I'll tell you nothing more. Let me leave, so I can go and conceal my infinite sorrow at the bottom of the sea. Only you, and the loathsome monsters seething in those black abysses, do not despise me. You are good. Farewell, you who have loved me!"

I (to her): "Farewell, again farewell! I shall always love you! . . . From today I abandon virtue."

That is why, O earth-people, when you hear the winter wind howl on the sea and near its shores, or over great towns which have long worn mourning for me, or across cold polar regions—you must say: "It is not the spirit of God passing, only the piercing sigh of Prostitution united with the heavy groans of the Montevidean."

Children, it is I who tell you this. So kneel down, filled with pity; and may men, more numerous than lice, say lengthy prayers.

———

By moonlight near the sea, in isolated country places, one sees (when sunk in bitter reflection) all things assume yellowish shapes, imprecise and fantastic. Tree shadows—now swift, now slow—race, chase, return in diverse forms, flattening themselves and sticking close to the ground.

In days gone by, borne on the wings of youth, this made me dream, seemed strange to me: now I'm used to it. The wind groans its languorous tones through the leaves, and the owl intones his deep lament which makes the hair of those who hear stand on end. Then dogs, driven wild, snap their chains and escape from far-off farms. They run hither and thither through the countryside, in the throes of madness. Suddenly they stop, stare in every direction with a fierce unease, their eyes ablaze, and, as elephants in the desert look up one last time at the sky before dying, desperately lifting their trunks, leaving their ears laid back, so the dogs lay back their ears, lift their heads, puff out their awful necks, and begin to bark in turn, sometimes like a child crying from hunger, or like a cat with wounded belly atop a roof, or a woman in labour, or a plague victim dying in hospital, or a young girl singing a sublime refrain. . . . They howl—at the northern stars, the eastern stars, the southern stars, and the stars in the west.

At the moon.

At mountains that resemble at a distance gigantic rocks looming from the darkness.

At the cold air they inhale in deep lungfuls, that inflames and reddens the insides of their nostrils.

At the silence of the night.

At owls bearing rat or frog in their beaks (sweet, live food for fledglings)—whose oblique flight grazes the dogs' muzzles.

At hares that vanish at the wink of an eye.

At the highwayman who gallops off on his horse after committing a crime.

At snakes rustling the heather, making the dogs' flesh creep and their teeth grind together.

At their own barking, by which they scare themselves.

At toads which they crunch with a single crack of the jaw (why have the toads strayed far from the swamp?).

At trees whose leaves, softly swayed, are so many mysteries they do not understand and want to seek out with their steady, intelligent eyes.

At spiders suspended between their own long legs, who scuttle up trees to escape.

At crows, that have found nothing to eat all day and return to the perch with weary wings.

At the rocks on the shore.

At the navigation lights to be seen on the masts of invisible vessels.

At the dull sound of the waves.

At the great fish, which while swimming show their black backs then sink into the depths.

And at Man, who makes them slaves!

—After which they resume their racing across the countryside, bounding with bleeding paws over ditches, paths, fields, grasses and steep rocks.

One would think them rabid, seeking some vast pond in which to slake their thirst. Their continuing howls terrify nature. Beware, the tardy traveller! The frequenters of cemeteries will hurl themselves upon him, ripping, devouring him with bloody, dripping jaws—the dogs' teeth are not carious. Wild animals, not daring draw near to partake of this feast of flesh, flee from sight, quaking.

After several hours the dogs, worn out rushing to and fro, half-dead, tongues lolling from their mouths, spring at each other not knowing what they do, and with incredible rapidity rip themselves into a thousand shreds. They do not act thus out of cruelty.

One day my mother, glassy-eyed, said to me: "Whenever you are in bed and hear the dogs' howling in the fields, hide under the bedclothes, don't deride what they do: they thirst insatiably for the infinite, like you, me, and the rest of us humans with our long, pale faces. I even allow you to stand at the window and gaze upon this quite exalted spectacle."

Since that time I have respected the dead woman's wish. Like the dogs, I too feel the longing for the infinite . . . I cannot, can not satisfy this need! I am son of man and woman, so they tell me. That astounds me . . . I thought myself more! Moreover, what does it matter whence I come? If it had been up to *me*, I'd far rather have been the son of a female shark, whose hunger is the friend of tempests, and of the tiger, whose cruelty is well-known: I would not be so wicked. You who look on me, keep your distance, for my breath exhales poisoned air. No one has yet seen the green fissures on my forehead; nor the bones protruding from my spare features, akin to the spiky fins of some huge fish,

or to rocks that cover the seashore, or to the steep Alpine mountains I often scaled when I had hair of a different hue on my
head.

And while through thundery nights I rove about the dwellings
of men, fiery-eyed, hair whipped by storm-winds, alone, like a
stone in the middle of the road—I cover my branded face with a
scrap of velvet black as the soot that clogs chimney flues. No eyes
must witness the ugliness which the Supreme Being, with a smile
of mighty spite, has set upon me.

Each morning when the sun rises for others, spreading joy
and wholesome warmth throughout all nature, none of my features stirs as I stare fixedly at space (full of shadows): I am crouched
near the back of my beloved cave, in a despair as intoxicant as
wine, and with my strong hands tear my breast to tatters. Yet I
do not feel rage-stricken! Nor do I feel that I alone suffer! But
I do feel I am breathing! As a condemned man soon to mount
the scaffold flexes his muscles, reflecting on their fate, so, upright
upon my straw pallet, my eyes shut, I turn my neck slowly, right
to left, left to right, for whole hours on end. I do not fall stone
dead. From time to time when my neck can no longer continue
to turn in one direction, and stops so as to resume its turning the
opposite way, I glance suddenly at the horizon, through the few
chinks left in the thick brushwood that covers the cave's entrance:
I see nothing! Nothing . . . except for the fields in a whirling
dance with the trees and long trails of birds traversing the
air. That disturbs my blood and brain. . . . So who deals those
blows on my head with an iron bar, like a hammer hitting an
anvil?

I propose, without my being upset, to declaim in loud tones the
cold and sober stanza you are about to hear. Pay heed to what it
contains, and beware of the painful impact it will not fail to leave
like a blight on your disordered imaginations. Do not believe I

am on the verge of death, for I am not yet a skeleton, and old age cleaves not to my brow. Let us consequently wave aside any idea of comparison with the swan at that moment when its life flies off, and before you, behold merely a monster whose face I am glad you cannot see: but the face is less horrible than the soul. I am not, however, a criminal. . . . Enough of this topic.

Not long ago I saw the sea again and trod the decks of ships, and my memories are as green as if I'd left the sea only yesterday. Nevertheless, if you can, on reading what I already regret offering you, be as calm as I, and do not blush at the thought of what the human heart is.

O octopus of the silken glance! you whose soul is inseparable from mine; you the most handsome inhabitant of the terrestrial globe, who govern a seraglio of four hundred suction-cups; you in whom are nobly enthroned as in their natural habitat, by common consent and an indestructible bond, the sweet virtue of communication and the divine graces—why are you not with me, your quicksilver belly against my breast of aluminium, both of us seated on some rock by the shore, to meditate upon this spectacle I adore!

Old ocean, with your crystal waves you resemble (by analogy) the parallel azure lines one sees upon the bruised backs of cabin-boys; you are an immense blue bruise slapped on the body of earth—I like this comparison. So, at first sight of you, a long-drawnout sigh of sadness that one might believe to be the murmur of your bland breeze passes over the deeply disturbed soul, leaving ineradicable scars, and you remind your lovers (though they don't always bear it in mind) of man's crude origins, when he became acquainted with the sorrow that is never to desert him. I hail you, old ocean!

Old ocean, your harmoniously spherical form that rejoices the grave face of geometry reminds me overmuch of man's tiny eyes—akin to the peccary's in minuteness and to those of the nightbirds in their circular perfection of contour. Yet down the ages man has deemed himself beautiful. As for me, I prefer to assume that man believes in his own beauty only out of *amour-propre*, but is not really goodlooking, and guesses as much; why else does he gaze on the face of his fellow with so great a contempt? I hail you, old ocean!

Old ocean, you are the symbol of identity: always equal unto yourself. In essence, you never change, and if somewhere your waves are enraged, farther off in some other zone they are in the most complete calm. You are not like man—who stops in the street to see two bulldogs seize each other by the scruff of the neck, but does not stop when a funeral passes. Man who in the morning is affable and in the evening ill-humoured. Who laughs today and weeps tomorrow. I hail you, old ocean!

Old ocean, it might well be possible that you conceal in your breast future utilities for man. You have already given him the whale. You do not easily let the avid eyes of natural science divine the thousand secrets of your inmost oeconomy: you are modest. Man boasts incessantly—over trifles. I hail you, old ocean!

Old ocean, the different species of fish that you nurture have not sworn brotherhood among themselves. Each species lives apart, on its own. The varying temperaments and conformations of each one satisfactorily explain what at first appears an anomaly. So it is with man, who has not the same motives as excuse. If a piece of land be occupied by thirty million human beings, *they* consider they have no obligation to concern themselves with the existence of their neighbours who are settled like roots in the adjacent patch of land. And descending from the general to the particular, each man lives like a savage in his den and rarely leaves it to visit his fellow—crouching alike in another lair. The great universal human family is a utopia worthy of the most paltry logic. Besides, from the spectacle of your fecund breasts emerges the notion of ingratitude, for one thinks immediately of those innumerable parents ungrateful enough towards the Creator to abandon the fruit of their sorry unions. I hail you, old ocean!

Old ocean, your physical magnitude is only discernible if one can imagine the energy needed to beget your entire mass. A glance cannot encompass you. To envision you, the sight must turn its telescope in one continuous movement towards the four points of the horizon, the same way that a mathematician, in order to resolve an algebraic equation, has to examine the various possible solutions before settling the problem. Man consumes nutritious substances and makes other attempts—worthy of a better fate—to appear fat. Let this adorable frog puff itself up as much as it pleases. Be calm: it will never equal you in volume. At least I suppose not. I hail you, old ocean!

Old ocean, your waters are bitter. They have the very same taste as the bile which criticism secretes upon the fine arts, the sciences, on everything. If someone has genius, one makes him out an idiot. If another has a handsome body, he becomes a hideous hunchback. Man must certainly feel his imperfections strongly indeed—threequarters of them, moreover, are his own fault—to criticise them thus! I hail you, old ocean!

Old ocean, men, despite the excellence of their methods, and being aided by scientific means of investigation, have still not managed to measure your dizzying unfathomed depths. You have some that the longest, heaviest plummets have recognised to be inaccessible. Fish have permission, but not man. I've often wondered which was the easier to acknowledge: the depth of the ocean or the depths of the human heart! Often, standing aboard ship, my hand to my brow, while the moon balanced askew between the masts, I've astonished myself, disregarding all save the goal I pursued, striving to solve this difficult problem! Yes, which is the deeper, the more impenetrable of the two: the ocean or the human heart? If thirty years' experience of life can tilt the scale toward one or the other of these solutions, I may be permitted to state that, despite the depth of the ocean, it cannot, within the context of such a comparison, match the depth of the human heart. I have had dealings with men who were virtuous. They would die at sixty, and everyone never failed to exclaim: "They did good on earth—that's to say they were charitable—that's all, not difficult, anyone could do as much." Who can understand why two lovers who idolised one another the night before, because of one word misinterpreted, split up, eastward one, west the other, goaded by hate, revenge, love and remorse, and never see each other again, both cloaked in lonely pride. This is a miracle renewed every day and is none the less miraculous for that. Who can understand why we relish not only the general misfortunes of our fellow men but also the particular ones of our dearest friends, while at the same time grieved by them? One indisputable example to conclude the series: Man hypocritically says Yes and thinks No. That is why the wild boars of humanity trust each other so much and are not egoists. Psychology still has a great deal of progress to make. I hail you, old ocean!

Old ocean, you are so powerful that men have learned this to their own cost. Well may they employ all the resources of their genius . . . incapable of ruling you. They have found their master. I say they have found something stronger than themselves. This something has a name. This name is: the ocean! The fear you inspire in them is such that they respect you. In spite of that, you make their heaviest machines waltz with grace, elegance and ease. You make them leap gymnastically into the sky, and dive marvellously down into the depths of your domain: a circus tumbler would be jealous. Happy are they whom you do not ultimately envelop in your foaming folds, so they can enter your aqueous entrails, railwayless, and see how the fish fare, and above all, how they themselves do. Man says: "I am more intelligent than the ocean." It's possible, even quite true; but the ocean is more formidable to him, than he to the ocean. No proof of this is necessary.

That patriarchal observer, contemporary of the first epochs of our suspended globe, smiles with pity when present at the naval encounters of nations. Here are a hundred leviathans sprung from human hands. The officers' bombastic orders, the shrieks of the wounded, the cannon blasts—all noise purposely made to annihilate a few seconds. The drama appears to be over, and the ocean has drawn everything into its belly. A formidable maw. It must be vast towards the bottom, in the direction of the unknown! Finally, to crown the foolish farce, which is not even interesting, one sees right there in the air some tired, straggling stork that, without its wingspan faltering, cries: "Look, that's not funny! There were black spots below. I shut my eyes and they'd gone." I hail you, old ocean!

Old ocean, great celibate—when you survey the solemn solitude of your stolid kingdoms, you rightly pride yourself on your innate magnificence and on the true eulogies that I hasten to attribute to you. Voluptuously swayed by the soft effluvia of your majestic deliberation—the grandest among those characteristics which the sovereign power has conferred upon you—in the midst of a sombre mystery, with the calm sense of your eternal strength, you unfurl all along your sublime surface your incomparable waves. Parallel, they follow each other, separated by short intervals. Hardly has one abated than another goes, growing, to meet it. They are accompanied by the melancholy sound of foam dissolving, to warn us that all is foam. (Thus humans, those living waves, die in a dreary way one after the other: but leave no frothy noise.) The bird of passage rests confidently on the waves, lets itself be borne by their motion, full of proud grace, until its wingbones have regained customary vigour to continue the aerial pilgrimage. I wish that human majesty were but the embodiment of the reflection of your own. I ask much, and this sincere wish casts glory on you. Your moral magnitude, image of the infinite, is vast as the philosopher's meditation, woman's love, the heavenly beauty of a bird, or the musings of the poet. You are more beautiful than the night.

Answer me, ocean, do you want to be my brother? Stir yourself, impetuously . . . more . . . still more if you want me to compare you to the vengeance of God. Extend your livid claws, tearing out a pathway in your own breast . . . that's it. Unroll your frightful breakers, hideous ocean—understood by me alone —before whom, at whose knees, I fall prostrate.

Man's majesty is borrowed; it shall not awe me: you, yes. Oh! when you advance, crest high and fearsome, surrounded by tortuous coils as by a royal court, mesmeric and savage, rolling your waves one on the other, conscious of what you are, while you force from the depths of your bosom as if overwhelmed by an intense remorse I cannot fathom, this perpetual muffled booming which men so much dread even when they contemplate you in safety, trembling on the shore: then I see that I do not possess the notable right of declaring myself your equal.

That is why in the presence of your superiority I would give you all my love (and no one knows how much love my aspirations towards the beautiful contain) if you did not make me dwell sadly upon my fellow men who, in highly ironic contrast to you, form the most buffoonish antithesis ever seen in creation. I cannot love you, I loathe you. Why do I return to you for the thousandth time, to your friendly arms that open to caress my burning brow —which sees fever flee upon their contact! Your secret destiny I know not: all that concerns you interests me.

Tell me whether you are the abode of the Prince of Darkness. . . . Tell me, ocean (me alone, so as not to sadden those who have as yet known only illusions); tell me if Satan's breath creates the storms that hurl your salty waters up to the clouds. This you must tell me because I would rejoice at knowing hell so close to man.

I want this to be the last stanza of my invocation. Consequently, just once more I would hail you and bid you farewell! Old ocean, with waves of crystal. . . . My eyes well with copious tears, and I have not strength to proceed, for I feel that the moment has come to return among men, with their brutal demeanour. But . . . take heart! Let us make a great effort, and with a sense of duty fulfil our destiny upon this earth. I hail you, old ocean!

───────────────

I will not be seen, in my last hour—I write this on my deathbed—surrounded by priests. I want to die cradled on the waves of the stormy sea or standing on a mountain . . . my eyes aloft—no: I know my annihilation will be total. Besides, I would have no remission to hope for.

Who is opening the door of my funeral chamber? I had said that none should enter. Whoever you are, keep away. But if you do discern some mark of sorrow or fear on my hyena's face (I use this metaphor although the hyena is handsomer than I, and more pleasant to look upon)—be undeceived. Approach, then.

A winter night it is, with the elements clashing on all sides: man is afraid, and the adolescent contemplates some crime against one of his friends, if he is as I was during my youth. May the wind—whose whinings have saddened humanity since wind and humanity existed—bear me (a few moments before my death-throes) on the bones of his wings, across the world, eager for my death. Once again I shall secretly gloat over the numerous examples of human wickedness (a brother loves to watch unseen the deeds of his brothers). Eagle, crow, the immortal pelican, the wild duck, the wandering crane, waking, shaking with cold, will see me pass in the glow of lightning, a horrid and happy apparition. They won't know what it means. On earth, the viper, the toad's vast eye, tiger, elephant; in the sea, whale, shark, hammer-head shark, shapeless ray, the tooth of the polar seal—all will wonder at this deviation from the law of nature. Man, trembling, groaning, will glue his forehead to the ground.

"Yes, I outdo you all in my innate cruelty—cruelty whose suppression does not lie with me. Is this the reason for your prostrating yourselves before me thus? Or else because you see me, new phenomenon, race like an appalling comet across blood-stained space?"

(A rain of blood falls from my vast body, akin to the blackish cloud that the hurricane thrusts ahead.)

"Fear naught, my children, I do not wish to curse you. The evil you have done me, the wrong I have done you, is too great, too great to be spontaneous. You have gone your way, I mine, both alike, both perverse. Therefore through this character resemblance we must needs have met: the resultant shock has been mutually fatal."

Then men, regaining courage, will lift their heads little by little, stretching out their necks like snails, to see who thus addresses them. Suddenly, their blazing distraught faces displaying the most frightful passions grimace fit for wolves to feel fear. All at once they rise upright like an immense spring. What curses! what rending voices! They have recognised me. Now the beasts of earth join together with men—make their weird hubbub heard. No more mutual hatred: the two hates are turned against the common foe, myself. Reconciliation by universal assent.

Supporting winds, raise me higher: I fear perfidy. Yes, let's gradually disappear from their sight—once again completely satisfied witness to the consequences of passion.

I thank you, O Rhinolophus, you whose snout is topped by a horseshoe-shaped crest, for having woken me with the motion of your wings. Indeed, I perceive it was unfortunately but a fleeting sickness, and with disgust I feel myself restored to life. Some say you approached me to suck what little blood is to be found in my body: why is this hypothesis not reality!

A family, seated round a lamp set on the table.

— My son, hand me the scissors there on that chair.

— They are not there, mother.

— Then go and look for them in the other room. Do you recall the time, my dear master, when we prayed to have a child in whom we would be born again and who would be our support in old age?

— I remember, and God answered our prayers. We need not complain of our lot on earth. Each day we bless Providence for her gifts. Our Edward possesses all his mother's graces.

— And his father's masculine qualities.

— Here are the scissors, mother. I found them at last.

He resumes his homework. . . .

But someone has appeared at the front door and for a few moments observes the tableau before his eyes:

— What does this scene mean? There are many people less happy than these. What argument do they themselves advance for loving life? Be off, Maldoror, leave this peaceful hearth: you have no place here.

He has withdrawn!

— I don't know why it is, but I feel human faculties start warring within my heart. My soul is uneasy without knowing why. It's so close.

— Wife, I feel the same as you do. I dread to think that some misfortune might befall us. Let's trust in God; in Him is the supreme hope.

— Mother, I can hardly breathe: my head aches.

— You too, son! I shall moisten your brow and temples with vinegar.

— No, mother dear. . . .

See, he slumps against the back of the chair, exhausted.

— Something makes me queasy, I can't explain it. The merest trifle vexes me now.

— How pale you are! This evening will not end before some fatal incident plunges the three of us into the lake of despair!

I hear in the distance prolonged screams of the most poignant anguish.

— My son!

— Oh mother, I'm scared!

— Tell me quickly if you are in pain.

— No, mother, I'm not . . . I'm not telling the truth.

The father cannot overcome his astonishment:

— Those cries are sometimes to be heard in the silence of starless nights. Although we can hear the cries, he who utters them is not nearby, since the groans can be heard three leagues off, borne on the wind from one city to another. I have often heard tell of this phenomenon but I've never had the chance myself to judge its truth. Wife, you mentioned misfortune. If truer misfortune existed within the long spiral of time, it is his misfortune who now disturbs the sleep of his fellow men.

I hear in the distance prolonged screams of the most poignant anguish.

— Heaven grant that his birth be not a calamity for his country, which has driven him from her breast. From land to land he goes, hated everywhere. Some say he has been stricken since childhood by a type of inherited madness. Others hold that he is of an extreme and instinctive cruelty of which he himself is ashamed, and that his parents died of grief because of it. There are those who maintain that he was branded with a nickname in his youth and that he has for the rest of his existence remained inconsolable, because his wounded pride saw in this a flagrant proof of men's wickedness, which shows itself from earliest years and increases thereafter. This nickname was *The Vampire*!

I hear in the distance prolonged screams of the most poignant anguish.

— They add that night and day without respite or rest, horrible nightmares have him bleeding from ears and mouth, and that spectres squat at the head of his bed, and, impelled despite themselves by an unknown force, fling in his face, now softly, now with voices like warcries, and with implacable persistence, this ever enduring, always hideous epithet which will perish only with the universe itself. Some have even asserted that love reduced him to this state, or that his cries show remorse for some crime shrouded in the night of his mysterious past. But the majority think an immeasurable pride tortures him, as it once did Satan, and that he would like to be God's equal. . . .

I hear in the distance prolonged screams of the most poignant anguish.

— My son, these are exceptional confidences: I pity your hearing them at your age, and I hope you will never imitate the man.

— Speak, Edward, say you will never imitate that man.

— Beloved mother, to whom I owe the light of day, I promise, if a child's hallowed promise has any meaning, never to imitate that man.

— That's fine, my son. One's mother must be obeyed in everything.

The screams are heard no more.

— Wife, have you finished your work?

— A few stitches left to put in this shirt, although we have stayed up rather late.

— And I've not finished a chapter I began. Let us take advantage of the last glimmers of lamplight—for there is hardly any more oil—and each complete our work. . . .

The child cries out:

— If God lets us live!

— Radiant angel, come to me. You shall stroll in the meadow, morning till night. You shall not work at all. My magnificent palace is built of silver walls, golden columns and diamond doors. You shall go to bed when you will, to the strains of celestial music, without having to say your prayers. When in the morning the sun displays his resplendent rays and the joyous lark transports its song out of sight in the skies, you may still stay in bed—until that wearies you. You shall tread the most precious carpets; you shall be constantly embalmed in an atmosphere composed of the perfumed essences of the most fragrant flowers.

— It is time to rest body and soul. Arise, mother of my family, on your strong ankles. It is fitting that your stiffened fingers abandon the needle of needless toil. One shouldn't go to extremes.

— Oh! how sweet your existence will be! I shall give you an enchanted ring. When you twist its ruby you'll be invisible like the princes in fairy tales.

— Put away your day-to-day utensils in the safety of the cupboard, while I for my part clear away my things.

— When you turn it back to its original position, you will reappear as nature fashioned you, O young magician. This is because I love you and strive for your happiness.

— Whoever you are, go away—don't grip my shoulders.

— My son, don't fall asleep, cradled on childhood's dreams: our evening prayers have not begun and your clothes are not yet set tidily on a chair . . . Kneel down! "Eternal Creator of the Universe, Thou showest Thine inexhaustible goodness even in the smallest things."

— Then do you not love limpid streams where thousands of little fish—red, blue, and silvery—are gliding? You shall catch them with a net so beautiful that it will of itself attract them until filled. From the surface you shall see shiny pebbles, more polished than marble.

— Mother, look at those claws: I distrust him. But my conscience is clear, for I've nothing with which to reproach myself.

— "Thou seest us prostrate at Thy feet, overwhelmed by the sense of Thy greatness. If any proud thought insinuate itself into our imagination, we reject it immediately with the spittle of disdain and surrender it irremissibly unto Thee."

— There you will bathe with little girls who will entwine you in their arms. Once out of the bath, they will deck you with wreaths of roses and carnations. They will have transparent butterfly wings, and long wavy hair that floats about the sweetness of their brows.

— Even though your palace were more beautiful than crystal, I would not leave this house to follow you. I think you only an impostor, since you talk to me so softly for fear of being overheard. Abandoning one's parents is an evil act. *I* shan't play the ungrateful son. As for your little girls, they are not so beautiful as my mother's eyes.

— "All our life is spent in praises of Thy glory. Such as we have been heretofore, so shall we be until that time when we receive from Thee the command to depart this earth."

— They will obey you at the slightest nod and have only your pleasure in mind. If you wish for the bird that never rests, they will bring it you. If you desire the coach of snow that in the twinkling of an eye bears one to the sun, they will bring it you. What will they not bring you! They will even bring you the kite, tall as a tower, that's hidden on the moon, and from whose tail birds of every species are suspended by silken threads. Heed yourself . . . take my advice.

— Do what you will. I don't want to interrupt prayers by calling for help. Although your body vanishes when I would ward it off, know that I do not fear you.

— "Before Thee nothing is great unless it be the flame issuing forth from a pure heart."

— Think over what I have told you. If not, you will regret it.

— "Heavenly Father, exorcise, avert the misfortunes that can swoop down upon our family."

— You will not be off then, evil phantom?

— "Preserve this beloved wife who has consoled me in my despondency. . . ."

— Since you reject me I shall make you weep and gnash your teeth like a hanged man.

— "And this loving son, whose chaste lips have scarcely opened to the kisses of life's dawn."

— Mother, he's choking me. . . . Father, help me! . . . I can no longer breathe! . . . Your blessing!

A cry of boundless irony rises up into the skies. See how eagles fall stunned from the topmost clouds, tumbling over one another, literally struck down by the column of air.

— His heart beats no more. . . . And she too has died, at the same instant as the fruit of her womb—fruit I no longer recognise, so greatly is he disfigured. . . . My wife! My son! I recall a distant time when I was husband and father.

He told himself, faced with the scene presenting itself to his eyes, that he would not endure this injustice. If the power the infernal demons have granted him (or rather that he summons from within himself) be effective, then before the night slips by this child should be no more.

He who knows not how to weep (for he has always suppressed the suffering within) noted that he found himself in Norway. On the Faroe Isles he participated in the search for seabirds' nests along sheer crevasses, and was amazed that the three-hundred metre rope which supports the explorer above the precipice was selected for its great strength. Whatever one says, he saw in this a striking example of human kindness, and could not believe his eyes. If *he* had had to prepare the rope, he would have slashed it at several spots so it would snap and plunge the hunter into the sea!

One evening he headed for a cemetery, and those youths who find pleasure in raping the corpses of beautiful women recently dead could, had they wished, have overheard the following conversation frittered away within the context of a plot that is to unfold simultaneously.

— Sexton, do you not wish to converse with me? A spermwhale rises gradually from the seabed and shows its head above the waters so as to see the ship that passes by these solitary latitudes. Curiosity was born with the universe.

— Friend, it is impossible for me to exchange ideas with you. Long have the moonbeams made the tombs' marble gleam. It is the silent hour when more than one human being dreams he sees chained women appear, dragging their shrouds covered with bloodstains—as a black sky is with stars. The sleeper utters groans like those of one condemned to death, until he wakes and realises that reality is thrice worse than dream. I must finish digging this grave with my tireless spade so it be ready tomorrow morning. To perform serious work one must not do two things at once.

— He thinks digging a grave is serious work! You think grave digging is serious work!

— When the brutal pelican brings itself to offer its breast for its brood to devour—having as witness only He who knew how to create such a love as would shame men—although the sacrifice be great, the act is quite natural. When a young man sees a woman whom he worshipped in the arms of his friend, he takes to smoking a cigar; doesn't leave the house, and clings with indissoluble friendship to sorrow: again, quite natural. When a boarder at a *lycée* is ruled for years (which are centuries), from morning till night and night till morning, by an outcast of civilisation whose eyes are constantly upon him, he feels tumultuous torrents of an undying hatred mount like heavy fumes to his head that seems about to burst. From the moment he was hurled into prison, until that time near to hand when he will leave it, a high fever yellows his face, knits his brows, and hollows his eyes. At night he muses, because he does not want to sleep. By day his thoughts vault over the walls of the abode of degradation, toward the moment when he escapes this perpetual cloister or they expel him from it like one stricken by plague. Quite natural too. Digging a grave is often beyond the forces of nature. Stranger, how would you like my pick to turn up this earth which first feeds us then gives us a comfortable bed sheltered from the winter wind furiously blowing about these freezing regions, when he who wields the pick with trembling hands, having all day long convulsively fingered the cheeks of those once living who return to his kingdom, sees before him in the evening, written in letters of flame on every wooden cross the terms of the fearful problem that mankind has not yet solved: the mortality or immortality of the soul. I have always preserved my love for the Creator of the universe, but were we to exist no more after death why, most nights, do I see each coffin open and its occupant softly lift the leaden lid so as to emerge and breathe the fresh air?

— Cease your work. Emotion saps your strength. To me you seem as feeble as a reed. It would be sheer madness to continue. I am strong, I'm going to take your place. You, stand aside. You shall advise me if I don't do well.

— How muscular his arms are, and what pleasure to watch him dig the soil with such ease!

— You must not let a useless doubt torment your thoughts. All these tombs that are scattered about the cemetery like flowers in a meadow (a simile lacking truth) are worthy of being measured by the serene orientation of the philosopher. Dangerous hallucinations may appear by day, but they come mainly at night. Do not, therefore, be amazed by fantastic visions your eyes seem to see. During the daytime when the mind is at rest, question your conscience: it will assuredly tell you that the God who created man with a particle of His own intelligence is possessed of limitless benevolence and will, after its earthly death, receive this masterpiece into His bosom. Why do you weep, gravedigger? Why these womanish tears? Remember this well: we are aboard this dismasted vessel in order to suffer. It is a credit to man that God has judged him capable of overcoming his deepest sufferings. Speak, if your tongue is made like other men's, and since, according to your most cherished wishes, there should be no suffering, tell me then what virtue is, that ideal each one of us strives to achieve.

— Where am I? Have I not changed character? I feel a strong breath of consolation brush my unruffled brow, like the spring breeze reviving hope in old men. What kind of man is this, whose sublime speech has said things not everybody would have uttered? What beauty—as of music—in the incomparable melody of his voice! I had rather hear him talk than others sing. Yet the more I observe him, the less candid his face. The general cast of his features contrasts queerly with these words which the love of

God alone could have inspired. Puckered by wrinkles, his brow
is branded with an indelible stigma. Is this stigma, which has
aged him before his time, honourable or infamous? Should his
wrinkles be regarded with veneration? I do not know, and dread
knowing. Though he says what he does not believe, I think
nonetheless he has reasons for acting as he has done, roused by the
tattered remnants of a charity destroyed within him. He is
absorbed in meditations unknown to me, and redoubles his
activity in difficult work he's not used to undertaking. Sweat
moistens his skin, he does not notice it. He is sadder than feelings
which the sight of a child in its cradle inspires. . . . Oh! how
gloomy he is! . . . Whence do you come? Stranger, let me touch
you, and let my hands, which seldom grasp those of the living,
venture upon the nobility of your body. Come what may, I'd
know where I stand. This hair is the finest I've ever touched in
my life. Who would be bold enough to claim I could not judge
the quality of hair?

— What do you want of me while I'm digging a grave? The
lion does not wish to be provoked as he gorges his fill. If you don't
know this, I shall teach you it. Come, hurry: perform what it is
you yearn for.

— What shudders at my touch, making me shudder myself,
is flesh and blood beyond doubt. It's true . . . I am not dreaming!
Who are you then, you who stoop there digging a grave while I,
like a sluggard who eats the bread of others, do nothing? It's the
time for sleep, or for sacrificing rest to learning. In any case, no
one strays from home, and men guard against leaving doors open,
so as not to let in burglars. They lock themselves up in their rooms
as best they can, while the embers in the old fireplace still manage
to warm the chamber with a remnant of heat. *You* do not behave
like other men. Your clothes suggest you are an inhabitant of some
distant country.

— Although I am not tired, it's useless to dig any more. Undress
me now, then place me inside it.

— Our conversation together these last few moments has been so odd I do not know how to answer you. . . . (I think he's joking.)

— Yes, yes, that's right, I was joking. Take no notice of what I said.

He collapsed and the gravedigger was quick to support him.

— What's the matter?

— Yes, yes, it's true, I lied. . . . I was exhausted when I laid down the pick. . . . It's the first time I've tackled such work. . . . Take no notice of what I said.

— My opinion steadily gains ground: here is someone with appalling sorrows. Heaven forfend that I question him. I would rather remain in doubt, such is the pity he inspires in me. Besides, he would not want to reply, that's certain. To open one's heart when in such an abnormal state is to suffer doubly.

— Let me leave this cemetery. I shall continue on my way.

— Your legs would not carry you. You would lose the way as you trudged on. I'm duty bound to offer you a homely bed: I have no other. Trust me, for hospitality will not demand infringing your secrets.

— O venerable louse, whose body is bereft of elytra, one day you bitterly reproached me for not caring sufficiently for your sublime understanding, which is no open book. Perhaps you were right, since I do not even feel gratitude towards this man. Lantern of Maldoror, whither do you guide his footsteps?

— To my home. Whether you be a criminal who has not taken the precaution of scrubbing his right hand with soap after committing his crime and is easily recognised upon inspection of this hand; or a brother who has lost his sister; or some dethroned monarch fleeing his kingdom, my truly awe-inspiring palace is worthy to receive you. It was not constructed of diamonds and precious stones; it's only a poor hut, poorly built, but this famous hut has an historic past that the present renews and incessantly continues. If it could speak it would astound you, you who seem to be astounded by nothing. How often have that hut and I seen funeral biers wind before us, hearses containing bones soon to be more worm-eaten than the back of my door against which I leant. My innumerable subjects increase daily. I need no census on set dates to realise that. Here, it is as with the living: each one pays a tax proportionate to the richness of the residence chosen; and should some miser refuse to hand over his quota I am authorised in such instances to act as bailiffs do: there's no lack of jackals and vultures longing to have a good meal. I have seen arrayed in death's ranks those who had been handsome; those whom death had not disfigured; men, women, beggars and kings' sons; the illusions of youth, the skeletons of the aged; genius and madness; sloth and its opposite; those who were false, those who were true; the mask of the haughty, the modesty of the humble; vice crowned with flowers and innocence betrayed.

— No, I certainly shan't refuse your bed—which is worthy of me—until daybreak, which will not be long. Thank you for your kindness . . . Gravedigger, it is fine to contemplate the ruins of cities, but finer far to contemplate the ruins of men!

The brother to the leech paced slowly through the forest. Again and again he would stop and open his mouth to speak. But each time his throat would contract and choke back the abortive attempt. At last he cried out:

"Man, when you come across a dog lying dead on its back, wedged against a sluicegate that prevents its being swept off, do not (like others) go and grasp a handful of maggots crawling from its bloated belly and gaze at them in astonishment, then open a claspknife and cut up a large number of them, telling yourself that you too will be no more than this dog. What mystery do you seek? Neither I nor the four flippers of the sea-bear of the Boreal ocean have been able to solve the riddle of life. Take care, night draws nigh and you have been there since morning. . . . What will your family, your little sister, say when they see you turn up so late? Wash your hands, take the road that leads to sleep. . . .

"Who is that being, there on the horizon, who dares approach me fearlessly with tormented, oblique leaps? And what majesty, mingled with serene mildness! His look, though soft, is profound. His enormous eyelids frolic in the breeze, and seem alive. He is beyond my ken.

"Meeting his monstrous eyes, my body quakes—for the first time since I sucked the dry dugs of what one calls a mother. There is a sort of halo of dazzling light about this being. When he spoke, all nature was stilled, and shared in a huge shudder. Since it pleases you to come to me, as if drawn by a magnet, I've no objection to that. How handsome he is! It pains me to say so. You must be strong, for you have a superhuman countenance, sad as the universe, beautiful as suicide. I abhor you to the utmost, and would rather see a serpent coiled round my neck from time immemorial than miss your eyes. . . .

"What! . . . It's you, toad! . . . Fat toad! . . . Ill fated toad! . . . Forgive me! . . . Forgive me! . . . Why are you on this earth where the accursed are? But what have you done to your viscous, foetid pustules that you should have so sweet a look? When, by a higher command, you came down from above on a mission to comfort the various breeds of existing creatures, you swooped upon earth with the speed of a kite, wings unwearied by this long, splendid errand. I saw you! Poor toad! How I mused then on the infinite, as well as on my frailty. 'One more being,' I told myself, 'who is superior to those on earth; and that by divine will. Why not I too? What place has injustice in the supreme decrees? Is the Creator mad? He is, though, the strongest, and his wrath terrible!' Since you appeared to me, monarch of marshes and ponds, clad in a glory that belongs only to God, you have, in some measure, consoled me. But my wavering wits are engulfed by such majesty! Who are you? Stay . . . Oh! stay longer on this earth! Fold your white wings, and do not look upward with anxious eyes. . . . If you leave, let us leave together!"

The toad sat down on his haunches (so like man's!) and while slugs, woodlice, and snails fled at the sight of their deadly enemy, thus uttered:

"Hear me, Maldoror. Note my face, calm as a mirror. And I believe I have an intelligence equal to yours. One day you called me the mainstay of your life. Since then I have not belied the trust you placed in me. True, I'm only a common inhabitant of the reeds, but thanks to your own contact, and taking after only what was beautiful in you, my mind has grown and I can talk to you. I came to snatch you from the abyss. Those who call themselves your friends, smitten with consternation, stare at you whenever they meet your pale and stooping figure at the theatre, in public places, in churches, or squeezing between your two sinewy thighs that horse who gallops only by night, bearing his phantom master swathed in a long black cloak. Abandon these thoughts which make your heart empty as a desert: they are more scorching than fire. Your mind is so sick that you do not realise it, and think yourself normal every time crazy words (though filled with an infernal grandeur) gush from your mouth. Wretch! What have you said since the day of your birth? O sad relic of an immortal intellect, created by God with such love! You have begotten only maledictions more frightful than the sight of famished panthers! *I* would sooner have my eyelids stuck together, my body armless and legless—or have murdered a man, than be *you*! Because I hate you. Why have this character which puzzles me? By what right do you come on earth to hold its inhabitants to ridicule, you rotting wreck buffeted by scepticism? If you don't like it here, you should go back to the spheres whence you came. A city-dweller ought not to live like a stranger in villages. We know that in space exist globes more spacious than ours, and whose creatures have an intelligence we cannot even begin to understand. Very well, be off then! . . . Leave this fleeting earth! . . . At last display your divine nature, hitherto hidden. And as soon as possible steer your ascending flight towards your own globe, which we do not covet at all, proud one that you are!—I have not yet succeeded in identifying you as man or more-than-man! Farewell, then. Hope no longer to encounter the toad on your journey. You have been the cause of my death. *I* set out for eternity, that I may beg your forgiveness!"

If it is sometimes logical to put one's faith in the appearance of phenomena, this first canto ends here. Be not too harsh with one who still only tunes his lyre: it makes so strange a sound! If, however, you would be impartial, you will already discern a strong hand in the midst of the imperfections. As for me, I shall resume work to produce a second canto in not too long a time. The end of the nineteenth century shall see its poet (though at the outset he should not begin with a masterpiece, but follow the law of nature).

He was born on South American shores, at the mouth of the River Plate, where two peoples once enemies now struggle to outdo each other in material and moral progress. Buenos Aires, queen of the south, and Montevideo, the coquette, extend friendly hands across the argentine waters of the great estuary. But everlasting war has imposed his destructive rule upon the fields, and joyfully reaps his countless victims.

Greybeard, farewell, and if you have read this, think of me. You, young man, do not despair, for despite your opinion to the contrary, you have a friend in the vampire. Counting the *acarus sarcoptes* that causes crabs, you have two!

2

What became of Maldoror's first lyric since his mouth, filled with leaves of belladonna, let it slip in a moment of meditation across the kingdoms of wrath? What happened to that canto? . . . We do not precisely know. Neither the trees nor the winds have retained it. And passing by this place, Morality, not foreseeing that in these incandescent pages she had a staunch supporter, saw it with firm and steady tread head for the obscure recesses and secret fibres of consciousness. Science has at least gained this much from it: since that time, toad-face man no longer recognises himself, and often falls into fits of rage which make him resemble a baboon. It is not his fault. Through the ages he had believed (eyelids fluttering under the mignonettes of modesty) that he was compounded only of good and a minimal amount of evil. Sharply I showed him, by laying bare in broad daylight his heart and life's weave, that on the contrary, he is compounded only of evil and a minimal amount of good which the legislators have difficulty managing to preserve.[1] I, who teach him nothing new, would not have him, through my bitter truths, suffer everlasting shame; but the fulfilment of this wish would not be consistent with the laws of nature. Indeed I rip the mask off his villainous, muddy face and make the sublime falsehoods with which he deceives himself fall one by one, like balls of ivory into a silver bowl. It is understandable, then, that he does not direct Calm to lay her hands upon his face even when Reason disperses the dark shades of Pride.

This is why the hero I bring on stage has incurred an irreconcilable hatred while attacking mankind that had thought itself invulnerable, by breaching it with absurd philanthropic tirades; these, like grains of sand, are heaped throughout his books, books whose comedy (when my senses take leave of me) I sometimes almost consider so droll—though irritating. He had anticipated it. Engraving the image of kindliness on the ornate exteriors of scrolled documents stored in libraries is not enough.

O human being, here you are now, naked as a worm faced with my diamond blade! Abandon your ways, there is no more time to put on proud airs: lying prone, I hurl up my prayer to you. There is one who observes the slightest stirrings of your guilty life; you are enmeshed by the subtle webs of his keen acumen. Do not trust him when he turns his back, for he is watching you. Do not trust him when he shuts his eyes, for he watches you still. It is hard to suppose that where guile and wickedness are concerned your formidable resolve may be to surpass the child of my imagination. His slightest blow tells. It's possible—cautiously—to teach those unaware of the fact, that wolves and bandits do not devour each other: it may not be their custom. Place your life in his hands, therefore, fearlessly into his care: he will direct it in the way he knows. Do not believe his purpose—which he makes scintillate in the sunshine—to reform you, for you scarcely interest him, to say the least: and I still do not come close to the whole truth, the benevolent bounds of my verification. But the fact is, he loves to do you harm, justifiably convinced that you will become as wicked as he, and will, when that hour tolls, accompany him into the yawning pit of hell. His place there has long been reserved, a spot where you see an iron gibbet from which chains and shackles hang. When destiny bears him there, the funereal funnel will never have tasted more savoury prey, nor will he have beheld a fitter abode. It seems to me that I speak in deliberately paternal manner, and that mankind has no right to complain.

———————————

I grasp the quill which is going to construct the second canto. . . an implement ripped from some russet sea-eagle's wing. . . .

But . . . what ails my fingers? As soon as I start work, their joints stay paralysed. Yet I need to write. . . . It's impossible! Well, I repeat: I need to write down my thoughts: I have the right, like others, to yield to this natural law. . . . But no, no, the pen remains inert! . . . Look—across the fields—see the lightning sparkle afar. The storm sweeps through space. It is raining . . . always raining. . . . How it rains! . . . Lightning flashes . . . swoops down through my half-open window, strikes my brow, and sends me sprawling on the floor. Poor youth! Your face was already adequately marked by the premature wrinkles and birthmark without needing (in addition) this long sulphurous scar. (I have just assumed that the wound has healed— which would not have happened so soon.)

Why this storm, and why the paralysis of my fingers? Is it a warning from on high, to prevent me from writing and to weigh well what risk I run by distilling the dribble from my outspoken mouth? Yet the storm has caused me no alarm. Why should I care about a legion of storms? These celestial policemen zealously perform their painful duty—judging by my wounded brow. I do not have to thank the Omnipotent for his astonishing adroitness. He aimed the bolt so that it would exactly bisect my face, from the forehead (where the wound was most dangerous) down. Let another congratulate Him! But the storms attacked someone stronger than they. So then, vile Eternal God, in viper's shape, not content with having set my soul on the frontiers of madness and those frenzied thoughts that kill slowly, you[2] had besides, after a close survey, to deem it befitting your majesty to make a goblet of blood gush from my brow! . . . Yet after all, who tells you anything? You know I do not love you; that on the contrary, I hate you: why do you insist? When will your behaviour stop shrouding itself in bizarre guises? Tell me frankly, as if to a friend: do you not suspect, in short, that you show in your hateful persecution a naive eagerness whose full absurdity none of your seraphim would dare point out? What anger seizes you? Know that if you let me live safe from your harassment,[3] my gratitude would be yours. . . .

Here, Sultan! set your tongue to get rid of the blood that sullies the floorboards. The bandage is done: my forehead, staunched, has been laved in salt water and I have bound strips across my face. The result is not boundless: four shirts soaked in blood and two handkerchiefs. At first sight one would not have thought Maldoror had so much blood in his arteries, for only a corpse's sheen shines on his face. Anyhow, there it is. Perhaps this was about all the blood his body could contain, and probably not much of it remains. . . .

Enough, you greedy dog, enough! Leave the floor just as it is, your belly's full. You must not go on drinking or you'll soon be sick. You've fed nicely, now off to your kennel! Consider yourself bathed in happiness, because for three long days you will not think of hunger, thanks to the globules you gulped down your gullet with solemnly visible satisfaction.

You, Leman—take up a broom. I would wield one too, but have not the strength. You understand, do you not, that I lack the strength? Sheathe your tears in their scabbard,[4] or else I shall think you have not the courage to gaze with sang-froid[5] upon this great gash caused by a torment already lost to me in the night of bygone times. Go and fetch two pails of water from the well. After washing the floor, put this linen in the next room. If the washerwoman calls again this evening, as she should, give them her. But as it has been pouring with rain for an hour and continues to rain, I do not think she will leave home. She will call tomorrow. If she asks you whence came all this blood, you are not bound to answer her. Oh! how weak I am! No matter; I shall still have the strength to lift the pen, and the courage to unearth my thought. What has the Creator gained by plaguing me—as if I were a child—with a thunderstorm? My resolve to write is undiminished. These bandages bother me, and the very air of my room breathes forth blood. . . .

May the day never come when Lohengrin and I go down the street side by side without looking at each other while brushing elbows like two (c)rushed[6] passers-by! Oh! let me flee forever, far from that supposition!

The Eternal created the world as it is: he would show much wisdom if, during the time strictly necessary to smash a woman's skull with a hammerblow, he were to forget his sidereal majesty and reveal to us the mysteries in whose midst our life chokes like a fish at the bottom of a boat. But he is great and stately; by the power of his conceptions he gets the better of us; were he able to parley with men, every disgrace would gush up to his face. . . . Yet—wretch that you are!—why do you not blush? It is not enough for the army of physical and spiritual sufferings that surround us to have been born: the secret of our tattered destiny has not been vouchsafed us. I know him, the Omnipotent . . . and he should know me too. If by chance we walk the same path, his piercing eye sees me approach from afar: he takes a short-cut to avoid the triple prick of platinum[7] that Nature gave me for a tongue!

It would please me, O Creator, if you let me vent[8] my feelings. Plying terrible ironies with a cool, firm hand, I warn you that my heart holds enough of them to make an attack on you till the end of my days. I shall hit your hollow carcass—so hard that I guarantee to rout out the remaining scraps of intelligence which you did not want to give to man, because you would have been jealous had you made him your equal, and which you had brazenly hidden in your bowels, wily villain, as though you did not know I would eventually have espied them with my ever-open eye, filched them from you, and shared them with my fellow men. I have done as I said, and now they fear you no more; they treat you as one power does another.

Grant me death, to atone for my audacity: I bare my breast and humbly wait. Come then, ridiculous reach of eternal retribution! . . . pompous unfurling of over-vaunted attributes! He has revealed his incapacity to halt the circulation of my blood, which flouts him. Yet I have proofs that he does not hesitate to snuff out—in their prime—the breath of other humans when they have hardly tasted the sensual pleasures of life. It's simply atrocious—but only according to *my* feeble opinion!

I have seen the Creator, spurring on his needless cruelty, setting alight conflagrations in which old people and children perished! It is not I who start the attack; it is he who forces me to spin him like a top, with a steel-thonged whip. Is it not he who supplies me with accusations against himself? *My* frightful zest will *not* run dry! It feeds on the crazed nightmares which rack my fits of sleeplessness.

It is because of Lohengrin that the above was written: so let us return to him. Fearing he might later become as other men, at first I had resolved to stab him to death when he had gone beyond the age of innocence. But I thought over—and in time wisely abandoned—my resolution. He does not suspect that his life was for a short while in danger. All was ready, and the knife had been bought. A darling, dainty stiletto—for I love grace and elegance even in the instruments of death; yet it was long and sharp-pointed. A single thrust in the neck carefully piercing one of the carotid arteries would, I think, have sufficed. I am pleased with my conduct: I should have repented later. So, Lohengrin, do what you will, act as you please, lock me up for life in a gloomy prison with scorpions for my cellmates; or gouge out one of my eyes till it drops to the ground—I shall never reproach you in the least. I am yours, I belong to you, I no longer live for myself. The pain you will cause me will not compare with the bliss of knowing that he who wounds me with murderous hands is steeped in an Essence[9] more divine than that of his fellows! Yes, it is still fine to give one's life for a human being and thus to preserve the hope that not all men are wicked,[10] since one of them, at last, has known how to draw upon himself, perforce, the distrustful contradictions[11] of my bitter sympathy! . . .

It is midnight. Not a single Bastille-Madeleine omnibus is to be seen. I am mistaken: here is one approaching suddenly, as if it were emerging from below ground. The few belated passers-by eye it attentively, for it seems unlike any other omnibus. Seated on the open upper deck are men with the immobile eyes of dead fish. They are crowded against one another and appear lifeless; besides, the regulation number of passengers has not been exceeded. Whenever the driver gives his horses the whip, one would think it was the whip that drove his arm, and not his arm the whip. What might this collection of bizarre, mute beings be? Are they inhabitants of the moon? There are times when one would be tempted to think so, but on the whole they resemble corpses.

The omnibus, in a hurry to reach the last stop, eats up the miles, and makes the cobbles crackle. . . . It hurtles past! But a misshapen mass chases doggedly after, in its wake, amid the dust.

"Stop, I beg you, stop! My legs are swollen from walking all day. . . . I've not eaten since yesterday . . . my parents have abandoned me . . . I don't know what to do any more . . . . I've made up my mind to return home and I'd soon get there if you'd let me have a seat. . . . I'm a small child—I'm eight—I'm relying on you. . . ."

It hurtles . . . hurtles past! But a misshapen mass chases doggedly after, in its wake, amid the dust.

One of the cold-eyed men nudges his neighbour and seems to be expressing displeasure at these argentine-toned moans that have caught his ear. The other, by way of assent, almost imperceptibly nods and then sinks once more into the fixity of his egoism, like a tortoise into its shell. The other passengers' features all register the same sentiments as the first pair's.

For two or three minutes the cries are still to be heard, every second more piercing. Along the boulevard windows can be seen opening—and a startled figure, lamp in hand, who, casting a glance down the roadway, impetuously re-closes the shutters—to reappear no more.

It hurtles . . . hurtles past! But a misshapen mass chases doggedly after, in its wake, amid the dust.

Rapt in reverie, one young man alone among these stony characters seems to feel any pity for misfortune. He dares not raise his voice on behalf of the child—who thinks that with his aching little legs he can catch up—for the other men give him contemptuous and authoritative looks, and he knows he can do nothing against them *all*. Elbows on knees and head in hands, he wonders, dumbfounded, if this is really what is called *Human Charity*. Then he acknowledges that it is but a vain word no longer to be found even in the dictionary of poetry, and frankly admits his error. He says to himself: "Why indeed concern oneself over a small child? Let's drop the subject."

However, a scalding tear rolls down the cheek of this youth who has just blasphemed. Wearily he passes a hand across his brow as if to brush aside a cloud whose opacity obscures his comprehension. He struggles hard (if unavailingly) in the century into which he has been hurled; he feels out of place there, yet cannot escape from it. Terrible prison! Hideous fate! Lombano, I have been pleased with you since that day. I had not ceased to watch you, while my face displayed the same indifference as the other passengers'.

The youth rises in a fit of indignation, and wants to alight so as not to participate, even involuntarily, in wrongdoing. I beckon to him and he sits down again beside me . . . .

It hurtles . . . hurtles past! But a misshapen mass chases doggedly after, in its wake, amid the dust.

The shouts suddenly stop, for the child has tripped over a jutting cobblestone and, falling, has hurt his head. The omnibus has disappeared into the distance and the street is silent once more.

It hurtles . . . hurtles past! But a misshapen mass no longer chases doggedly after, in its wake, amid the dust.

See this passing ragman, crouched over his feeble lantern: he has more heart than all his kin on the omnibus. He has just lifted up the child—you may be sure that he will heal it and not forsake it as did its parents.

The omnibus hurtles . . . hurtles past! But from the spot on which he stands, the ragman's piercing gaze chases doggedly after it, in its wake, amid the dust! . . .

Stupid and idiotic species! You will regret such conduct, I tell you! You will regret it, yes, regret it! My poetry shall consist of attacks, by all means,[12] upon that wild beast, Man, and the Creator, who should never have begotten such vermin! Volume shall pile upon volume until the end of my life, and there, ever-present in my consciousness,[13] shall this single aim be discerned!

Taking my daily stroll, I'd walk down a narrow street, and every day a slender ten-year-old girl would follow me at a respectful distance along that street, eyeing me with a pleasant and inquisitive air.[14] She was tall for her age, and slim. Flowing black hair centrally parted fell in separate plaits on to her marble shoulders.

One day she was following me as usual when a vulgar muscular woman[15] seized hold of her hair as a whirlwind seizes a leaf, laid two brutal slaps across her proud, silent cheek, and hauled this stray soul back home. In vain I feigned unconcern: she never failed to pursue me with her—now inopportune—presence. Whenever I strode down another road to continue on my way she would stop at the bounds of that narrow street, trying desperately to control herself, motionless, like the statue of Silence, and would not cease staring after me until I disappeared.

Once the girl walked ahead of me in the street, and kept in step. When I went fast to overtake her she almost ran so as to maintain the same distance between us, but if I slowed down to ensure enough space separated us, then she too would slow down, doing so with childish charm. On reaching the end of the street she turned slowly round in order to block my path. I had no time to step aside and found myself face to face with her. Her eyes were red and swollen. I readily observed that she wished to talk to me and did not know how to set about it. Suddenly turning pale as a corpse she asked: "Would you be so kind as to tell me the time?"

I told her I carried no watch, and made off hastily.

Since that day, child of uneasy and precocious fancy, you have seen no more in that narrow street the mysterious youth whose heavy boots beat painfully upon the paving-stones of winding crossroads. The vision of that fiery comet shall shine no more—like a sorry subject of zealous curiosity—across the façade of your disappointed observation.[16] And you will often think—too often, perhaps forever—of him who seemed not to concern himself with the good or ill of presentday life, and wandered haphazardly, with staggering stride, his face horribly dead, hair standing on end, and arms—as though seeking there the bloody prey of hope, swimming blindly in the ironic waters of the aether, continually buffeted about through the huge regions of space by the implacable snowplough cow-catcher[17] of fatality. You shall see me no more, and I shall no more see you! . . .

Who knows? Perhaps that young girl was not what she appeared to be. Perhaps under an artless exterior she concealed immeasurable guile, the weight of eighteen years, and the charm of vice. Vendors of love have been seen gaily leaving their own British Isles and crossing the Channel. While wheeling in gilded swarms their wings would sparkle in the Parisian light, and when you beheld them, you'd say: "But they are still only children, not more than ten or twelve years old." Actually they were twenty.

On this supposition, oh! cursed be the byways of that gloomy street! And horrible, horrible what happens there! I believe her mother hit her because she did not ply her trade with sufficient skill. It is possible that she was a mere child, and if so the mother was guiltier still. As for me, I don't want to believe this assumption—only a hypothesis—and prefer to love in this romantic character a soul that unveils itself too soon. . . . 'Ah! girl, I urge you to reappear before my eyes no more if ever I pass through this alley again. Or it could cost you dear!

Already blood and hate rush to my head in boiling floods. *I* generous enough to love my fellow men! No, no! I swore to do so from the day of birth: it's *they* who do not love me! Worlds shall be seen to destroy themselves, and granite glide like the cormorant on the waves' surface before I touch the vile hand of a human being! Avaunt! . . . Away with that hand! . . . Young girl, you are no angel, and in short, will become as other women. No, no, I implore you—appear no more to my scowling, suspicious gaze.[18] In a moment of aberration I might seize your arms and twist them as one wrings water from washing, or snap them with a crack like two dry branches, forcing you afterwards to eat them. Taking your head between my hands in soft, fond manner, I might sink my greedy fingers into the lobes of your innocent brain, thence to extract (with a smile on my lips) a blubber effective for bathing my eyes—sore from the eternal insomnia of life. I might, by sewing together your eyelids, deprive you of the spectacle of the universe and make it impossible for you to find your way: *I* should not act as your guide. Lifting up your virginal body with an arm of iron, I might grasp you by the legs, whirl you around me like a slingshot, concentrate my strength on describing the final circle and fling you against the wall. Each drop of blood will spatter a human breast to startle men and set before them the example of my wickedness! Without respite they will tear from themselves shred after shred of flesh, but the drop of blood remains in the same place, indelible, and gleams like a diamond. Never fear, I shall order half-a-dozen servants to keep watch over the revered relics of your body and to safeguard them from the greed of ravenous dogs.

Doubtless the body has stayed caked across the wall like an

overripe pear and has not dropped to the ground. But dogs know how to perform high leaps,[19] if one isn't careful.

How nice he is, this child seated on a bench in the Tuileries Gardens! His fearless eyes flash forth at some invisible object far off in space. He can't be more than eight years old and yet does not enjoy himself as one might expect. He ought at the very least to laugh and stroll with some friend instead of staying alone: but it is not his nature.

How nice he is, this child seated on a bench in the Tuileries Gardens! Moved by a hidden purpose, a man comes and sits beside him on the same bench, with questionable demeanour. Who is he? No need to tell you, for you'll recognise him by his devious conversation. Let us listen, let's not disturb them.

— What were you thinking about, child?

— I was thinking of heaven.

— It's unnecessary for you to think of heaven: there's already enough to consider about earth. Are you tired of living, you who have barely been born?

— No, but everyone prefers heaven to earth.

— Well, not I. For since heaven, as well as earth, has been made by God, you may count on encountering up there the very same evils as here below. After your death, you will not be rewarded according to your deserts, for if injustices are done you on this earth (as you will find out later by experience) there is no reason why, in the next life, you will not be further wronged. The best thing for you to do is not to think of God and, since it is refused you, to make your own justice. Were one of your playmates to harm you, would you not be happy to kill him?

— But that's forbidden.

— Not as forbidden as you believe. It's only a matter of not letting oneself be caught. The justice laws purvey is worthless: what counts is the legal skill of the injured party. If you hated one of your playfellows, wouldn't you be unhappy upon reflecting that at every moment you might have the thought of him on your mind?

— That is true.

— So there's one of your companions who would make you unhappy all your life. For seeing that your hatred is only passive, he will merely continue to flout and harm you with impunity. There is, then, only one way of putting a stop to the situation, and that is to get rid of the enemy. Which is what I wanted to drive at—so as to make you aware of the foundations upon which present society is based. Each man must mete out his own justice: if he does not, he is simply an imbecile. He who gains victory over his fellow men is the slyest and strongest. Some day wouldn't you like to dominate your fellow men?

— Yes, yes.

— Then be the strongest and most wily. You are still too young to be the strongest, but from today forth you can use cunning, the finest weapon of men of genius. When David the shepherd struck giant Goliath on the forehead with a stone thrown from a sling, is it not wonderful to note that David vanquished his opponent solely by guile, and that had they, on the contrary, grappled together, the giant would have crushed him like a fly? The same applies to you. In open warfare you could never defeat men over whom you desire to exert your will, but by your cunning you could battle alone against all. Do you desire riches, fine palaces and fame? Or did you mislead me when assuring me of such lofty pretentions?

— No, no, I didn't mislead you. But I would like to acquire what I desire by other means.

— In that case you will gain nothing whatever. Righteous and simple-minded methods lead nowhere. One must bring into play more forceful levers, weave more skilful plots. Before you become famous because of your virtue and achieve your end, a hundred others will have time to bound over your back and reach the winning post before you, so that then there will be no room for your narrow ideas. One must know how to clasp the horizon of the present with more grandeur. For example, have you never heard tell of the boundless glory victories bring? Yet victories do not come about of themselves. Blood, much blood, must be spilled to breed them and lay them at the conquerors' feet. Without the corpses and strewn limbs you see spread across the plain where carnage was so wisely wrought, there would be no war, and without war, no victory. You see when one wants to become famous one must wallow gracefully in rivers of blood fed by cannon-fodder. The end justifies the means. The first thing in becoming famous is to have money. Now since you have none, you must murder to get it. But as you are not strong enough to wield a dagger, be a thief, while waiting for your limbs to develop. And so that they develop the faster I advise you to do gymnastics twice daily, one hour in the morning, one in the evening. In this manner you can attempt crime, with some success, as soon as you are fifteen instead of waiting until twenty. The love of fame excuses everything, and later perhaps, when master of your fellow men, you will do them almost as much good as you did them ill in the beginning! . . .

Maldoror perceives that inside his youthful interlocutor's head the blood boils: the nostrils flare, lips froth forth a fine white spray. He takes the boy's pulse: its beat races. Fever has overtaken this frail frame. Maldoror fears the consequences of his words. He makes himself scarce—the wretch—vexed at not being able to converse longer with this child. When in maturity it is so difficult to master the passions, balanced between good and evil, what about a mind still brimming with inexperience? And what relative amount of energy does it further require? The child will get off with three days' stay in bed. Heaven grant that maternal care may bring peace to this sensitive flower, fragile envelope of a fine soul!

Over there in a grove surrounded by flowers slumbers the hermaphrodite, sound asleep upon the sward, drenched with his tears.

The moon's disc is clear of the cloud mass and with pale beams she caresses this smooth youthful form. His features manifest the most manly vigour coeval with a heavenly virgin's grace. Nothing in him appears natural, not even the muscles of his body, which force their way across the harmonious contours of feminine forms. One arm curves over his forehead, the other hand rests against his breast as if to repress the beat of a heart closed to all confidences and fraught with the weighty burden of an eternal secret. Weary of life and ashamed to walk among beings who do not resemble him, despair has won his soul and he wanders alone like a beggar in the valley. How does he find the wherewithal to exist? Compassionate souls watch over him closely, without his suspecting such surveillance, and do not abandon him: he is so good! so resigned!

Sometimes he talks readily to those of sensitive disposition, without touching their hands, and standing his distance for fear of an imagined danger. If asked why he has taken solitude for companion, he raises his eyes heavenward and has difficulty holding back a tear of reproach against Providence; but he does not answer this imprudent question, which sheds upon his snowy eyelids the blush of a morning rose. Should the colloquy continue, he waxes restless, turning his gaze toward all four cardinal points of the compass as if seeking to flee the presence of an invisible, approaching foe. A brusque wave of farewell and he makes off on the wings of his awakened modesty and disappears into the forest. He is generally taken for a madman.

One day four masked men, upon orders received, threw themselves upon him and bound him hand and foot, so that he could move only his legs. The whip's harsh lash slashed at his back, and they told him to be on his way without delay—along the road that leads to Bedlam.[20] He began to smile while scourged and spoke to them with such feeling, such intelligence concerning so many human sciences he had studied—displaying vast erudition for one who had not yet crossed the threshold of youth. And his discourse on humanity's destiny, during which he laid absolutely bare the poetic nobility of his soul, made his captors—shaken to the core by what they had done—unbind his battered limbs and fall on their knees begging forgiveness. This was granted, and they left, marked by a reverence not usually bestowed on men.

Since this incident, which was much discussed, everyone guessed his secret but feigns ignorance of it so as not to increase his sufferings; and the government granted him a respectable annuity to make him forget that they had once wanted to commit him forcibly, without preliminary examination, to a madhouse. Half of his money he spends: the rest he gives to the poor.

Whenever he sees a man and a woman stroll along some lane of plane-trees he feels his body cleave in twain from head to foot and each new part strain to clasp one or other of the strollers; but it is only a hallucination and reason is not slow to regain her sway. This is why he mingles neither with men nor women: his excessive modesty, which dawned on him because of this idea of being but a monster, prevents his bestowing his glowing compassion upon any man.

He would fain believe he was profaning himself, and fancy he profaned others. His pride repeats to him this axiom: "Let each keep to himself."[21] Pride, I said, because by joining his life with that of a man or a woman he fears sooner or later to be taxed with, taunted for, an enormous fault—the conformation of his own organism.[22] So he shelters behind his self-respect, offended by this blasphemous assumption which arises solely from himself, and persists in remaining alone and without solace in the midst of torments.

Over there in a grove surrounded by flowers slumbers the hermaphrodite, sound asleep upon the sward, drenched with his tears.

Through the branches of the trees the awakened birds gaze rapturously on this melancholy visage, and the nightingale is unwilling to utter its cavatinas of crystal. The wood has become as august as a grave because of the nocturnal presence of the hapless hermaphrodite.

O errant traveller, by your spirit of adventure that has caused you from tenderest years to leave behind father and mother; by the torments you suffered from thirst in the desert; by the fatherland you seek perchance after wandering long, outlawed, in strange lands; by your steed, your staunch friend, who has borne with you the exile and inclement climes in which your vagrant mettle led you roving; by the dignity man gains through voyages over distant territories and uncharted seas, amid polar ice-floes or under the influence of a torrid sun—touch not with your hand, as does a rustling gust of breeze, these locks of hair spread on the soil and threading with the green grass. Stand several paces back, and thus you will do well. These tresses are sacred: the hermaphrodite himself wished it. He does not want human lips piously kissing hair scented by the mountain breeze, nor his brow, aglow now like the stars of the firmament. But it is better to believe that while traversing space a star itself has descended out of orbit on to this majestic brow, and encircles it with a diamond's brilliance as a halo.

Night, waving sadness aside, adorns herself in all her charms to celebrate the sleep of this incarnation of modesty, this perfect image of angelic innocence: the buzz of insects is less audible. The branches bend their lofty tufts over him to protect him from the dew, and the wind, twanging the strings of its tuneful harp sends blithe strains across the universal silence towards those lowered eyelids which, motionless, seem to witness the cadenced concert of suspended worlds.

He dreams he is happy; that his corporeal nature has changed; or at least that he has flown off upon a purple cloud to another sphere peopled by beings of the same kind as himself. Alas! May his illusion last till dawn's awakening! He dreams the flowers dance round him in a ring like immense demented garlands, and impregnate him with their balmy perfumes while he sings a hymn of love, locked in the arms of a magically beautiful human being. But it is merely twilight mist he embraces, and when he wakes their arms will no longer be entwined. Awaken not, hermaphrodite. Do not wake yet, I beg you. Why will you not believe me? Sleep . . . sleep forever. May your breast heave while pursuing the chimerical hope of happiness—that I allow you; but do not open your eyes. Ah! do not open your eyes! I want to leave you thus, not to witness your awakening.

Perhaps one day, with the aid of a voluminous tome and in moving pages I shall recount your tale, shocked by its contents and the lessons it brings forth. So far, I have been unable to, for each time I try, copious tears fall upon the paper and my fingers tremble, and not through old age. But in the end I want to have courage enough. I am indignant at having no more nerve than a woman and swooning like a little girl whenever I consider your deep misery.

Sleep . . . sleep forever, but do not open your eyes. Ah! do not open your eyes! Hermaphrodite, farewell! I shall not fail to pray Heaven daily for you (were it for myself, I would not pray at all). Peace be in your bosom![23]

Whenever a woman's soprano voice emits its vibrant and melodious notes—on hearing this human harmony—my eyes are filled with a latent flame and flash forth grievous sparks, while my ears seem to ring with the clangour of the cannonade. Whence can come this deep loathing for all that stems from man? If the chords wing from the heart of an instrument I listen delightedly to these exquisite notes escaping, cadenced across the buoyant billows of the aether. Perception imparts to my ear only an impression of a sweetness able to melt nerves and thought; an unutterable torpor with its magic poppies enwraps the active potency of my senses and the lively vigour of my imagination, like a veil softly filtering the light of day.

They say I was born deaf![24] In the early stages of my childhood

I could not hear what was said to me. When with the greatest difficulty they managed to teach me to talk, only after reading what they would write down on a piece of paper was *I* then able to communicate my train of thought.

One day—ill fated day!—I was growing up in beauty and innocence, and everyone admired the intelligence and goodness of this divine youth. Many a conscience blushed to contemplate the limpid features wherein his soul had its throne. They used to draw near him only with reverence, since they discerned in his eyes the glance of an angel. But no—I knew only too well that the carefree roses of adolescence ought not to bloom perpetually, woven in wayward wreaths about his brow, the modest and noble brow bussed frenziedly by every mother. The universe with its starry vault of annoying and impassive globes started to seem not, perhaps, as imposing as I had dreamed.

So one day, then, tired of trudging along the steep track of earthly voyage and of staggering like a drunkard through life's dark catacombs, I slowly raised my morose eyes (ringed with huge bluish circles) toward the concave firmament, and, though so young, dared penetrate the mysteries of heaven! Not finding what I sought I raised my dismayed gaze higher, still higher, until I caught sight of a throne fashioned of human excrement and gold upon which, with idiotic pride, body swathed in a shroud made of unwashed hospital sheets, sat he who calls himself the Creator!

He held in his hand a corpse's decaying torso and bore it in turn from eyes to nose, from nose to mouth: once in his mouth one can guess what he did with it. His feet were immersed in a vast pool of boiling blood, to whose surface two or three cautious heads would suddenly rise like tapeworms from a full chamberpot, and immediately slip back again quick as arrows: a well-applied kick on the bridge of the nose was the familiar reward for breach of rules (caused by the need to breathe in another element—for after all, these men weren't fish!) Amphibians at best, they swam between two waters in that loathsome liquid!

And then the Creator (having nothing left in his grasp) would with the first two claws of his foot seize another swimmer by the neck as in a vice, and raise him from the reddish slime (delicious sauce!) into the air, there to be dealt with like the others. First of all he would devour head, legs, and arms, and lastly the trunk, until nothing was left—for he crunched the bones. And so on throughout the other hours of his eternity. Sometimes he would exclaim: "I have created you, so I have the right to do with you what I will. You have done nothing against me, that I do not deny. And for my pleasure, I make you suffer." And he would resume the cruel repast, lower jaw moving, moving his beard clotted with brains.

O reader, does not the latter detail make your mouth water? Such brains are not there for everyone to eat—so good—absolutely fresh—and caught only a quarter of an hour ago from the lake of *fish*.

Limbs paralysed and my throat dumb, I contemplated this spectacle for some time. Thrice I almost fell head over heels, like a man who undergoes too strong an emotion; thrice I managed to regain balance. Not a fibre of my body remained immobile, and I quaked like the lava inside a volcano. In the end, my tight chest unable to exhale the lifegiving air quickly enough, my lips parted and I cried out . . . a cry so earsplitting . . . that I heard it! The trammels in my ears came loose abruptly, the eardrums cracked at the shock of this mass of resounding air forced vigorously forth from me, and there occurred a new phenomenon within the organs condemned by nature. I had just heard a sound! A fifth sense revealed itself in me!

But what pleasure could I have found in such a discovery? Henceforth human sound reached my ear only with the sensation of pain which pity for a great injustice engenders. Whenever anyone addressed me I recalled what I had seen that day, above the visible spheres, and the translation of my stifled feelings into an impulsive howl whose tone was identical with that of my fellows! I was unable to reply, for the tortures wrought upon man's weakness in that hideous sea of crimson brushed past my brow, bellowing like flayed elephants, and with their fiery wings sheared my charred hair.

Later when I was better acquainted with humanity, the feeling of pity was united with an intense fury against this tigress step-mother whose callous offspring know only how to curse and do evil. They say (a brazen lie!) that with them evil is merely the state of exception!

All that is long since over: for a long time now I have spoken to no one. O you—whoever you are—when you are beside me, let not the cords of your glottis utter any modulation; may your motionless larynx not strive to outdo the nightingale. And on no account try to make known your soul to me by the use of speech. Maintain a religious silence that nothing interrupts: humbly cross your hands on your breast and lower your eyes. I have told you that since the vision vouchsafing me the supreme truth, night-mares enough have day and night sucked greedily at my throat—so I might still have the courage to revive even in thought the sufferings I experienced during that infernal hour whose memory pursues me without pause.

Oh! whenever you hear the snowy avalanche hurtling from the cold mountain top; the lioness in the arid desert howling at the disappearance of her cubs; the tempest accomplishing its destiny; the condemned man in his dungeon moaning on the eve of the guillotine; and the ferocious devil-fish recounting to the ocean wave his victories over swimmers and castaways—say then, are not these majestic voices more beautiful than the sneering laughter of man?

There exists an insect men foster[25] at their own expense. They owe it nothing yet they fear it. This insect, which does not care for wine but prefers blood, would, were its lawful needs not satisfied, be capable (by an occult power) of becoming big as an elephant and trampling men like ears of corn. One must also note how they respect it, how they surround it with canine veneration, how highly they esteem it above the animals of creation. They give it the head for throne and it hooks its claws into the roots of the hair, with dignity. Later, when plump and well advanced in years, it is—to emulate the custom of bygone peoples—killed, in order to be spared the onslaughts of old age. They give it, as unto a hero, imposing obsequies, and the coffin conveying it straight to the cover of the tomb is carried shoulder-high by the leading citizens. Upon the damp soil which with skilled shovel the gravedigger turns over they turn multicoloured phrases concerning the immortality of the soul, the nothingness of life, the inexplicable will of Providence—and the marble closes shut forever on this laboriously filled existence now no more than a corpse. The crowd disperses and the shades of night quite soon cover the cemetery walls.

But console yourselves, humans, for this painful loss. Here, advancing, comes the innumerable family it has bountifully bequeathed to you, that your despair might be less bitter, and assuaged by the agreeable presence of these peevish little freaks which will duly grow into splendid lice endowed with remarkable beauty, monsters with the look of the sage. It brooded with maternal wing over several dozen cherished eggs, in your hair— dried up by the eager suction of such formidable strangers. The time promptly came when the eggs hatched. Be not alarmed, these youthful philosophers will not take long growing into this ephemeral life. They will grow so much that they'll make you feel it—with their claws and suckers.

You others do not know why they don't devour the bones of your skull but content themselves with extracting (in pomp and by pump)[26] the quintessence of your blood. Wait a moment, I shall tell you: it is because they lack the strength. Be assured that if their jaws were proportionate to their infinite desires, your brains, retinas, spines, the whole body, would be consumed.

Like a drop of water. Take a microscope and observe a louse at work on the head of a young street-beggar: you will be amazed. Unfortunately, these raiders of the long-haired scalp are small. Of no avail to conscript them: they are not of the necessary height required by law. They belong to that Lilliputian world of the stunted, and the blind do not hesitate to rank them among the infinitely tiny. Alas for the whale that fights a flea, it would be devoured in the twinkling of an eye, despite its size. Not even the tail would be left to tell the tale. The elephant lets itself be stroked. But not the tick. I don't advise you to try out this perilous test. Beware if your hand be hairy—or simply made of flesh and bone. Your fingers would be finished. They'd crack as if put to the torture. The skin would disappear as if by strange magic. Lice are incapable of wreaking as much ill as their imaginations contemplate. If you find a louse in your way, be off, and do not lick the papillae of its tongue. You would meet with an accident. That has been known. No matter, I am already content with the amount of harm the louse does you, O human race; I only wish it could do still more.

For how long will you maintain the decrepit cult of this god who is impervious to your prayers and the generous offerings you proffer him in expiatory holocaust? Look, this horrible manitou is not beholden to you for the great bowls of blood and brains you spill upon those piously bedecked, flower-wreathed altars of his. He is not grateful . . . for earthquakes and tempests have continued to rage from the Beginning. And yet (spectacle worth noting), the more indifferent he proves himself, the more you admire him. It's clear that you mistrust his attributes—which he conceals; and your argument rests on the assumption that only a deity of extreme power can display such contempt towards the faithful who submit to his worship. For this reason, in every land diverse gods are extant—here the crocodile, there the whore—but when it comes to the louse, that sacred name, all peoples, universally kissing the chains of their slavery, together kneel down in the majestic court before the pedestal of the misshapen, blood-thirsty idol. That nation not obeying its own instincts for grovel-ling, and which made a show of revolt, would sooner or later disappear from the earth like an autumn leaf annihilated by the vengeance of that inexorable god.

O louse with shrivelled eye—as long as rivers spill their shelving waters into the abysses of the sea; as long as the stars gravitate along their orbits' paths; as long as the mute void has no horizon; as long as humanity rends its own flanks in deadly wars; as long as divine justice casts down its vengeful bolts upon this selfish globe; as long as man disregards his Creator and (not without reason) flouts him, so doing with some contempt—your reign over the universe will be assured, and your dynasty extend its links from age to age. I salute you, rising sun, celestial liberator, you invisible enemy of man. Continue telling Filth to unite with man in tainted embraces and to swear to him by oaths not blown to dust that she shall remain his faithful lover for eternity. From time to time, kiss this grand wanton's robe, in memory of the important services she does not fail to render you. If she did not seduce man with her lascivious teats, probably you could not exist—you, the product of this rational and consistent[27] coupling. O son of Filth! tell your mother that if she abandons man's bed to wander alone and friendless along desolate ways she will see her existence imperilled. May the bowels which bore you nine months in their perfumed maw stir a moment at the thought of the dangers that their tender fruit (fruit so nice, tranquil, but already cold and ferocious) would consequently encounter. Filth, mighty empress, preserve for my hate's eyes the sight of your famished progeny and the imperceptible[28] increase of their muscles. To attain this end you know you need only glue yourself closer to man's flanks. This you can do conveniently enough for decorum, since both of you have long been married.

For myself, if I may be allowed to add a few words to this hymn of glorification, I shall speak of the pit I have had dug, forty

leagues square and correspondingly deep. Therein lies in foul
virginity a living mine of lice. It fills the bottom layers of the pit,
and thence writhes in vast dense veins in every direction. Here's
how I built this artificial mine. I snatched a female louse from the
hair of humanity. Three successive nights I was seen to lie with
her, and then I cast her into the pit. Human fertilisation, which
would have been ineffective in other such cases, was this time
accepted by fate, and a few days afterwards thousands of monsters
swarming in a compact knot of matter saw the light of day. This
loathsome cluster became in time more and more immense, all
the while acquiring the liquid attribute of mercury, and spread
out into several tributaries which now feed upon themselves (the
birthrate is higher than the mortality rate) whenever I do not
throw them for fodder a newborn bastard whose death its mother
desired, or an arm that during the night, thanks to chloroform, I
am going to hack from some young girl. Every fifteen years the
generations of lice that feed on man appreciably decrease and
themselves foretell infallibly the impending era of their complete
destruction. For man, more intelligent than his enemy, manages
to conquer him. Well then, with devilish shovel which increases
my strength, I quarry lumps of lice big as mountains from this
inexhaustible mine, break them up with axe blows, and transport
them at dead of night into the main thoroughfares of cities. There,
on contact with human temperature, they split up as in their first
formative days in the tortuous galleries of the subterranean
mine, dig themselves beds in the gravel, and stream into human
dwellings like harmful spirits. The house guardian barks dully,
for it seems to him that a legion of unknown beings is piercing
the pores of the walls and bringing terror to the sleepers' bedsides.
Perhaps, unwittingly, you have heard at least once in your life
this sort of doleful, drawn-out howl. He tries with helpless eyes
to penetrate the darkness of the night, for his dog's brain cannot
understand it—this hum irritating him—and he feels betrayed.
Millions of enemies thus sweep down on every city like a cloud

of locusts. Enough for fifteen years. They will combat man, in-
flicting burning wounds upon him. After this space of time I shall
send others. When I am crushing the lumps of live matter, one
fragment may happen to be denser than another. Its atoms
struggle furiously to detach their cluster in order to go tor-
menting humanity; but cohesion in its hardness resists. By a
supreme convulsion they generate such a stress that the stone,
unable to disperse its living constituents, hurls itself high into the
skies as if blown up by gunpowder and falls back, burying itself
deep below the soil. Sometimes the musing peasant perceives a
meteorite cleave vertically through space, heading at its lowest
point for a field of maize. He does not know whence comes the
stone. You now have a clear and succinct explanation of the
phenomenon.

Were the earth covered in lice like grains of sand on the sea-
shore, the human race would be annihilated, stricken with terrible
grief. What a sight! And I, with angel's wings, motionless in the
air to view it!

O stern mathematics, I have not forgotten you since your learned
teachings, sweeter than honey, filtered through my heart like a
refreshing wave. From the cradle I instinctively aspired to drink
from your spring more ancient than the sun, and, most faithful
of your initiates, still I continue to tread the sacred court of your
grave temple. There was a haze in my spirit, something indefinable, smoky-thick, but I knew how to cross—religiously—the
steps that lead to your altar, and as wind drives off the fritillary,
so you have cleared this dim mist. In its place you set excessive
coolness, a consummate prudence, and an implacable logic. With
the aid of your strengthening milk my intellect developed rapidly
and acquired immense proportions amid the entrancing clarity
that you prodigally present to those who love you with a sincere
love.

Arithmetic! Algebra! Geometry! Grand trinity! Luminous

triangle! He who has not known you is a dolt! He deserves the test of the greatest tortures, for in his ignorant thoughtlessness there is blind contempt. But he who knows and appreciates you wants naught else of the world's chattels; is content with your magical ecstasies[29]; and, borne on your sombre wings, desires nothing more than to rise in gentle flight, describing an ascendant helix, toward the spherical vault of the heavens. Earth shows him only illusions and moral phantasmagorias, but you, O concise mathematics, by the rigorous series of your tenacious propositions and the constancy of your iron laws, dazzle the eyes, shining forth a powerful reflection of that supreme truth whose imprint is discernible in the order of the universe. Yet the order that surrounds you, represented particularly by the perfect regularity of a square—Pythagoras' friend—is greater still, for the Almighty revealed himself and his attributes completely in this memorable task which consisted in bringing forth from the bowels of chaos your treasures of theorems and your magnificent splendours.

In bygone days as in modern times, more than one great mind saw its genius awe-stricken on contemplating your symbolic figures traced upon fiery paper and living with a latent breath like so many mysterious signs not understood by the vulgar and profane, signs merely the brilliant revelation of eternal axioms and hieroglyphics pre-existent to the universe, and which will outlast it. On the precipice-brink of a fatal questionmark, the mind wonders how mathematics happen to contain so much commanding importance and so much incontestable truth, while comparison between mathematics and man only uncovers the latter's false pride and mendacity. Then this superior intellect, saddened, and through the noble intimacy of your counsels made still more sharply to feel humanity's pettiness and incomparable folly, bows grizzled head upon emaciated hand and remains rapt in supernatural meditations. To you he bends the knee, and his reverence pays homage to your divine features as though to the very image of the Almighty.

During my childhood you appeared to me one moonlit May night, in a verdant meadow by the banks of a limpid brook, all three equal in grace and modesty, all three full of majesty, like queens. You took a few steps towards me, with long robes floating like mist, and enticed me to your proud breasts, as a blessed son. Then I readily drew close, my hands clenched on your white bosom. I fed gratefully upon your fruitful manna and felt humanity grow within me, and improve. Since that time, O rival goddesses, I have not abandoned you. Since that time, how many energetic projects, how many sympathies—whose outlines I thought I had graven upon my heart's pages as on marble—have you not slowly erased from my disillusioned reason as daybreak dispels the shadows of night! Since that time I have seen death—with a view (visible to the naked eye) to populating the tombs—ravage battlefields fertilised by human blood, and make morning flowers sprout over the funereal bones. Since that time I have witnessed the revolutions of our globe; earthquakes, volcanoes with their blazing lava, the desert simoon and the storm's shipwrecks—of these my presence has been impassive spectator. Since that time I have seen several generations of humans in the morning raise their wings and eyes toward space with the inexperienced joy of the chrysalis hailing its last metamorphosis, and in the evening, before sunset, die, heads drooping like wilted flowers which the wind's plaintive whistling sways.

Yet *you* remain the same forever. No change, no pestilential blast grazes the steep rocks and vast valleys of your identity. Your modest pyramids will endure longer yet than the pyramids of Egypt, those anthills reared by stupidity and slavery. The end of time will see—still erect on the ruins of the ages—your cabalistic numbers, laconic equations, and sculptural lines enthroned on the avenging right hand of the Almighty, while the stars plunge desperately like waterspouts into the eternity of a horrible, universal night, and humanity, grimacing, dreams of settling accounts with the last judgment.

Thank you for the countless[30] services you have rendered me. Thank you for the unfamiliar qualities with which you have enriched my intellect. But for you, perhaps I might have been defeated in my struggle against man. But for you, he would have made me roll in the sand and kiss the dust of his feet. But for you, he would have scored my flesh and bones with treacherous claw. But I stood on my guard like an experienced athlete. You gave me the coolness arising from your sublime conceptions that are free of passion. I made use of it when disdainfully rejecting the ephemeral joys of my short voyage, and in order to turn away from my door the sympathetic yet mistaken offers of my fellows. You gave me the stubborn prudence deciphered at each step in your admirable methods of analysis, synthesis, and deduction. I made use of it to outwit the pernicious wiles of my mortal enemy, attacking him adroitly in turn and plunging into man's vitals a keen dagger to stay embedded in his body forever, for it is a wound from which he shall not recover.

You gave me logic, the very soul of your wise instruction, and through its syllogisms whose involved maze makes them still more comprehensible, my intellect felt its bold strength redouble. With the aid of this redoubtable ally, I discovered in mankind (while swimming down to the depths opposite the reef of hatred) black, vile wickedness wallowing amid noxious miasmas and contemplating its navel. I was the first to discover in the darkness of man's bowels this baneful vice—evil!—stronger in him than good.

With the poisoned weapon you lent me I forced to descend from his pedestal constructed by man's cowardice—the Creator himself! He gnashed his teeth and bore this ignominious injury, for he had to reckon with an adversary stronger than he. But I cast him aside like a ball of string, that I might descend in my flight. . . . Descartes the thinker once made the reflection that nothing solid had been built upon you—an ingenious way of making it clear that your inestimable worth could not be discovered all at once by just anybody. Indeed, what could be more solid than the three aforenamed principal qualities which rise up intertwined like a unique crown upon the majestic summit of your colossal architecture? A monument ceaselessly growing via daily discoveries in your diamond-mines, and scientific explorations among your superb domains.

O holy mathematics, would you might, by your perpetual commerce, console my remaining days for the wickedness of man and the injustice of the Most High!

"O lamp with silver tip, companion of the cathedral dome, my eyes catch sight of you in mid-air, and seek the reason for this suspension. They say that during the night your rays illumine the rabble—those who come to worship the Almighty—and that you show the repentant the path to the altar. See here, it's quite possible—but . . . need you render such services to those to whom you owe nothing? Leave the columns of the basilicas plunged in darkness, and whenever a tempest blast upon which, borne in space, the devil whirls, bursts with him into the holy place spreading terror—instead of your struggling bravely against the prince of evil's foul squall, extinguish yourself suddenly beneath his feverish breath so that, unseen, he can select his victims from the kneeling believers. If you do this, you know I shall owe all my happiness to you. While you are shining thus, shedding your blurred but adequate beams, I dare not respond to the promptings of my nature, and stay under the sacred porch staring through the half-open portals at those in the Lord's bosom, who escape my vengeance.

"O poetic lamp! you who would be my friend if you could understand me—why, when in the night hours my feet tread the basalt of churches, do you begin gleaming in a way which, I must say, seems to me unwonted? Your beams then take on the white hues of electricity; the eye cannot look at you; and with a new and powerful flame, as if prey to a holy wrath, you light up the most trifling details of the Creator's kennel. And when after blaspheming I withdraw, you imperceptibly become modest and lambent, sure of having accomplished an act of justice. Tell me something—would it be because you know the byways of my heart that whenever I happen to appear where you keep vigil you hasten to point out my pernicious presence, and draw the worshippers' attention toward the place where the enemy of man has just shown up? I incline to this opinion for I too begin to understand you, and I know who you are, old hag, who watch over the sacred mosques where your curious master struts like a cockscomb.

"Vigilant wardress, you have undertaken a crazy mission. I warn you, the first time you pick me out for my fellowmen's attention by amplifying your phosphorescent rays—since I dislike this optical phenomenon (not mentioned, moreover, in any physics book)—I shall seize you by the skin of your teats, hook my claws into the scabs on your scurvy nape, and cast you into the Seine. (I don't maintain that whenever I am doing nothing to you you knowingly behave in a harmful way towards me.) *There*, I'll allow you to shine as long as it pleases me; there you will flout me with an inextinguishable smile; there, convinced of the inefficacy of your criminal oil, you will bitterly piss it forth."

Having thus spoken, Maldoror does not leave the temple. He stands staring at the lamp in that holy place. . . . He thinks he sees a kind of provocation in the lamp's attitude, which by its inopportune presence causes him the utmost annoyance. He tells himself that if any spirit is enclosed inside this lamp, it is cowardly not replying sincerely to a straightforward attack. With wiry arms he flails the air and wishes the lamp would turn into a man: he promises himself *he'd* give the fellow a bad time! But the means by which a lamp changes into a man are unnatural. He is not resigned to this, and along the courtyard of that wretched pagoda goes looking for a flat, sharp-edged pebble. This he throws powerfully through the air . . . the chain is severed at its centre like

grass by the scythe and the cult's instrument falls to the ground
spilling its oil over the flagstones. . . . He seizes the lamp to
carry it outside but it resists, grows in size. He seems to see wings
at its sides, and the upper part assumes the form of an angel's
torso. The whole thing tries to rise, to take flight, but with firm
hand he holds it back. A lamp and an angel forming one and the
same body—that's something one doesn't often see. He recognises
the shape of the lamp; he recognises the shape of the angel; but
cannot separate them in his mind. Indeed, in reality they merge
one with the other, and form only one free and independent body.
But he believes some cloud has veiled his eyes and has made him
lose a little of the excellence of his sight. Nevertheless, he readies
himself courageously for the fight, for his adversary feels no fear.

Naive folk recount (to those who wish to believe them) that
the sacred portal closed of its own accord, swinging on its creaky
hinges so none could witness this impious struggle whose vicissitudes were going to unfold within the precincts of the violated
sanctuary.

The cloaked man, while meeting with grievous wounds from
an invisible sword, strove to pull the angel's face close to his
mouth. He thought only of that, and all his struggles were to
that end.

The other loses strength and seems to foresee its fate. It wrestles
only feebly, and the moment approaches when its adversary will
be able to clasp it at his ease, if that is what he wants to do.

Now the moment has come. His muscles throttle the throat
of the angel, which can no longer breathe, and he tilts its face,
forcing it against his odious breast. For one instant he is moved by
the fate awaiting this heavenly being, which he would gladly
have made his friend. But he tells himself this is the Lord's envoy,
and can no longer curb his wrath. The worst has happened:
something horrible is going to rejoin the cage of time! He leans
over and applies his saliva-steeped tongue to an angelic cheek
whose owner glances at him beseechingly. For some time he runs

his tongue over that cheek. Oh! Look! . . . Look there! . . . The
pink and white cheek has turned black as coal! Tainted miasmas
it exhales. This is gangrene—no longer any doubt about it. The
gnawing sickness spreads across the whole face and from there
wreaks havoc on the lower regions: soon the entire body is only
an enormous loathsome wound.

Maldoror, appalled (for he did not think his tongue contained
so virulent a poison), snatches up the lamp and flees from the
church. Once outside, he sees in the air a blackish shape with
singed wings, which painfully wends its way heavenward. They
both look at one another as the angel ascends towards the serene
heights of good and Maldoror, on the contrary, sinks down into the
vertiginous abysses of evil. . . . What a look! All that humanity
has thought for sixty centuries, and will yet think in times to come,
could readily be contained therein, so many things did they say
in that supreme farewell! But you understand that here were
thoughts more elevated than those springing from the human
intellect; firstly on account of the two characters involved, and
then because of the circumstances. This look binds them in an
eternal friendship.

Maldoror is astonished that the Creator can have missionaries
so noble of soul. For a moment he believes himself mistaken and
wonders whether he should have followed the path of evil as
he has.

The unease has gone. He keeps to his resolve, and according to
him, it will be glorious sooner or later to conquer the Most
High—to reign in His place over the entire universe and legions
of angels as beautiful as that one. Which, without speaking, gives
Maldoror to understand that it will, as it mounts toward heaven,
resume its pristine form; lets fall a tear which refreshes the brow
of him who has given the angel gangrene; and gradually disappears like a vulture, rising amid the clouds. The culprit looks
at the lamp, the cause of the foregoing. He runs through the
streets like a madman, makes for the Seine, and hurls the lamp

over the parapet. For a few moments it whirls round, then finally sinks into the muddy waters.

Since that day, each evening about nightfall a bright lamp with two dainty angel's wings instead of a handle may be seen bobbing and floating gracefully upon the river's surface near the Pont Napoleon. It proceeds slowly along the waters, passes beneath the arches of the Pont de la Gare and the Pont d'Austerlitz, and continues its silent course down the Seine as far as the Pont de l'Alma. There it turns back upstream with ease and after four hours returns to its starting point. And so on, throughout the night. *Its beams, white as electric light,* eclipse the gas lamps that skirt both river banks and between which it advances like a queen, solitary, unfathomable, *with an inextinguishable smile, nor does its oil spill bitterly forth.*

At first, boats pursued it, but it would baffle these vain attempts and escape from every chase by diving coquettishly to surface a long way further on. Now, whenever the superstitious boatmen see it they row in the opposite direction and refrain from their shanties.

When crossing a bridge by night, take care: you are sure to see the lamp shine here or there, though they say it does not show itself to everyone. When a human being who has something on his conscience is crossing a bridge, the lamp suddenly goes out and the passer-by, scared, peers vainly, desperately, at the surface— and the silt—of the river. He knows what this means. He would like to think he has seen the heavenly radiance, but tells himself that the light came from the fore-part of a ship or was reflected from the gas lamps, and he is right. . . . He know she is the reason for its disappearance, and, sunk in sad reflections, hastens his step homeward. Then the lamp with silver tip reappears upon the surface and continues its progress in capricious and elegant arabesques.

Hear, mankind, the thoughts of my childhood, when I used to wake with red prick:[31] "I have just woken, but my mind is still sluggish. Each morning I feel a heaviness in my head. It is rare for me to find rest at night, for frightful dreams torment me when I succeed in falling asleep. By day my mind wearies itself with bizarre meditations while my eyes stray at random through space; and at night I cannot sleep. Then when *am* I to sleep? Nature must, however, claim her rights. As I scorn her, she makes my face pale and my eyes glow with the sharp flame of fever. Moreover, I would ask for nothing better than *not* to exhaust my wits by continual reflection, but even when I do not wish it, my dismayed senses drive me invincibly towards this inclination. I have realised that other children are like me, yet they are paler still and their brows are furrowed like those of our elder brothers, men.

"O Creator of the universe, this morning I shall not fail to offer you the incense of my childish prayer. Sometimes I forget it, and I have noticed that on those days I feel happier than usual. My breast expands, free of all constraint, and I breathe the balmy air of the fields more comfortably. While whenever I perform the distressing duty prescribed by my parents of addressing you daily with a canticle of praises—accompanied by the inseparable boredom its laborious invention causes me—I am sad and irritated for the rest of the day because to me saying what I don't believe does not seem logical and natural, and I seek retreat in boundless seclusion. If I ask the solitudes to explain this my strange condition of soul, they do not answer me.

"I would like to love and worship you but you are too powerful and there is fear in my hymns. If you can destroy or create worlds by a single manifestation of your thought, my feeble prayers will be of no use to you. If, when you please, you send cholera to ravage cities, or death to carry off in its claws—without any distinction—the four ages of life, I do not wish to ally myself with so redoubtable a friend. Not that hatred governs the line of my argument: on the contrary, I fear your own hate, which at a capricious command can issue from your heart and become vast as the wingspan of the Andean condor. Your ambiguous amusements are not within my grasp and I would probably be their first victim. You are the Omnipotent. This title I do not dispute since you alone have the right to bear it, and your desires with their baleful or happy consequences have no end but yourself. That is precisely why it would pain me to walk beside you, you with your cruel tunic of sapphire—not as your slave, but liable to be so from one moment to the next.

"True that, whenever you delve within yourself to examine your sovereign conduct, if the phantom of a past injustice committed against wretched mankind (which has always obeyed you as your most loyal friend) rears before you the immobile vertebrae of a vengeful spine, your haggard eyes let fall appalled tears of belated remorse, and then, as your hair stands on end, you believe yourself sincerely resolving forever to suspend among the undergrowths of nothingness the inconceivable tricks of your tiger's imagination, which would be comical if it were not lamentable. But I know that constancy has not implanted the harpoon of her eternal abode in your bones like tenacious marrow, and that you and your thoughts often enough relapse into the black leprosy of error, into the dismal lake of gloomy maledictions. I want to believe that the latter are unconscious (although their venom is no less fatal for being suppressed) and that good and evil fused together gush from your royal gangrenous bosom in impetuous surges as torrent does from rock—through the secret spell of a blind force. But of this nothing provides me with proof.

"I have seen your filthy teeth chatter with rage, and your august face (overlaid with the moss of ages) redden like a blazing coal because of some microscopic trifle men had committed, too often to be able to halt longer before the signpost of this simple-minded hypothesis.

"Each day, hands clasped, I offer up to you the strains of my humble prayer, because I must. Yet let not your Providence consider me, I beg you; cast me aside like an earthworm crawling beneath the soil. I'd have you know that I would rather feed greedily on the seaweed from wild and unknown islands, which in these waters tropical waves sweep along upon their foamy laps, than be aware that you are watching me and digging your sneering scalpel into my conscience. Which has just revealed all my thoughts to you—and I hope that your prudence readily applauds the good sense whose ineradicable imprint they retain.

"Apart from these reservations placed upon the kind of more-or-less-intimate relationship I must maintain towards you, my mouth is ready at no matter what hour of the day to exhale, like an artificial afflatus, the flood of lies that your vainglory sternly requires of each human, from the moment when dawn breaks bluish—seeking light in the twilight's satin folds, even as I, stirred by the love of virtue, seek the good. My years are few, yet I already feel that virtue is only a combination of high-sounding syllables: nowhere have I found it. You lay your personality too open; you should conceal it more artfully. But perhaps I am mistaken and you do this on purpose—for you know better than others how to behave. *Men* stake their fame in imitating you; that is why divine providence does not recognise her tabernacle in their wild eyes: like father, like son. Whatever one thinks of your intelligence, I talk of it simply as an impartial critic. I am quite willing to have been led into error. I do not wish to show you the hate I bear you, on which, as over a dear daughter, I gloat lovingly; better to hide it from your eyes and before you to take on solely the aspect of a strict censor charged with controlling your lewd acts. Thus you will end all active dealings with it; forget it; and completely destroy that ravenous bug gnawing your liver. I would rather have you listen to words of reverie and sweetness. . . .

"Yes, you it is who created the world and all in it. You are perfect. Lacking no virtue. You are the most powerful, this everyone knows. Let the entire universe at all times intone your everlasting hymn of praise! The birds glorify you while winging

through the countryside. The stars belong to you. . . . So
be it!"

After these beginnings, you need not be surprised to find me as
I am!

I sought a soul that might resemble mine, and I could not find it.
I scanned all the crannies of the earth: my perseverance was useless. Yet I could not remain alone. There had to be someone who
would approve of my character; there had to be someone with
the same ideas as myself.

It was morning. The sun in all his magnificence rose on the
horizon, and behold, there also appeared before my eyes a young
man whose presence made flowers grow as he passed. He
approached me and held out his hand: "I have come to you, you
who seek me. Let us give thanks for this happy day." But I
replied: "Go! I did not summon you. I do not need your friendship. . . ."

It was evening. Night was beginning to spread the blackness
of her veil over nature. A beautiful woman whom I could scarcely
discern also exerted her bewitching sway upon me and looked at
me with compassion. She did not, however, dare speak to me.
I said: "Come closer that I may discern your features clearly, for
at that distance the starlight is not strong enough to illumine them."
Then, with modest demeanour, eyes lowered, she crossed the
greensward and reached my side. I said as soon as I saw her:
"I perceive that goodness and justice have dwelt in your heart:
we could not live together. Now you are admiring my good looks
which have bowled over more than one woman. But sooner or
later you would regret having consecrated your love to me, for
you do not know my soul. Not that I shall be unfaithful to you:
she who devotes herself to me with so much abandon and trust—
with the same trust and abandon do I devote myself to her. But
get this into your head and never forget it: wolves and lambs look
not on one another with gentle eyes."

What then did I need, I who rejected with such disgust what was most beautiful in humanity! I would not have known how to formulate what I needed. I was not yet accustomed to take rigorous stock of my mind's phenomena by means of the methods philosophy recommends.

I sat on a rock near the sea. A ship had just put out from shore at full sail: an imperceptible dot had appeared on the horizon and was gradually approaching, growing rapidly, pushed on by the squall. The storm was going to begin its onslaughts and already the sky was darkening, turning into a blackness almost as hideous as man's heart.

The vessel, which was a great warship, had dropped all her anchors to avoid being swept on to the rocks along the coast. The wind whistled furiously from all four points of the compass, and made mincemeat of the sails. Claps of thunder crashed amid the lightning but could not outdo the sound of wailing to be heard from the foundationless house—a floating sepulchre. The lurching masses of water had not managed to break the anchor chains, but had dashed open a way into the ship's sides: an enormous breach, for the pumps were quite unable to expel the vast quantities of salt water which smashed foaming over the deck like mountains.

The distressed ship fires off her alarm gun but slowly, majestically, founders.

He who has not seen a vessel founder in the midst of a hurricane, sporadic lightning, deepest darkness—while those aboard are overcome by the despair with which you are familiar-knows not life's mischances. Finally from within the ship a universal shriek of sheer woe bursts forth, while the sea redoubles its redoubtable attacks. Human strength giving way was the cause of that cry. Each man enfolds himself in the cloak of resignation and puts his fate into God's hands. They huddle at bay like a flock of sheep.

The distressed ship fires off her alarm gun but slowly, majestically, founders.

All day long they have had the pumps in action. Futile efforts. And to cap this gracious spectacle, night has fallen, dense, implacable. Each man tells himself that once in the water he will no longer be able to breathe; for no matter how far back his memory ferrets, he owns no fish as ancestor. Yet he urges himself to hold his breath as long as possible, to prolong his life by two or three seconds: that is the vengeful irony he aims at death.

The distressed ship fires off her alarm gun but slowly, majestically, founders.

He is unaware that the vessel as she sinks causes a powerful convolution of swell upon swell; that miry mud mingles with the turbid waters, and that a force coming from below—backlash of the tempest raging above—drives the element to violent jolting motions. Thus despite his reserve of composure mustered beforehand, the man marked for drowning should (on further reflection) feel glad to prolong his life amid the whirlpools of the abyss by even half a normal breath, for good measure. It will be impossible for him to defy his supreme wish, death.

The distressed ship fires off her alarm gun but slowly, majestically, founders.

An error. She fires no more shots, she does not founder. The cockle-shell has been completely engulfed. O heaven! how can one live after tasting so many delights! It has just been my lot to witness the death-throes of several of my fellow men. Minute by minute I observed the vicissitudes of their last agonies. Heard now above the market din would be the bawling of some old woman driven mad by fear; now, the solitary yelps of a suckling infant, making nautical orders hard to hear. The vessel was too far off for me clearly to distinguish the groans borne on the gale, but by an effort of will I drew nearer to them, and the optical illusion was complete. Every quarter of an hour or so, whenever a gust of wind stronger than the rest, keening its dismal dirge amid the cries of startled petrels, struck and cracked the ship's length and increased the moans of those about to be offered up to death-by-holocaust, I would jab a sharp iron point into my cheek, secretly thinking: "They suffer still more!" Thus, at least, I had grounds for comparison.

From the shore I apostrophised them, hurling imprecations and threats at them. It seemed to me that they must have heard me! It seemed to me that my hatred and my words, covering the distance, destroyed the laws of acoustics and, distinctly, reached those ears deafened by the wrathful ocean's roar! It seemed to me that they must have thought of me and vented their vengeance in impotent rage!

From time to time I would cast my gaze towards the cities asleep upon terra firma, and seeing no one suspected that a few miles offshore a ship was sinking—with a crown of birds of prey and a pedestal of emptybellied aquatic giants—I took courage and regained hope. I was now certain of her loss! They could not escape! By way of extra precaution, I had been to fetch my double-barrelled musket, so that were any survivor to try swimming ashore from the rocks, thus escaping imminent death, a bullet in the shoulder would shatter his arm and prevent him from effecting his purpose.

During the fiercest part of the storm I saw a forceful head, its hair on end, cleaving the waters with desperate exertions. Tossed about like a cork, it gulped litres of water and sank into the gulf, but soon reappeared, hair streaming, and fixed its gaze on the shore, seeming to defy death.

His composure was admirable. A great gory wound caused by the outcrop of some hidden reef scarred his intrepid and noble countenance. He could not have been more than sixteen, for by the lightning flashes which lit the night the peachbloom on his upper lip was barely visible. And now he was no more than two hundred metres from the cliff and I could take a good look at him. What courage! What indomitable spirit! How his head's steadiness seemed to taunt destiny while vigorously ploughing through the waves whose furrows parted intractably before him! I had resolved beforehand: I owed it to myself to keep my promise: the last hour had tolled for all, none should escape it. That was my resolution. Nothing would change it. . . .

There was a sharp report and the head sank at once to reappear no more.

From this murder I did not derive as much pleasure as one might think. And precisely because I was sated with perpetual killing, henceforth I would do it through sheer habit—impossible to abandon, but affording only the scantest climax. The senses were blunted, calloused. What pleasure could I feel at the death of this human being when there were more than a hundred about to present me with the spectacle of their last struggles against the waves once the ship had gone down? With this death I had not even the lure of danger, for human justice, cradled by the hurricane of this frightful night, slumbered in the houses a few steps from me.

Today when the years hang heavy on me, I sincerely state for a supreme and solemn truth: I was not as cruel as men later related; but sometimes their wickedness wreaks its enduring ravages for years on end. So my fury knew no limit; I was seized with an access of cruelty and struck awe in anyone (of my own race) who might happen to meet my haggard eyes. Were it a horse or dog, I would let it by: did you hear what I just said? Unfortunately on the night of the storm I was seized by one of my fits of wrath, my reason had flown (for as a rule I would be cruel but more discreet), and everything falling into my hands at that time had to perish. I do not intend to justify my misdeeds. The fault is not entirely with my fellow men. I simply state what *is*, while awaiting the last judgement. (Which makes me scratch my nape in anticipation. . . .) What care I for the last judgement! My reason never deserts me as I claimed—to mislead you. And when I commit a crime I know what I am doing: I would not wish to do otherwise!

Standing on the rock while the hurricane lashed at my hair and cloak, I ecstatically watched the full force of the storm hammering away at the ship, under a starless sky. In triumphant fettle I followed all the twists and turns of the drama—from the instant the vessel cast anchors until the moment she was swallowed up within that fatal garment which dragged those whom it clothed like a cloak, down into the bowels of the sea. But the time was approaching when I myself would play a part as actor in these scenes of disordered nature.

When the spot where the vessel had battled clearly showed that she had gone to spend the rest of her days in the stalls of the sea, some of those who had been borne overboard by the breakers reappeared on the surface. They clung to one another, grappling in twos and threes: this was *not* the way to save their lives, for their movements were hampered and they sank like cracked beakers. . . .

What is this army of marine monsters swiftly slicing through the waves? There are six of them, with sturdy fins that cut a path through the heaving waves. The sharks soon make merely an eggless omelette of all the human beings who flail their four limbs in this unsteady continent, and share it out according to the law of the strongest. Blood mingles with the waters and the waters with blood. Their savage eyes sufficiently illumine the scene of carnage. . . .

But what is this new turmoil in the water, yonder on the horizon? A waterspout approaching, perhaps. What strokes! I realise what it is. An enormous female shark is coming to partake of the duck liver pâté, to eat the cold boiled beef. She is raging, ravening. A battle ensues between her and the others to contest the few palpitating limbs that here and there bob silently on the surface of the crimson cream. To left and right her jaws slash, dealing mortal wounds. But three live sharks surround her still, and she is forced to thrash around in all directions to foil their manoeuvres.

With a mounting emotion hitherto unknown to him the spectator upon the shore follows this new variety of naval engagement. His eyes are fixed on this valiant female shark with her vicious teeth. He hesitates no longer. Musket to shoulder, and adroit as ever, he plants his second bullet in the gills of one of the sharks as it shows itself a moment above a wave. Two sharks remain, displaying even greater tenacity.

His mouth full of bile, the man throws himself off the rock's summit into the sea and swims towards the pleasantly-tinted carpet, gripping the steel knife he always carries. From now on each shark has one enemy to reckon with. He heads for his weary opponent and, taking his time, buries the sharp blade in its belly. Meanwhile the mobile fortress easily disposes of her last enemy. . . .

Swimmer and female shark he has rescued confront each other. For some minutes they stare warily at one another, each amazed to find such ferocity in the other's stare. They swim, circling, neither losing sight of the other. Each thinking: "Till now I was wrong—here is someone wickeder than I!" Then of one accord, in mutual admiration, they slid toward each other— the female parting the water with her fins, Maldoror smiting the surge with his arms—and held their breaths in deepest reverence, both longing to look for the first time on their living image. Three metres separated them. Effortlessly, abruptly, they fell upon each other like magnets, and embraced with dignity and recognition, in a hug as tender as a brother's or sister's.

Carnal desires soon followed this demonstration of affection. A pair of sinewy thighs clung to the monster's viscous skin, close as leeches; and arms and fins entwined about the loved one's body, surrounded it with love, while throats and breasts soon fused into a glaucous mass reeking of sea-wrack. In the midst of the tempest that continued raging. By lightning's light. The foamy wave their nuptial couch—borne on an undertow as in a cradle—they rolled over and over towards the unknown depths of the briny abyss—and came together in a long, chaste, hideous coupling! . . .

At last I had found someone who resembled me! . . . Now I would no longer be alone in life! . . . She had the same ideas as I! . . . I was facing my first love!

———

The Seine sweeps away a human body. On such occasions she assumes a solemn look. The swollen corpse floats upon the waters, disappears beneath the arch of a bridge. But it can be seen again further off, slowly rolling over like a millwheel and submerging at intervals. With the aid of a pole a boat-owner gaffs it as it passes and pulls it to the bank. Before being taken to the Morgue, the body is left for a while on the embankment so they can try reviving it. A massive crowd gathers round the body. Those unable to see because they are at the back jostle those in front as best they can. Each thinks: "I'm not one to drown myself." They pity the young suicide, admire him, but do not imitate him. Yet *he* found it quite natural to give himself death, deeming nothing on earth able to content him, and aspiring higher.[32] His face is distinguished, his clothing sumptuous. Not yet seventeen? That is young to die!

The paralysed crowd continues to stare fixedly at him. . . . Night is falling. Everyone silently draws back. No one dares turn the drowned man upside down so that he can vomit the water from his body. They are afraid of appearing too responsive, and no one has moved—they shelter in stiff collars. One goes off, shrilly whistling an absurd Tyrolean tune; another snaps his fingers like castanets. . . .

Maldoror, on horseback, and plagued with gloomy thoughts, rides past the place at lightning speed. He catches sight of the drowned man: that is enough. Immediately he halts his steed and has descended from the stirrup. He lifts the youth without disgust and makes him vomit quantities of water. At the thought that this inert body might revive beneath his hands, Maldoror feels his heart give a leap. And this excellent impression (and pressure) give him fresh heart. Vain efforts! Vain efforts, I said, and it's true. The corpse remains inert and lets itself be turned in all manner of ways. He chafes its temples, massages this limb and that, breathes mouth-to-mouth for an hour, pressing his lips against those of the stranger. At last the hand he has laid upon the youth's chest seems to feel a slight beating. The drowned man lives!

At this supreme moment it could be noted that several wrinkles left the horseman's brow, making him look ten years younger. But alas! the wrinkles will return, tomorrow perhaps, or maybe as soon as he departs from the Seine's banks.

Meanwhile the drowned man opens lack-lustre eyes and thanks his benefactor with a pallid smile. But he is still weak and can make no movement.

How fine to save a life! And how the act atones for sins!

The man with lips of bronze, until then engrossed in saving the youth from death, looks at him more closely: the features seem not unfamiliar. He tells himself there is little difference between the fair-haired victim of asphyxia and Holzer. See how effusively they embrace! No matter. The man with jasper eyes persists in keeping up a stern appearance. Without a word he hoists up his friend to ride pillion and the steed gallops off.

O Holzer—you who thought yourself so rational and so strong —have you not seen by your very own example how hard it is in a fit of despair to keep the cool head of which you boast? I hope you will never again cause me such sorrow, and I for my part promise you never to attempt my life.

———

There are times in life when verminous-scalped man trains his wild[33] and staring gaze upon the green membranes of space, for ahead of him he seems to hear the ironic jeers of a phantom. He reels and bows his head: what he has heard is the voice of conscience. Then quick as a madman he rushes in amazement from the house, taking the first route available, and tears along the rugose plains of the countryside. But the yellow phantom does not lose sight of him and just as rapidly pursues.

Sometimes on a stormy night while legions of winged squids (at a distance resembling crows) float above the clouds and scud stiffly toward the cities of the humans, their mission to warn men to change their ways—the gloomy-eyed pebble perceives amid flashes of lightning two beings pass by, one behind the other, and, wiping away a furtive tear of compassion that trickles from its frozen eye, cries: "Certainly he deserves it; it's only justice." Having spoken thus it reverts to its timid pose and trembling nervously, continues to watch the manhunt and the vast lips of the vagina of darkness whence flow incessantly, like a river, immense shadowy spermatozoa that take flight into the dismal aether, the vast spread of their bat's wings obscuring the whole of nature and the lonely legions of squids—grown downcast viewing these ineffable and muffled fulgurations.

But meanwhile the steeplechase with the two indefatigable runners continues, and the phantom belches forth torrents of flame at the human antelope's calcined back. If, during the discharge of this duty he meets Pity wishing to bar his path, he yields to her pleas with repugnance and lets the man escape. The phantom clucks his tongue as if to inform himself that he is giving up the pursuit, and returns to his kennel until further notice. His voice is that of the damned, and is heard at the remotest reaches of space; and when his horrible howls penetrate the human heart, it's said that the latter would rather have "death for mother than remorse for son."[34] He buries his head up to the neck in the earthy intricacies of a hole; but conscience volatilises this ostrich's trick. Like a drop of ether the excavation evaporates; light appears with its retinue of rays like a herd of curlews raining down on clumps of lavender, and the man again finds he is confronting himself with wide-open, colourless eyes.

I saw him make for the seashore, climb a jagged promontory

ringed by brows of spume,[35] and like an arrow dart headlong into the waves. Now for the miracle: next day the corpse reappeared on the surface of the ocean, which bore this fleshy flotsam back to shore. The man freed himself from the mould of sand hollowed by his body, wrung the water out of his dripping hair and dumbly, with lowered brow, resumed life's journey.

Conscience judges our thoughts and most secret acts sternly, and does not err. As she is often powerless to avert evil she ceaselessly runs man like a fox to earth, above all after dark. Avenging eyes which ignorant science calls *meteors* diffuse a livid flame, whirl round each other and utter words of mystery . . . which he understands! Then the bedstead is jarred by jolts from his body (burdened by insomnia's weight) and he listens to the sinister breathing of the night's vague murmurs. The angel of sleep himself, brow mortally stricken by an unknown stone, abandons his task and re-ascends to heaven.

Well then, this time I present myself in man's defence; I, the contemner of all the virtues; I, whom the Creator has been unable to forget since the glorious day when, casting off their plinth heaven's annals—in which were listed, by some infamous form of skulduggery *his* power and *his* eternity—I applied my four hundred suction-cups to the hollow of his armpit and made him shriek hideously. . . . The screams turned into vipers on leaving his mouth, and went to lie in ambush by day and by night, in scrub and inside ruined walls. These screams, creeping now, and endowed with countless coils, small flattened heads, and treacherous eyes, have sworn to bar the path of human innocence; and when the latter wanders through the tangled undergrowth or upon the other side of the slopes or over the sand dunes, she will not take long to change her outlook. If, however, there is still time to do so; for occasionally man perceives the poison seeping into the veins of his leg via an almost imperceptible bite before he has had time to retrace his steps and make off. Thus does the Creator, maintaining an admirable coolness even when confronted with the most atrocious sufferings, know how to extract harmful germs from the very bosoms of earth's inhabitants.

How astonished he was to see Maldoror, changed into an octopus, clamp eight monstrous tentacles about his body: any one of these strong thongs could easily have spanned the circumference of a planet. Caught off guard, he struggled for several moments against this viscous embrace which was contracting more and more. . . .

I feared some mischief on his part. After abundant suckling on the globules of this sacred blood, I detached myself abruptly from his majestic body and hid in a cavern which remained my home thereafter. After fruitless searches he could not find me. All this was long ago; but now I think he knows where I dwell; he takes care not to go back there. We both live like two neighbouring monarchs who know their respective strengths, cannot vanquish one another, and are weary of the useless battles of the past. He fears me and I him: each, while unconquered, has sustained heavy blows from his adversary, and there we let things rest. I am ready, however, to resume the fray whenever he wishes. But let him not await some moment favourable to his secret plans. I shall always stand on my guard, keeping an eye on him. Let him never more send conscience and her tortures to earth. I have shown men the weapons with which she can advantageously be fought. They are not yet familiar with her, though you know that to me she is but a straw in the wind. That's as much store as I set by her. If I wished to take advantage of the occasion that presents itself, by refining these poetical discussions, I would add that I attach more value to the straw than to conscience, for straw is of use to the kine champing it, while conscience knows only how to display her steel claws. Claws which experienced a painful setback the day they came up against me.

As conscience had been sent by the Creator, I thought fit not to let her stand in my way. Had she introduced herself with the modesty and humility appropriate to her station and from which she ought never to have departed, I would have harkened to her. I did not like her pride. I held out one hand and my fingers pulverised her claws: they crumbled to dust under the increasing pressure of this new kind of mortar. I extended my other hand and tore off her head. Then, whipping her, I hounded the woman from my house and have not seen her since. Her head I kept as a souvenir of my victory. . . .

Holding a head whose skull I gnawed, I stood like the heron on one foot at the brink of a precipice scored into the mountain-side. Men saw me descend to the valley, while the skin of my chest was still and calm as the lid of a tomb!

Holding a head whose skull I gnawed, I swam in the sea's most dangerous whirlpools, skirted deadly reefs, and plunged deeper than the currents, to be an alien spectator at battles between marine monsters. I bore off from shore till land was lost to my piercing gaze, and hideous stingrays with their paralysing magnetism prowled round my limbs (which smote the waves with sturdy strokes), not daring to draw nearer. I was seen returning safe and sound to the beach while the skin of my chest was still and calm as the lid of a tomb!

Holding a head whose skull I gnawed, I climbed the winding stairs of a high tower. Weary-limbed I reached its vertiginous platform. I gazed upon the countryside, the sea; gazed upon sun and firmament. My foot spurning the granite (which did not budge), I defied death and divine vengeance with a supreme howl and hurled myself like a paving-stone into the maw of space. Men heard the painful and reverberant crash that resulted from the ground's encounter with the head of conscience, which I had dropped in my fall. They saw me descend, slow as a bird, borne on an invisible cloud, and pick up the head—to force it to witness a triple crime I was to commit that very day, while the skin of my chest was still and calm as the lid of a tomb!

Holding a head whose skull I gnawed, I headed for the spot on which stand the stakes supporting the guillotine. Beneath the blade I placed the graceful, smooth necks of three young girls. Executioner now, I let go the rope with the apparent experience of a whole lifetime, and the triangular knife, dropping obliquely, lopped three heads that looked at me meekly. Then I laid my own beneath the heavy razor and the headsman made ready to accomplish his duty. Thrice the blade, with renewed vigour, sliced down between its slots; thrice my physical body—especially at the base of the neck—was shaken to its foundations, as when in dream one fancies oneself crushed by a collapsing house. The dumbfounded multitude made way so I could leave the grisly place—and saw my elbows part its undulating waves, as I moved forward, full of life, my head held erect, while the skin of my chest was still and calm as the lid of a tomb!

I had said that I wished to defend man this time, but I fear my apologia may not be the expression of truth, and prefer, consequently, to hold my tongue. Mankind will applaud this measure with gratitude!

It is time to curb my inspiration and to pause a while along the way, as when one looks at a woman's vagina. It is good to inspect the course already run, and then, limbs rested, to dart forward with an impetuous bound. To complete a stage of a journey in a single breath is not easy, and the wings become very weary during a high flight without hope and without remorse. No . . . let us lead the haggard mattock-and-trench mob no deeper through the explosible mines[36] of this impious canto! The crocodile will change not a word of the vomit that gushed from his cranium. It can't be helped if some furtive shadow, roused by the laudable aim of avenging the humanity I have unjustly attacked, surreptitiously opens the door of my room and, brushing against the wall like a gull's wing, plunges a dagger into the ribs of the wrecker, the plunderer of celestial flotsam![37] Clay might just as well dissolve its atoms in this manner as in another.

3

Let us recall the names of these imaginary beings of angelic nature whom my pen, during the second canto, has drawn from a brain brilliant with a radiance emanating from themselves. They die stillborn, like sparks whose rapid obliteration the eye can scarcely trace, upon the burnt paper. Leman! . . . Lohengrin! . . . Lombano! . . . Holzer! . . . for an instant, covered again with the insignia of youth you appeared on my charmed horizon. But I let you fall back like diving-bells into chaos. You shall leave it never more. For me it is enough to have retained the memory of you. You must make room for other substances, less beautiful perhaps, and spawned by the stormy excesses of a love that has resolved not to slake its thirst anywhere near the human race. A ravenous love, that would devour itself did it not seek nourishment in celestial fictions: creating, in time, a pyramid of seraphim more numerous than insects swarming within a drop of water, it will intertwine them into an ellipse which it will cause to whirl around itself. Meanwhile, if the traveller, pausing at the sight of a cataract, raises his head, he will see in the distance a human being being borne towards the cave of hell by a garland of living camellias! But . . . silence! The floating image of the ideal fifth outlines itself slowly, like the blurred folds of an aurora borealis, upon the vaporous map of my intelligence, and takes on a growing, definite consistency. . . .

Mario and I were riding along the beach. Our horses, their necks taut, cut through the membranes of space and struck sparks from the shingle. The wintry blast hit us full on, flapping our cloaks, and sweeping back the hair on our twin heads. The seagull strove vainly with screams and wing-beats to warn us of the storm's possible proximity, and cried out: "Where are they going at that mad gallop?" We said nothing; sunk in reverie, we let ourselves be carried away, flying off on this furious course. The fisherman, seeing us pass swift as the albatross, and realising that he saw speeding past him *the two mysterious brothers* (as they had been called, since they were always together), hastened to cross himself and hid with his helpless, fear-stricken dog deep beneath a rock.

The inhabitants of the coast had heard tell of strange things concerning these two characters, who would appear on earth amid clouds during eras of great calamity, whenever a dread war threatened to plant its harpoon in the breasts of two enemy countries, or when cholera was preparing to catapult putrescence and death into entire cities. The oldest beachcombers would frown gravely, affirming that the two phantoms—whose vast black wingspan each of them had noticed during hurricanes, above sand-bank and reef—were the spirit of the land and the spirit of the sea, who would parade their majesty amid the skies during great revolutions of nature, united in an eternal amity the glory and rarity of which have bred astonishment in the generations' indefinable chain.

It was said that, flying side by side like two Andean condors, they liked to glide among the strata of the atmosphere adjacent to the sun; that in these regions they fed upon the purest essences of light; but that they would decide only reluctantly to lower the incline of their vertical flight towards the dismayed orbit where the human globe deliriously turns—inhabited by cruel spirits who massacre one another on fields where battle roars (when they do not kill each other treacherously, secretly, in the midst of towns, with the dagger of hatred or ambition), and who feed upon beings as full of life as themselves but placed a few rungs lower on the ladder of existence.

Or else, when the pair firmly resolved—in order to excite men to repentance through the strophes of their prophecies—to swim with great strokes towards the sidereal regions where, amid dense exhalations of avarice, pride, cursing, and mockery reeking like pestilential vapours from its hideous surface, that planet moved, seeming as small as a *boule* and almost invisible because of the distance, they would not fail to find occasions on which they bitterly regretted their (misunderstood and decried) benevolence and would go and hide in volcanoes' depths to converse with the everlasting lava that boils in the vats of the central vaults, or to the sea bed, there to let their disillusioned gaze rest pleasantly upon the most ferocious monsters of the deep, which to them appeared models of mildness compared with the bastards of mankind.

When, with her propitious obscurity, night fell, they leapt from porphyry-crested craters of submarine currents, and left very far behind them the rocky chamber-pot in which heaves the constipated anus of the human cockatoo—until they could no longer discern the suspended silhouette of the filthy planet. Then—grieved by their fruitless attempt—amid the compassionate stars and under the eye of God—the angel of the land and the angel of the sea kissed, weeping! . . .

Mario and he who galloped beside him were not unaware of the vague and superstitious rumours which the coastal fishermen recounted in whispers, behind bolted doors and windows, during their evenings round the hearth, while the night wind, wanting to warm itself, vents its whistlings about the straw shacks, vigorously shaking these frail walls whose foundations are encrusted with fragments of shells washed ashore by the dying wrinkles of the waves.

We did not speak. What do two hearts that love each other say? Nothing. But our eyes expressed everything.

I warn him to wrap his cloak closer about him, and he points out to me that my horse is moving too far ahead of his. Each takes as much interest in the other's life as in his own. We do not laugh. He endeavours to smile at me, but I see that his countenance bears the weight of the terrible impressions engraved there by reflection—constantly bent over the sphinxes which with sidelong glance baffle the mortal intellect and its great agonies. Seeing his manoeuvres are useless, he averts his eyes, champs his earthly bit with the spittle of rage, and looks at the horizon that flees at our approach.

In my turn I try to remind him of his gilded youth which seeks only to progress like a queen through the palace of pleasures. But he notices that my words emerge with difficulty from my emaciated mouth, and that the years of my own springtime have passed, sad and glacial like a relentless dream which brings to banqueting tables and satin beds wherein (paid with glistening gold) the pale priestess of love slumbers, the bitter delights of disenchantment, old age's pestilential wrinkles, solitude's shocks, and the torches of woe.

Seeing my manoeuvres are useless, I am not surprised I cannot make him happy. The Almighty appears before me adorned with his instruments of torture, in all the glorious aureole of his horror; I turn away my eyes and look at the horizon that flees at our approach. . . .

Our horses galloped along the shore as if fleeing from the human eye. . . .

Mario is younger than I. The weather's humidity and the salty spray that splashes up at us bring the cold in contact with his lips. I tell him: "Take care! . . . Take care! . . . keep your lips tightly closed. . . . Don't you see the keen, chapping claws that score your skin with smarting wounds?" He stares straight at me and retorts, with tongue movements: "Yes, I see them, those green claws, but I shan't unsettle the natural disposition of my mouth to dispel them. See if I'm lying. Since it seems to be the will of Providence, I'll conform to it. Providence's will could have been better." And *I* cried out: "I admire this noble vengeance." I wanted to tear out my hair but with a stern glance he forbade me and I respectfully obeyed him.

It was growing late, and the eagle was returning to its eyrie hollowed from the rock's anfractuosities.

Mario told me: "I am going to lend you my cloak to protect you from the cold: I don't need it." I retorted: "Woe betide you if you do as you say. I don't want another to suffer in my stead, and above all not you." He did not reply, because I was right, but for my part I began to console him, on account of the over-impulsive tone of my words. . . .

Our horses galloped along the shore as if fleeing from the human eye. . . .

I again raised my head like a ship's prow lifted by an enormous wave, and said to him: "Do you weep? Tell me if you can, king of snows and mists. I see no tears on your face—beautiful as the cactus-flower—and your eyelids are dry as the riverbed. Yet I discern in your eyes' depths a vat full of blood, in which your innocence boils—its neck bitten by the large species of scorpion. A violent wind rakes the fire which reheats the copper tun, and scatters dim flames even outside your sacred orbit.[38] My hair neared your rosy brow and I smelled burning because the hair had caught fire. Close your eyes, or else your face, cindered like volcanic lava, will crumble to ash upon my palm."

He, however, turned towards me, paying no heed to the reins he held in his hand, and gazed at me with great tenderness while closing, opening, his lily eyelids like the ebb and flow of the sea. He badly wanted to answer my bold question, and did so thus: "Take no notice of me. Just as the river-mists creep up along the hillside and then, at the summit, melt into the atmosphere forming clouds, so your anxieties on my behalf have imperceptibly increased without reasonable motive, and form—beyond your imagination—the delusive body of a desolate mirage. I assure you that there is no fire in my eyes, although I do feel as if my skull had sunk into a helmet of blazing coals. How can you suppose the flesh of my innocence aboil in that vat, for I hear only very faint and confused cries which to me are but the wailings of the wind passing over our heads? It is impossible for a scorpion to have set up house and set its sharp pincers into my seamed eye-socket. I think, rather, that these are powerful pliers which pulverise the optic nerves. I am, however, of your opinion that the blood filling the vat has been extracted from my veins by an invisible executioner, during last night's sleep. I have awaited you a long time, beloved son of the ocean; and my drowsing arms engaged in a vain combat with whoever crept into the vestibule of my house. . . . Yes, I feel that my soul is bolted into my body and cannot free itself to flee far from beaches beaten by the human sea, and be no longer witness to the ghastly pack of calamities which without respite, across the quagmires and abysses of boundless dejection, pursues the human izard. But I do not complain. I received life like a wound, and I have forbidden suicide to heal the scar. I want the Creator—every hour of his eternity—to contemplate its gaping crevasse. This is the punishment I inflict upon him.

"Our steeds slow down the pace of their brazen hooves; their bodies tremble, like a hunter startled by a drift of peccaries. They must not start listening to what we say. Their intelligence would grow by dint of attention and they might perhaps be able to understand us. Woe betide them, for they would suffer still more! Indeed, only consider the wild boars of mankind: does not the degree of intelligence that separates them from the other beings in creation seem to have been afforded them only at the irremediable price of incalculable sufferings? Follow my example, and let your silver spurs sink into your steed's flanks. . . ."

Our horses galloped along the shore as if fleeing from the human eye. . . .

Here comes the madwoman, dancing, while she dimly remembers something. Children drive the crone off with volleys of stones as if she were a crow.[39] She brandishes a stick and looks like chasing them, then sets off again on her way. She has left a shoe behind and of this she remains unaware. Long spider's legs stir upon her nape: these are naught but her hair. Her face no longer resembles the human face and she bursts into fits of laughter like a hyena. She lets slip shreds of sentences which, re-stitched, would afford very few any clear meaning. Full of holes, her dress flaps fitfully about her bony and mudstained legs. She drives herself onward like a poplar leaf blown along by the whirlwind of unconscious powers—she, her youth, her illusions and the past happiness she glimpses again through the mists of a demolished mind. She has lost her pristine grace and beauty; her bearing is base and her breath reeks of brandy.

If men were happy on this earth, one ought then to be astonished. The madwoman makes no reproaches, she is too proud to complain and will die without having revealed her secret to those interested in her but whom she has forbidden to address her.

Children drive the crone off with volleys of stones as if she were a crow.

She has dropped a scroll of paper from her bosom. A stranger picks it up, locks himself in his room all night and reads the manuscript which runs as follows:

"After many barren years Providence sent me a daughter. For three days I knelt in churches and did not cease giving thanks to the great name of Him who had at last answered my prayers. I suckled the one who was more than my life on my own milk, and saw her grow apace, endowed with every quality of soul and body. She would say to me: 'I'd like a little sister to play with. Ask God to send me one, and to pay him back I'll wind him a garland of violets, mint, and geraniums.' My only answer was to raise her to my breast and kiss her lovingly.

"She was already interested in animals, and would ask me why the swallow is content to skim across the cottages of humans without daring to enter in. But I would lay a finger at my lips as if to tell her to keep quiet about this serious question whose details I did not yet want her to understand, in order not to impress an extreme sensation upon her childish imagination; and I hastened to change the subject—one painful to discuss for any being belonging to that race which has extended an unjust domination over the other animals in creation. When she spoke to me of the graves in the cemetery, saying that in this atmosphere one inhaled pleasant scents of cypress and immortelle, I refrained from contradicting her, but I did tell her that it was the town of birds, that there they sang from dawn till dusk, the graves their nests, where at night, lifting up the marble slabs, they slept with their kin.

"I sewed all the dear little clothes she wore, as well as the lace things with a thousand arabesques, which I reserved for Sundays. In winter she had her rightful place on the hearth, for she took herself very seriously, and during the summer the meadow once more knew the dulcet pressure of her footsteps when with her silken net fastened to a cane's tip she would venture forth after the independent hummingbirds and the butterflies with their teasing zigzags. 'What have you been up to, little vagabond, while your soup waited an hour with its spoon growing impatient?' But she would exclaim, flinging her arms round my neck, that she would not go back there any more. The next day she would wander off anew through the daisies and mignonettes; amid the sunbeams and the mayflies' swirling flight; knowing only the prismatic glass of life—not yet its gall; happy to be bigger than the titmouse; making fun of the warbler for not singing as well as the nightingale; slyly sticking out her tongue at the nasty crow who would watch her paternally; and graceful as a kitten.

"I was not to delight in her presence for long. The time was approaching when, in an unexpected manner, she would bid farewell to life's charms, and abandon forever the company of turtle-dove, hazel-grouse, and greenfinch, the prattle of tulip and anemone, the counsels of the marsh-grass, the rasping wit of the frogs and the freshness of the brooks. They told me what had happened, for I did not witness the incident which resulted in my daughter's death. If I had, I would have defended that angel at the price of my very blood. . . .

"Maldoror was passing by with his bulldog. He saw a young girl sleeping in a plane tree's shade and at first he took her for a rose. . . . None can conjecture whether the sight of this child or his resultant resolution rose foremost to his mind. He undressed rapidly, like a man who knows what he is about. Naked as a stone, he flung himself upon the young girl's body and pulled up her dress to attempt her virtue . . . in broad daylight! Not at all embarrassed, not he! Let us not dwell on this foul deed. His mind discontent, he dressed hurriedly, glanced cautiously at the dusty, deserted track, and ordered the bulldog to choke the blood-stained child with a snap of its jaws. He pointed out for the mountain dog the spot where the suffering victim gasped and wailed, and drew aside out of sight so as not to witness the sharp teeth sinking into those rosy veins.

"Carrying out this order appeared to be hard for the bulldog. He thought his master was telling him to do what had already been done, and this wolf with monstrous muzzle in turn satisfied himself by violating this delicate child's virginity. The blood from her lacerated abdomen ran once again down her legs and on to the meadow. Her moans mingled with the animal's whining. The maid held up the gold cross she wore round her neck, so that he might spare her; she had not dared exhibit it to the savage eyes of him who had first thought of taking advantage of her tender years. But the dog well knew that if he disobeyed his master a knife thrown out of a sleeve[40] would swiftly, without warning, rip open his guts.

"Maldoror (how loathsome to utter the name!) heard the death-pangs and was amazed that the victim was so hard to kill[41] and was still not dead. He approached the sacrificial altar and saw the behaviour of his bulldog—surrendering to the lowest instincts and raising its head from the girl as a drowning man raises his above the wrathful waves. He kicked the dog and split open one eye. The crazed bulldog raced off across the countryside dragging after him—along a stretch of track that however short would always be too long—the little girl's dangling body, which was only disentangled thanks to the jerky motions of the flight; but the dog was scared to attack his master, who was not to see him again.

"Maldoror drew from his pocket an American penknife with ten or a dozen blades serving diverse purposes. He opened the angular paws of this steel Hydra and, equipped with one like a scalpel, and seeing that the greensward had not yet disappeared—dyed by so much spilled blood—readied himself without blanching to grope bravely inside the unhappy child's vagina. From this enlarged trough he removed the internal organs, one after the other: intestines, lungs, liver, and finally the heart itself were ripped from their roots and pulled out through the frightful aperture into the light of day. The sacrificer perceived that the girl—a drawn chicken—had died long ago. He cut short the increasing persistence of his ravages and let the corpse again sleep in the plane tree's shade.

"The knife was found lying a few steps away. A shepherd witnessed the crime—whose perpetrator was not discovered—and only told of it long afterwards when he had ascertained that the criminal had safely reached the frontier and that he himself need no longer dread the retribution certain to overtake him should he reveal all.

"I pitied the madman who committed this heinous, unprecedented crime which the legislators had not predicted. I pitied him because it is unlikely that he was in his right mind when he wielded the dozen-edged dagger, ploughing completely through the stomach lining. I pitied him because if he were not mad his shameful conduct must have hatched out a great hatred for his fellows in order to rage so rabidly against the flesh and blood of a harmless child, who was my daughter. I attended the burial of these human remnants with mute resignation; and every day I come to pray over a grave."

On concluding his reading, the stranger can no longer keep his senses, and faints. He comes to, and burns the manuscript. He had forgotten this souvenir of his youth (habit blunts the memory!); and after twenty years' absence he returned to this fatal land. He will not buy a bulldog!... He will not talk to shepherds!... He will not go and sleep in the plane trees' shade!...

Children drive the crone off with volleys of stones as if she were a crow.

Tremdall has shaken for the last time the hand of him who is voluntarily leaving, forever fleeing, forever fleeing the image of man the pursuer.[42] The Wandering Jew[42a] tells himself that if earth's sceptre belonged to the race of crocodiles he would not flee thus. Tremdall, standing in the valley, has raised one hand to his eyes to focus the solar rays and make his sight keener, while his other hand palpates the bosom of space, arm horizontal and immobile. Leaning forward (the statue of friendship) he watches (with eyes mysterious as the sea) the gaiters of the traveller (aided by his iron-shod staff) climbing up the gradient of the hill. The earth seems to give way beneath Tremdall's feet and even had he so wished he could not have held back his tears and his feelings:

"He is far away. I see his silhouette mounting a narrow path. Where's he going with that heavy step? He himself does not know.... Yet I am convinced I am not sleeping. What is it approaching and going to meet Maldoror? How huge this dragon is ... bigger than an oak! You would say that its whitish wings, jointed by tough ligaments, had nerves of steel so easily do they smite the air. Its body starts with a tiger's torso and ends in a long serpent's tail. I have not been accustomed to such sights. What is that on its brow? I see written there in a symbolic language a word I cannot decipher. With a final wingbeat it draws close to him whose tone of voice I know well. And says: 'I was awaiting you, and you me. The hour is come. Here I am. Read on my brow my name writ in hieroglyphics.'

"But no sooner had Maldoror seen the enemy than he turned into an enormous eagle, and now he prepares for battle, contentedly clacking his curved beak as if to say that singlehanded he undertakes to devour the dragon's hindquarters. See how they describe ever-diminishing concentric circles, sounding out each other's tactics before fighting. They're wise to do so. The dragon seems the stronger to me. I would like him to win victory over the eagle. I shall undergo strong emotions during this spectacle in which a part of my own being is involved. Potent dragon, I shall spur you on with my cries if necessary, since it is in the eagle's own interest that he be defeated.

"Why are they waiting to attack? I am in mortal dread. Come, dragon, you first, begin the onslaught. You've just struck him a hard blow with your talons: not at all bad. I assure you the eagle must have felt it—the wind bears off some of his beautiful feathers, bloodstained now. Ah! The eagle tears out one of your eyes with his beak, and you, you had only ripped his skin. You should have paid heed to that. Bravo, take your revenge, break one of his wings! Needless to say, your tiger's teeth are pretty good. If only you could get near the eagle while he wheels in space, hurtling down towards the fields! I notice this eagle, even when falling, fills you with caution. He is on the ground, he won't be able to fly up again. The sight of all these gaping wounds intoxicates me. Fly in at ground level, around him, and finish him off if you can with blows of your scaly serpent's tail. Take heart, good dragon, dig your strong claws in, and may blood mingle with blood and form streams where no water runs. Easy to say but not to do. Due to the untoward reverses of this memorable struggle the eagle has just devised a new defence strategy; he is cagey. He is squatting securely in an unshakeable position upon his remaining wing, his two thighs, and his tail which

previously served him as rudder. He defies exertions more extraordinary than those he has so far faced. Now he turns as quick
as a tiger, with no sign of exhaustion; now he lies on his back with
his two powerful feet in the air and coolly, ironically, stares at
his adversary. In the long run I *must* know who will be the victor:
the battle cannot last for ever. I am thinking of its consequences!
The eagle is terrible and makes tremendous leaps that jar the
earth, as if he were about to take flight—yet he knows this is
impossible. The dragon distrusts these leaps: he thinks that at
any moment the eagle will attack him on the side where he has
lost an eye. . . . Alas for me! That is what does happen. How did
the dragon let himself be seized by the breast? He may try in vain
to use cunning and force, for I see that the eagle, all his limbs
clinging leech-like to the dragon's, and despite fresh wounds he
sustains at the base of his neck, is burying his beak deeper and
deeper into the dragon's belly. Only his body is visible. He seems
to be at ease—in no hurry to emerge. Doubtless he seeks something,
while the tiger-headed dragon utters bellows that awaken the
forests. Here is the eagle now, withdrawing from this cavern.
Eagle, how vile you are! You are redder than a lake of blood!
Although in your virile beak you hold a palpitating heart, you
are so covered in wounds that you can hardly stand upright upon
your feathered feet, and stagger without unclenching your beak,
beside the dragon who is dying in frightful agonies. Victory has
been hardwon; no matter, you gained it: one must at least relate
the truth. . . . In shedding your eagle's shape you act according
to the rules of reason, as you move off from the dragon's
carcass.

"Thus then, Maldoror, did you conquer! Thus then, Maldoror,
did you conquer *Hope*! Henceforth despair shall feed upon your
purest substance! Henceforth, by deliberate steps, you return
to the course of evil! In spite of my being, so to speak, indifferent
to suffering, the last blow you dealt the dragon has not failed to
affect me. Judge for yourself whether I suffer! But you scare me.

See—see in the distance that man fleeing. Through him (excellent seedbed!) malediction has sprouted its bushy foliage. He is accursed, and curses. Where do your sandals bear you? Where are you going, hesitating like a sleepwalker atop a roof? May your perverse destiny be fulfilled! Farewell, Maldoror! Farewell until eternity, when we shall not meet together again!"

It was a spring day. Birds spilled out their warbling canticles, and humans, having answered their various calls of duty, were bathing in the sanctity of fatigue. Everything was working out its destiny: trees, planets, sharks. All except the Creator!

He was stretched out on the highway, his clothing torn. His lower lip hung down like a soporific cable. His teeth were unbrushed, and dust clogged the blond waves of his hair. Numbed by a torpid drowsiness, crushed against the pebbles, his body was making futile efforts to get up again. His strength had left him, and he lay there weak as an earthworm, impassive as treebark. Gouts of wine swamped the ruts trenched by his shoulders' nervous twitches. Swine-snouted brutishness shielded him with protective wing and cast on him its loving look. Like two blind masts his slack-muscled legs swept the soil. Blood flowed from his nostrils: his face had hit a stake as he fell. . . . He was drunk! Dreadfully drunk! Tight as a tick which has guzzled three tuns of blood in the night! He filled the echoes with garbled comments I will desist from repeating here; even if the Supreme Drunkard has no self-respect, *I* must respect men. If you were to know that the Creator . . . got drunk! Pity this lip besmirched by the goblets of orgy!

A passing hedgehog sank its spines into his back, saying: "Take that! It is noon—work, sluggard, and eat not the bread of others. Wait a while and see what happens when I call the crook-beaked cockatoo."

A passing woodpecker and screech-owl buried their beaks right into his belly, saying: "Take that! What are you doing

here on earth? Have you come to present the animals this lugubrious comedy? I swear to you that neither mole nor cassowary
nor flamingo will imitate you."

A passing ass kicked him on the temple, saying: "Take that!
What did I do to you that you should give me such long ears?
The very crickets scorn me."

A passing toad shot a gob of spittle into his face, saying: "Take
that! If you had not made my eye so huge, and had I perceived
the state in which I see you now, I would chastely have hidden
your limbs' beauty beneath a shower of buttercups, myosotis,
and camellias, that none might see you."

A passing lion bowed a royal head, saying: "For my part I
respect him although his splendour appears to us momentarily
eclipsed. You others who affect haughtiness and are merely
cowards for having attacked him while he slept, how would *you*
in *his* stead enjoy enduring abuse from passers-by—abuse you have
not spared him?"

A passing man stopped in front of the unappreciated Creator
and, to applause from crab-louse and viper, crapped three days
upon that august countenance! Woe unto man for that insult: for
not respecting his defenceless and almost lifeless enemy laid out
in a mishmash of mud, blood, and wine! . . .

Then God the Supreme, woken at last by all these mean insults,
got up again as best he could, reeling, and went to sit on a rock,
arms a-dangle like a consumptive's testicles. He looked upon the
whole of nature, which belonged to him, with lack-lustre spiritless
gaze.

O human beings, you are *enfants terribles*; but I beg you spare
this Great Being who has not yet done sleeping off the effects
of filthy liquor, and who, not having enough strength left to
stand erect, has fallen heavily back against this rock on which,
like a traveller, he is seated.

Observe this passing beggar. He saw that the dervish was
holding out a wasted arm and, without knowing on whom he

bestowed alms, threw a scrap of bread at that hand beseeching pity. The Creator expressed his gratitude by a movement of the head.

Oh! you will never know how difficult a thing it becomes, constantly to be holding the reins of the universe! Sometimes the blood rushes to the head as one strives to wrest from nothingness a last comet with a new race of spirits. The Mind, overstimulated to its very core, retreats like one defeated, and once in a lifetime may well fall into the aberrations you have witnessed!

A red lamp, ensign of vice, hung on the end of a rod and swung its carcass which the four winds lashed, above a massive wormeaten door. A grubby corridor stinking of human thighs gave on to a courtyard where cocks and hens, thinner than their own wings, grubbed for meal. Along the wall that served as the courtyard's enclosure, on the west side, various openings covered by barred grills had been meanly cut. Moss overlaid this main part of the building which had, no doubt, been a convent, and like the rest of the block was now used as an abode by all those women who would daily display, in exchange for a small sum, the interiors of their vaginas to any who entered.

I was on a bridge whose piers sank into the scummy water of a surrounding moat. From its raised vantage-point I beheld on the plain this structure askew with age, and the minutest details of its inner construction. Now and then the grill of a crib would rise gratingly as if from the upward impetus of a hand that outraged the iron's nature: a man's head would appear at the half-cleared aperture, then his shoulders thrust forward and on them flaking plaster would fall before, by arduous heaving, his body followed, covered in cobwebs. Placing his hands like a crown upon refuse of every kind piled on the ground, while his leg was still caught in the twisted rails, he would reassume his normal posture, go to dip his hands in a rickety bucket whose soapy water had seen whole generations rise and fall, and then hurry away as quickly as possible from these suburban slum alleys to breathe the pure air near the town centre. When the client had left, a stark naked woman would emerge in the same manner, and make for the same bucket. There from various parts of the courtyard the cocks and hens would come thronging, attracted by the seminal odour, and knock her to the ground despite her vigorous struggles, trampling over her body as on a dunghill and pecking the flaccid lips of her swollen vagina till the blood came. Hens and cocks, gullets glutted, would go back to scratching at the courtyard grass; the woman, clean now, would get up trembling, covered in wounds, as when one wakes from a nightmare. She would drop the rag she had brought for drying her legs and, having no further need of the communal bucket, return to her lair as she had left it, to await another job.

These scenes made me, too, long to enter that house! I was about to descend from the bridge when I saw upon the entablature of a pillar the following inscription in Hebrew characters: "Ye who pass over this bridge, go not yonder. There crime sojourns with vice. One day his friends in vain awaited a youth who had crossed that fatal gate."

Curiosity prevailed over fear: after a few moments I reached a grating whose grill had solid, closely criss-crossed bars. I wanted to peer inside through this thick mesh. At first I could see nothing: but it did not take me long to distinguish the objects in the dark chamber, thanks to the fading beams of the sun soon about to disappear below the horizon.

The first and sole thing which met my gaze was a flaxen pole composed of interlocking cones. This pole was moving! It was walking round the room! Its jolts were so forceful that the floor shook; with either tip it tore enormous breaches in the wall and seemed like a battering-ram one slams against the gate of a beleaguered town. Its efforts were useless: the walls were built of ashlar, and whenever it beat at the partition-wall I saw it bend like a steel blade and rebound like a rubber ball. So the staff was not made of wood! Then I noticed it coiled and uncoiled with ease, like an eel. Although tall as a man it did not stand straight. Sometimes it tried to, and would present one end at the barred grating. It would make impetuous bounds, fall to the ground again, and be unable to stave in the obstacle. I began to observe it more and more intently and I saw that it was a hair! After a great struggle with the matter penning it in like a prison, it leaned upon the bed that was in the room, root resting on a rug and tip set against the bed-head. After a few moments of silence punctuated by broken sobs, the hair raised its voice and spoke as follows:

"My master left me behind in this room. He does not come looking for me. He rose from this bed whereon I lie, combed his perfumed locks, and did not think I had earlier fallen to the ground. Yet had he picked me up I would not have found this act of plain justice astonishing. He is abandoning me mewed up within this room after being himself enveloped in a woman's arms. And what a woman! The sheets are still moist from their lukewarm contact and in their disorder bear the impress of a night spent in love. . . ."

And I wondered who his master might be! And I glued my eye to the grating still more eagerly!

"While all of nature chastely slumbered, *he* coupled with a dissolute woman in impure and lewd embraces. He so debased himself as to let faded, shrivelled cheeks, contemptible for their habitual shamelessness, meet his august countenance. He did not blush, but *I* blushed for him. It is obvious that he felt happy sleeping with this bride of one night. The woman, amazed at this guest's majestic demeanour, seemed to be enjoying matchless ecstasies and was frenziedly kissing his neck."

And I wondered who his master might be! And I glued my eye to the grating still more eagerly!

"I, meanwhile, was conscious of inflamed pustules in growing numbers—owing to my master's unwonted ardour for the fleshly lusts—that encircled my root with their deadly venom, absorbing through their suckers the generative substance of my life. The more the couple abandoned themselves to their crazed motions, the more I felt my strength ebb. At the moment in which carnal desires reach a paroxysm of passion I perceived that my root was crumpling, doubling up like a soldier wounded by a bullet. Life's torch extinguished in me, I broke away from his illustrious head like a dead branch. I fell to the ground without heart, without strength, without vitality, but feeling a deep pity for him to whom I belonged—and yet with everlasting sorrow at his voluntary lapse! . . ."

And I wondered who his master might be! And I glued my eye to the grating still more eagerly!

"If at least his soul had encompassed the innocent bosom of a virgin. She would have been worthier of him and the degradation less. His lips kiss that sullied brow which men have ground with dusty heels! . . . His impudent nostrils inhale the emanations of those two dank armpits! . . . I saw the membranes of the latter contract in shame, while for their part the nostrils jibbed at this foul respiration. But neither he nor she paid any heed to the armpits' solemn warnings, to the nostrils' wan and dismal aversion. She lifted her arms higher, and with a stronger thrust he buried his face in their hollows. I was forced to be party to that profanation. I was forced to be spectator of that outrageous contortion; to take part in the strained amalgam of these two beings whose different natures were separated by a measureless gulf. . . ."

And I wondered who his master might be! And I glued my eye to the grating still more eagerly!

"When satiated with sniffing at the woman, he wanted to rip out her muscles one by one. But since she was a woman he spared her, preferring to inflict pain on someone of his own sex. He summoned to the neighbouring crib a young man who had come to the brothel to while away some carefree moments with one of the women, and enjoined this young man to come and stand one pace in front of him. I had been lying a long time on the ground.

Not having the strength to raise myself up on my smarting root, I could not see what they did. All I know is, hardly was the young man within arm's reach before shreds of flesh fell from either end of the bed and came to rest beside me. They whispered to me that my master's claws had torn them from the youth's shoulder. The youth, after several hours of fighting a stronger foe, rose from the bed and retired majestically. He was literally flayed alive from head to foot; along the flagstones of that room he dragged his hide—turned inside out. He kept saying to himself that his disposition was full of goodness, that he liked to believe his fellow men good too; for this reason he had acquiesced in the wish of the distinguished stranger who had called him to approach, but never, *never*, had he expected to be tortured by an executioner. 'By such an executioner,' he added, after a pause. At length he made his way to the grating, which out of pity split itself right down to ground-level when confronted with this body bereft of epidermis. Without abandoning his skin, which might still be of use to him, if only as a cloak, he tried to leave this cutthroats' den. Once he was clear of the room I could not see whether he had had the strength to regain the bolt-hole. Oh! how the cocks and hens, despite their hunger, respectfully shunned that long trail of blood upon the sodden earth!"

And I wondered who his master might be! And my eyes were glued to the grating still more eagerly! . . .

"Then he who should have further reflected upon his dignity and justice wearily propped himself up on an exhausted elbow. Alone, gloomy, disgusted, and hideous! . . . He dressed slowly. Nuns, buried centuries ago in the convent catacombs, after being rudely awakened by the sounds of that horrible night reverberating throughout a crib situated above the vaults, took each other by the hand and formed a funereal ring around him. While he sought the rubble of his former splendour; while he washed his hands with spittle and wiped them on his hair (it was better to wash them with spittle than not at all, after spending a whole night in vice and crime), the nuns intoned woeful prayers for the dead, as when someone is lowered into the grave. Indeed, the young man could not have survived the torture inflicted upon him by a divine hand, and his death-throes came to an end during the chanting of the nuns. . . ."

I recalled the inscription on the pillar, and I understood what had become of the pubescent dreamer whose friends still awaited him every day since the time of his disappearance. . . .

And I wondered who his master might be! And my eyes were glued to the grating still more eagerly!

"The walls drew aside to let him pass. The nuns, seeing him take flight into the air with the wings which he had hitherto hidden under his emerald robe, silently took up position once again beneath the tomb-lids. He departed to his heavenly abode, leaving me here: it's not fair. The other hairs stayed on his head, and *I* lie here in this gloomy room, its flooring covered in clotted blood and scraps of dry meat. This room is accursed now, since he wormed his way into it. No one enters it. Yet I am imprisoned here. The worst has happened, then! Never more shall I see the angelic legions marching in serried phalanxes, nor stars wandering through the gardens of harmony. Well, so be it. . . . I shall know how to bear my misfortune with resignation. But I shall not fail to tell men what happened in this crib. I shall give them permission to reject their dignity like a needless garment, since they have my master's example I shall advise them to suck the prick of crime, since *another* has already done so. . . ." The hair fell silent.

And I wondered who his master might be! And my eyes were glued to the grating still more eagerly!

Immediately there was a clap of thunder. A phosphorescent flash irrupted into the room. Through some instinctive admonition I shrank back despite myself. Although I stood back from the grating I heard another voice, this time fawning and low for fear of being overheard:

"Don't bound about so! Be quiet. . . ! be quiet! What if someone were to hear you? I will put you back among the other hairs, but first let the sun sink below the horizon so that the night may cover your tracks. . . . I have not forgotten you, but someone would have seen you leave and I'd have been compromised! Oh! if you only knew how I have suffered since that moment! When I returned to heaven my archangels surrounded me full of curiosity: they would not ask me the reason for my absence. They, who had never dared gaze up at me, cast aghast looks at my drawn face, striving to guess the riddle although they did not get to the bottom of the mystery, and whispered among themselves opinions fearfully anticipating some unwonted change in me. They wept silent tears; they felt vaguely that I was no longer the same, had become inferior to my identity. They would have liked to know what fatal resolution had made me cross the frontiers of heaven in order to hurl myself upon earth and taste ephemeral delights which they themselves deeply despised. They observed on my brow a drop of sperm and a drop of blood. The former had spurted forth from the courtesan's thighs! The latter had gushed from the martyr's veins! Hateful stigmata! Resolute rosettes! My archangels had recovered the dazzling debris of my opal tunic—hanging in the copses of space—where it floated over multitudes agape. They were unable to mend it and my body remains naked before their innocence: memorable punishment for lost virtue. See the furrows which have made a bed for themselves in my colourless cheeks: it is the drop of sperm and the drop of blood slowly trickling down my wizened wrinkles. When they arrive at the upper lip they make a great effort and enter the sanctuary of my mouth drawn as if to a magnet by my irresistable weasand. They choke me, these two implacable drops. Hitherto I had believed myself the Almighty—but no—I must bow before Remorse who screams at me: 'You're nothing but a sorry scoundrel!'

"Don't bound about so! Be quiet. . . be quiet! What if

someone were to hear you? I will put you back among the other hairs, but first let the sun sink below the horizon so that the night may cover your tracks. . . .

"I saw Satan, the great enemy, straighten the bony structure of his frame, heave from his larval torpor and erect, triumphant, sublime, harangue his reassembled hosts—and hold me up to ridicule as I deserve. He said he was greatly amazed that his haughty rival, caught *in flagrante delicto* through the success (at last achieved) of perpetual espionage, could so debase himself as to kiss the robe of human debauch after a long voyage across the reefs of the aether, and to cause the death in agony of a member of humanity. He said that this young man trapped in the toils of my subtle tortures might perhaps have become a genius and solaced men on earth for misfortune's blows with admirable songs of poetry, of courage. He said that the nuns of the convent-brothel could sleep no more and wander about the courtyard gesticulating like automata, trampling buttercups and lilacs underfoot; that they have gone mad from indignation, but not mad enough to forget what caused this disease of their brains. . . . (Here they come, again wrapped each in their white shroud; they do not speak together; they hold one another by the hand. Their hair falls in disorder upon their bare shoulders; each has a bouquet of black flowers drooping against her breast. Nuns, go back to your vaults, night has not yet quite descended; it is only dusk. . . . O hair, you can see for yourself: on all sides I am assailed by the unfettered sense of my depravity!) He said that the Creator who boasts of being the Providence of all that exists conducted himself with considerable levity (to say no more) in presenting such a sight to the starry worlds—for he clearly affirmed his intention of reporting among the orbicular planets just how, by my own example, I uphold virtue and goodness in the vastness of my kingdoms. He said that the great esteem in which he had held so noble an enemy had vanished from his imagination and that though it might be an act of execrable mischief, he preferred to

set his hand on a young girl's breast than to spit in my face
(covered as it was by three commingled layers of blood and sperm)
in order not to sully his slavering saliva. He said he believed himself rightly superior to me, not through vice, but virtue and
modesty; not through crime, but justice. He said that for my
countless sins I ought to be tied to a hurdle, burned slowly over a
red-hot brazier, and afterwards hurled into the sea—if the sea
would have me. That, since I boasted of being just—I, who for a
trifling revolt that had had no serious consequences, had condemned him to everlasting torments—I should, then, administer
strict justice upon myself and impartially judge my conscience
fraught with iniquities. . . .

"Don't bound about so! Be quiet . . . be quiet! What if
someone were to hear you? I will put you back among the other
hairs, but first let the sun sink below the horizon so that the night
may cover your tracks."

He paused for a moment. Although I could not see him I
understood from this necessary hiatus that his breast heaved on
emotion's swell, as a whirling cyclone sweeps up a school of
whales. Divine bosom one day besmirched by the bitter contact
of a shameless woman's teats! Royal soul surrendered in one for-
getful instant to the crab of debauch, the octopus of weakness of
character, the shark of individual abasement, the boa of absent
morals, and the monstrous snail of idiocy! The hair and its master
embraced each other tightly like two friends who meet again
after a long absence. The Creator continued—as the accused
appearing before his own tribunal:

"And what will men think of me, of whom they used to have
so high an opinion, when they learn about the vagaries of my
behaviour, the hesitation of my footsteps along the muddy
labyrinths of Matter, and the direction of my gloomy route over
the stagnant waters and dank reeds of the pool where amid the
mists dark-footed crime howls and turns blue! . . . I see that in
future I shall have to work hard at rehabilitating myself so as to

regain their esteem. I am the Most High and yet on one count I remain inferior to men, whom I created with a handful of sand! Tell them a brazen lie, tell them I never left heaven, have been constantly caught up with the cares of the throne, among the marbles, statues, and mosaics of my palaces. I appeared before the heavenly sons of men and said to them:

" 'Drive evil from your dwellings and let the cloak of virtue enter your abode. Let him who raises his hand against one of his fellows—fatally wounding his breast with murderous steel—not hope for the workings of my mercy, and let him dread the scales of justice. He will go to hide his sadness in the woods, but the leaves' rustle across the glades will sing the ballad of remorse in his ears and he will flee from those regions, his flank pricked by briar, holly, and alpine sea-holly, his swift steps impeded by the suppleness of liana and the sting of scorpion. He will head for the shingly beach but the rising tide with its spindrift and dangerous onrush will warn him that it is aware of his past; and he will hasten his blind dash towards the cliff summit whilst the strident equinoctial winds striking into the gulf's natural grottoes and the quarries cut below a wall of echoing rock, will bellow like huge herds of pampas buffaloes. The coastal lighthouses will chase him with their caustic beams to hyperborean reaches, and the will-o'-the-wisp of the maremmas—mere fiery vapours—by their fantastic dances will cause his pores' hairs to twitch with fear, and turn the irises of his eyes green. . . . May modesty thrive within your cottages and be safe in the shadows of your fields. Thus shall your sons wax fair and obey their parents with gratitude; otherwise, puny and stunted like the parchment in libraries, and led on by revolt, they shall march with great strides against the day of their birth and the clitoris of their "impure mother". How will men want to obey these stern laws if the legislator himself is the first to refuse to conform to them? . . . And my shame is vast as eternity!' "

I heard the hair humbly forgive his master for his confinement, since the latter had acted with caution, not thoughtlessness. And the last pale ray of sun playing on my eyelids receded from the mountain ravines. Turning towards the hair, I saw him coil up like a shroud. . . .

Don't bound about so! Be quiet! . . . be quiet! What if someone were to hear you? He will put you back among the other hairs. And now that the sun has set on the horizon, climb, both of you—cynical greybeard and sweet hair—out of the brothel, while night, spreading her shadow over the convent, covers the full length of your furtive steps upon the plain. . . .

Then the louse, jumping out suddenly from behind the headland and putting up its claws, said to me: "What think you of that?"

But I had no wish to answer him. I left, and reached the bridge. I obliterated the original inscription and replaced it with this: "It is painful as a dagger, keeping such a secret in one's heart, but I swear never to reveal what I witnessed when for the first time I entered this terrible dungeon."

I threw over the parapet the pocket-knife I had used to carve the letters, and made some brief speculations upon the dotage of the Creator who, alas!, would be causing humanity to suffer for a long time to come (eternity is long), either through cruelties inflicted or through the vile spectacle of the chancres spawned by a great vice. I closed my eyes like a drunken man at the thought of having such a being for an enemy, and was on my way again sadly, through the labyrinthine streets.

———

4

A man or a stone or a tree is about to begin the fourth canto. When the foot slithers on a frog one feels a sensation of disgust, but one's hand has barely to stroke the human body before the skin of the fingers cracks like flakes from a block of mica being smashed by hammer blows; and even as the heart of a shark an hour dead still palpitates on the deck with dogged vitality, so are we stirred to our very depths long after the contact. Such is the horror man inspires in his own neighbour! Perhaps I am mistaken to propose this, but perhaps too I am telling the truth. I know of, conceive, a sickness more terrible than the eyes swollen from long meditations upon the strange nature of man: but I am seeking it still . . . and have been unable to find it! I do not consider myself less intelligent than anyone else, and yet who would dare assert that I have succeeded in my investigations? What a lie would escape his lips!

The ancient temple of Denderah lies an hour and a half away from the left bank of the Nile. Today countless phalanxes of wasps have taken possession of its gutters and cornices. They swarm round the columns like dense waves of black hair. Sole inhabitants of the cold porch, they guard entrance to the ante-chambers as a hereditary right. I liken the humming of their metallic wings to the incessant clash of ice-floes flung against one another during the breaking-up of the polar seas. But if I ponder the conduct of him on whom Providence has conferred this earth's throne, the three pinions of my grief give vent to a louder murmur!

When at night a comet suddenly appears across part of the sky after an absence of eighty years, it displays to earth-dwellers and to the crickets its brilliant and nebulous tail. Doubtless it has no consciousness of this long journey. Not so with me: elbows propped on my bolster, while the jagged outlines of a barren and bleak horizon loom into being in the depths of my soul, I am engrossed in dreams of compassion and I blush for mankind!

Cut in two by the North wind, the sailor, having kept his night watch, hastens to get back to his hammock: why is this consolation not offered me? The idea that I have voluntarily fallen as low as my fellow men and have less right·than anyone else to utter complaints about our lot (which remains shackled to the hardened crust of a planet) and our perverse soul's essence, pierces me like a forge nail. One has seen fire-damp explosions annihilate entire families; but their sufferings were brief because death was almost instantaneous amid the rubble and poisonous gases: *I* exist forever, like basalt! In the middle as in the beginning of life, the angels resemble themselves: how long ago it is since I resembled myself!

Man and I, immured in the limits of our intelligence as a lagoon often is within a belt of coral islands, instead of joining our respective forces to defend ourselves against mischance and ill-fortune, move away from one another trembling with hate, and take opposite directions as if each had wounded the other on the point of a dirk! It might be said that the one understands the contempt he inspires in the other; driven by the incentive of a related dignity, we take pains not to lead our adversary into error; each keeps to his separate way and is aware that were peace declared it would be impossible to preserve. Well, agreed! Let my war against man last forever, since each recognises his own degradation in the other . . . since the pair are mortal foes. Whether I win a Pyrrhic victory or succumb, the combat will be noble: I alone against humanity. I shall not use weapons made of wood or iron; my foot shall spurn the layers of

minerals extracted from the earth: the harp with its potent
and seraphic sonority shall at my touch become a formidable
talisman.

In more than one ambush man, that sublime ape, has already
pierced my breast with his porphyry spear: a soldier does not
display his wounds, however glorious they may be. This terrible
war will bring sorrow to both parties: two friends stubbornly
trying to destroy one another, what a drama!

Two pillars, that it was not difficult—and still less possible—to
take for baobab trees, were to be seen in the valley, taller than two
pins. Actually they were two enormous towers. And although
at first glance two baobabs do not resemble two pins, nor even
two towers, nevertheless, while cleverly pulling the strings of
prudence one can affirm without fear of error (for if this affirmation were accompanied by a single iota of fear it would no longer
be an affirmation; although the same name expresses these two
phenomena of the spirit which present characteristics distinct
enough not to be lightly confused) that a baobab is not so different
from a pillar as to prohibit comparison between these architectural
forms . . . or geometric forms . . . or both . . . or neither . . .
or rather, raised and massive forms. I have just found—I don't
even claim the contrary—the proper adjectives for the nouns
pillar and baobab: let it be known that it is not without joy
mingled with pride that I address the remark to those who, after
waking again, have taken the very commendable resolution to
scan these pages while the candle burns—if it be night, or while
the sun shines—if day.

And again, even if a higher power should command us in the
plainest, most precise terms to cast back into the abyss of chaos
the judicious comparison which everyone has certainly been
able to savour with impunity, even then, and then above all, let
none lose sight of this principal axiom: habits acquired through
the years, books, contact with one's fellows, and the innate

character of each person who develops in a quick efflorescence—
these would impose on the human spirit the irreparable stigma
of relapse into the criminal use (criminal, that is, if one momentarily
and spontaneously sees it from the higher power's point of
view) of a rhetorical figure many despise, but which many
eulogise.

If the reader finds this sentence too long, I trust he will accept
my apologies; but let him expect no servilities from me. I can
acknowledge my faults, but not make them graver by my
baseness.

My reasonings will sometimes clash head on with the jester's
bells of folly and the serious appearance of what is, in short,
merely grotesque (although according to certain philosophers it
is quite difficult to distinguish the jester from the melancholic,
life itself being a comic drama or a dramatic comedy); however,
everyone is allowed to kill flies and even rhinoceroses in order to
rest occasionally from over-arduous work. Here is the most
expeditious, though not the best, way to kill flies: one crushes
them between thumb and forefinger. Most writers who have
treated this subject thoroughly have calculated with great plausi-
bility that in a number of cases it is preferable to cut off their
heads.

Should anyone reproach me for speaking of a radically frivo-
lous subject such as pins, let him note without prejudice that the
greatest effects have often been produced by the smallest causes.
And so as not to deviate still further from the framework of this
piece of paper, is it not evident that this laboured piece of literature I am bent on composing since the start of this stanza would,
perhaps, be relished less had it taken as fulcrum some knotty
problem of chemistry or internal pathology? Besides, nature
caters to all tastes; and at the beginning when I compared pillars
to pins with so much accuracy (indeed, I did not think that one
day I would be upbraided for it), I based my observation on the
laws of optics, which have established that the further the line of

sight from the object, the smaller the image reflected on the retina.

Thus that which our minds' bent for farce takes to be a wretched witticism is generally, in its author's imagination, only an important truth majestically proclaimed! Oh! that asinine philosopher who burst out laughing when he saw a donkey eating a fig! I invent nothing: ancient books have related in the greatest detail this wilful, shameful deprivation of human nobility. *I* know not how to laugh. I have never been able to laugh, although I have tried it a number of times. It is very difficult to learn how to laugh. Or rather, I think that a feeling of repugnance for this monstrosity forms an essential characteristic of my personality. Well, I have witnessed something even more outrageous: I have seen a fig eating a donkey! And yet I did not laugh; frankly, no buccal portion stirred. I was seized by so strong an urge to weep that my eyes let fall a tear, "Nature! Nature!" I cried out, sobbing, "The sparrow-hawk rends the sparrow, the fig eats the donkey, and the tapeworm devours man!"

Without resolving to go further, I am really wondering whether I spoke of the way to kill flies. I did, didn't I? It is no less true that I did *not* speak of the destruction of the rhinoceros! If certain of my friends were to claim the contrary I would not listen to them, and would recall that praise and flattery are two great stumbling-blocks. However, so as to satisfy my conscience as much as possible, I cannot help pointing out that this dissertation on the rhinoceros would lead me beyond the bounds of patience and composure and in itself would probably (let us in fact have the audacity to say "certainly") dishearten present generations. Not to have spoken of the rhinoceros after the fly! At least for a passable excuse I should promptly have mentioned (and did not do so!) this unpremeditated omission, which will astonish no one who has seriously studied the real and inexplicable contradictions that inhabit the lobes of the human brain. To a noble, simple intellect, nothing is unworthy: the least phenomenon of nature, if it hold mystery, gives the sage inexhaustible food for thought. If anyone sees a donkey eat a fig or a fig eat a donkey (these two incidents do not often occur, except in poetry) you may be sure that after two or three minutes' reflection in order to know what course to take, he will abandon the way of virtue and begin to crow with laughter like a cock![43]

Again, has it not been correctly proved that cocks open their beaks to imitate man and pull a cockeyed face? What I call grimace in birds bears the same name among men! The cock does not stray from its nature—less from incapacity than pride. Teach them to read and they rebel. This is no parrot—which would be in ecstasies before its ignorant or unforgivable weakness! Oh! loathsome degradation! How like a goat one is when one laughs! The calm brow has disappeared to make way for two enormous fishes' eyes which (is it not deplorable?) . . . which . . . begin to shine like lighthouses!

I often happen to state, solemnly, the most clownish propositions. . . . I do not find that that provides a peremptorily sufficient reason for expanding the mouth! "I cannot help laughing", you will answer me; I accept this absurd explanation, but let it be a melancholy laugh, then. Laugh, but weep at the same time. If you cannot weep with your eyes, weep with your mouth. If this is still impossible, urinate. But I warn you, some sort of liquid is needed here to attenuate the drought which sidesplit-pundit laughter carries in her womb.[44] As for me, I shall not let myself be put out by the comical clucking[45] and odd bellows of those who always find some fault in a character unlike their own, because this is one of the innumerable intellectual modifications that God, without departing from the primal model, created to regulate our bony frames.[46]

Until today poetry was on the wrong track. Rising up to heaven or grovelling on the ground, it has misunderstood the principles of its existence and has been, not without reason, constantly derided by upright folk. It has not been modest . . . the finest quality that ought to exist within an imperfect being! *I* want to display my good qualities, but am not hypocrite enough to hide my vices! Laughter, evil, pride, folly, will appear in turn, between compassion and love of justice, and will serve—to mankind's stupefaction—as examples. Everyone will recognise himself herein, not as he should be but as he is. And perhaps this simple ideal conceived by my imagination will yet surpass all that poetry has hitherto deemed most imposing and most sacred. For if in these pages I let my vices leak out, people will only believe more strongly in the virtues I cause to glitter here and whose halo I'll set so high that the greatest geniuses of the future will sincerely express their grateful recognition of me.[47] Hypocrisy will thus be driven firmly from my abode. And so as to scorn accepted opinions, there will be in my lyrics an impressive proof of force and authority.

He sings for himself alone and not for his fellow men. He does not weigh his inspiration upon human scales. Free as the storm, some day he shall run aground upon the indomitable shores of his terrible will! He fears nothing, unless it be himself! In his supernatural battles he shall successfully assault man and the Creator, as when the xiphias sinks its sword into the whale's belly. Accursed —by his children and by this emaciated hand of mine—be he who persists in not understanding the implacable kangaroos of laughter and the bold lice of caricature! . . .

Two enormous towers were to be seen in the valley; this I stated at the start. Multiplying them by two, the product was four . . . but I could scarcely perceive the need for this arithmetical process. I continued on my way with fevered brow, crying out incessantly: "No . . . No . . . I can scarcely perceive the need for this arithmetical process!" I had heard the clanking of chains, and sad groans. May no one, passing this spot, find it possible to multiply the towers by two so that the product be four! Some surmise that I love mankind as if I were its own mother and had borne it nine months in my perfumed womb: this is why I never again pass through the valley whence rise the two units of the multiplicand!

A gibbet grew from the ground. One yard below its bar, hung by his hair, swung a man whose hands were tied behind his back. His legs had been left loose to aggravate his anguish and lead him to long for any torment other than that of trussed arms. The skin on his brow, so tensely stretched by his own weight on the pulley, pulled his face (forced by ill-luck to lack its natural look) into resembling the silted stone of a stalactite. He had suffered this torture three days. Was howling, "Who'll untie my arms, my hair! With each move I dislocate my bones, but my hair is severed more sorely from my scalp. Hunger and thirst aren't the principal problems preventing sleep. Impossible for my existence to prolong itself beyond the bounds of another hour! Someone slit my throat with a sharp flint!"

Each word was prefaced and followed by piercing shrieks.

I bounded from the bush behind which I had sheltered, and rushed towards that puppet or slice of pork slung from the scaffold. But two drunk women came dancing from the opposite side, one holding a sack and two whips tipped with lead, the other, a tub full of tar, and a pair of brushes. The elder woman's frayed grey locks floated in the wind like fragments of a torn veil, while the other's clogs clattered like the slaps of a stranded tuna's tail on a ship's poop deck.

Their eyes blazed with so black, so strong a flame, that at first I did not believe they belonged to my species. They laughed with such selfish self-assurance, and their appearance inspired such repugnance, that I didn't for one instant doubt I was confronting two of the most hideous specimens of the human race. Again I hid behind the bush, and kept quite quiet, like the *acantophorus serraticornis*, which shows only its head outside its nest. At tide speed they approached. Applying my ear to the soil, I distinctly discerned the pounding sound of their liquidly lyrical lope.

When these two female orang-outangs got to the gallows, they sniffed the air for a few seconds. They then registered by absurd gibbers, the truly remarkable degree of stupefaction resultant from their perception that nothing about the place had changed. Death, the dénouement they here desired, had not occurred. They did not deign to look up and see if the salami still swung in the same spot. One said: "Can you possibly be breathing still, my beloved spouse? You *are* an old diehard." As when two choristers in a cathedral intone in turn verses of a psalm, the second continued: "You don't want to die, my precious son? Tell me what sort of witches' ruse you used to scare off the vultures! And how skinny your carcass is, it swings in the wind like a lantern!"

Both took brushes to tar the hanging body. . . . Then whips, which they raised together. It was impossible not to admire the vigorous precision with which the metal strips, instead of slipping upon the skin's surface (as when in nightmare one battles a black-amoor and makes vain attempts to seize his hair), struck, thanks to the tar, into the flesh's core, slashing furrows as deep as the bones' more resistant obstacle could reasonably allow. I have refrained from the temptation of taking a voluptuous view of this very bizarre episode—though less profoundly comical than anyone had a right to expect. Yet despite good resolutions made before-hand, how could their female force, or the muscles of their fore-arms, be ignored? Imperative to mention that skill in their manner of selecting the most sensitive parts, face and groin, if I lay claim to tell absolute truth.

Unless, by application of my lips one upon the other, mainly in horizontal mode (but then everyone knows this to be the normal method giving rise to the said pressure), I prefer to preserve a tearful silence, mysteriously mute, whose painful manifestation may prove impossible to conceal—not only as well as but still better than my speech (for I assume I am right in thinking that although one should certainly not deny on principle, at risk of wrecking those most elementary rules of aptitude, the hypothetical possibilities of error), the deadly results caused by that fury which sets in motion the dry metacarpus and sturdy joints: however even without adopting the position of impartial observer or experienced moralist (almost as important for me to learn I do not admit, at least in sum, this more or less faulty limitation), doubt, on that score, would lack facilities to put down its roots—for at present I do not presume it to be the prey of a supernatural power—and would inevitably perish, perhaps not precipitately, failing some sap that might at once fulfil both the conditions of nutrition and absence of toxic matter. It's understood, or if not do not read me, that the shy thespian I set on stage is merely my own opinion: far be it from me, then, to think of relinquishing undoubted rights! My intention is certainly not to assault that affirmation, in which glitters the criterion of certitude, that it is a simple means of making oneself plain: it would consist (and I interpret it with few words, fitter than a thousand) in not arguing—more difficult to put into practice than the average mortal generally prefers to believe. Argue is the grammatical term, and many persons will find it prudent not to take issue, without a dossier of data, with what I have just committed to paper. But things notably differ if it's permissible to grant to one's own instinct the employment of a rare sagacity in service of its circumspection, when (rest assured) it formulates judgments otherwise apparently so impudent they border on braggadocio.

To end this little incident, itself deprived of pith by a flippancy as irremediably deplorable as it is fatally full of interest (and no one, provided he has deeply plumbed his most recent memories will have failed to verify as much), it is well, if faculties possessed are poised in perfect equilibrium, or better still, if the balance of lunacy does not too greatly outweigh the scale on which rest Reason's noble and magnificent qualities, that is to say, somewhat to clarify the matter, since until now I've been nothing if not concise, a fact some may not admit because of my periphrases, which are only illusive for they fulfil their function: with the scalpel of analysis to track down the fleeting appearances of truth as far as their final trenches. If the intellect sufficiently subdues deficiencies under whose weight it has been in part stifled by habit, nature, and education, it is well, I repeat for the second and last time, for by dint of repetition we shall end, and this is true more often than not, in incomprehension—to return with my tail (if it's even true I have one) between my legs, to the solidly dramatic tale within this stanza.

Useful to drink a glass of water before I undertake to pursue my work. I prefer to drink two, rather than do without. Thus, during the pursuit of a runaway slave through the forest, at a suitable moment each member of the posse suspends musket upon lianas and all unite in common need to slake their thirst and ease their hunger in the shade of a clump of shrubs. But the pause is only seconds long, the chase is resumed with frenzy and the yells re-echo. So, even as oxygen is recognisable through its property (possessed without pride) of relighting a match which presents several glowing points, you will recognise the accomplishment of my duty by the zeal I reveal in returning to the point.

When the two females found it impossible any longer to grip their whips, which fatigue let slip from their hands, they judiciously ended the gymnastic labours they had been performing for the past two hours, and withdrew with a joy not devoid of further, future threats. I advanced toward him who called to me for help with glazing gaze (his loss of blood was so profuse that weakness prevented speech, and though I am no doctor, I diagnosed a haemorrhage apparent in face and groin). After unbinding his arms I cut his hair with a pair of scissors.

He told me that one evening his mother had summoned him to her bedroom and ordered him to strip and spend the night with her there, in the one bed. Without awaiting a reply this matron had doffed all her clothes, posturing before his eyes with the most shameless gestures. At which he withdrew to bed. But by his constant refusals he had drawn on himself his wife's wrath, she who'd deluded herself with hope of reward if she could succeed in getting her husband to agree to lend his body to the old hag's lusts. The pair plotted together to hang him from a gibbet prepared earlier, in some deserted spot, and leave him to die slowly, exposed to every wretchedness and danger. They finally managed, not without many considered reflections full of insurmountable difficulties, to lure their chosen victim to the refined torture—unfinished until the unexpected aid of my intervention. The liveliest signs of gratitude marked his every expression, lending additional value to his confidences. I carried him to the nearest cottage, for he had fainted, and left the peasants only after leaving them my purse, to purchase comforts for the wounded man, and after I made them promise to lavish upon the unfortunate—as though on their own son—the proofs of patient understanding.

In turn, I told them the tale, and made for the door to take up my journey, but after going a few hundred yards I automatically retraced my steps, set foot once more in the cottage, and, addressing its simple tenants, cried: "No, no . . . don't imagine all this surprises me!"

And this time I departed for good, though the soles of my feet could not plant themselves firmly down: no one else could have noticed this fact!

The wolf no longer passes below the gallows which the joined hands of a mother and a wife set up one spring day, a path he used, in his haunted imagination, to take, on the way to an illusory meal. When he sees on the skyline this black scalp, racked by the wind, he plays down his power of inertia, and takes flight with incomparable speed. Are we to see in this psychological phenomenon an intellect superior to that of ordinary instinctive mammals? Without even conjecturing or attesting anything it seems to me that this animal understood the nature of crime! How could he fail to, when human beings themselves have rejected so indescribably the realm of Reason in order to let live—in place of this dethroned Queen—nothing but savage revenge!

I am filthy. Lice gnaw me. Swine, when they look at me, vomit. The scabs and sores of leprosy have scaled off my skin, which is coated with yellowish pus. I know not river water nor the clouds' dew. From my nape, as from a dungheap, an enormous toadstool with umbelliferous peduncles sprouts. Seated on a shapeless chunk of furniture, I have not moved a limb for four centuries. My feet have taken root in the soil forming a sort of perennial vegetation—not yet quite plant-life though no longer flesh—as far as my belly, and filled with vile parasites. My heart, however, is still beating. But how could it beat if the decay and effluvia of my carcass (I dare not say body) did not abundantly feed it?

In my left armpit a family of toads has taken up residence, and whenever one of them moves it tickles me. Take care lest one escape and come scratching with its mouth at the interior of your ear: it could next penetrate into your brain.

In my right armpit there is a chameleon which endlessly chases the toads so as not to die of hunger: everyone has to live. But when one side completely foils the tricks of the other, they find there's nothing better than making themselves at home and sucking the dainty grease that covers my sides: I am used to it.

A spiteful viper has devoured my prick and taken its place. This villain made a eunuch of me. Oh! if only I could have defended myself with my paralysed arms—but I rather think they have turned into logs. Be that as it may, it is vital to note that in them blood no longer pulses redly.

Two small fullgrown hedgehogs flung to a dog—which did not decline them—the contents of my testicles; inside the scrupulously scrubbed scrotal sac they lodged.

My anus has been blocked by a crab. Encouraged by my inertia, it guards the entrance with its pincers and causes me considerable pain!

Two jellyfish crossed the seas, at once enticed by a hope which did not prove mistaken. They closely inspected the twin buttocks which comprise the human rump and, fastening on to these convex contours, so squashed them by constant pressure that the two lumps of flesh disappeared while the two monsters which issued from the kingdom of viscosity remained, alike in colour, form, and ferocity.

Speak not of my spinal column, since it is a sword. Yes, yes . . . I wasn't paying attention . . . your question is fair. You want, don't you, to know how a sword comes to be set vertically down my back? I myself remember it none too clearly. Yet if I decide to treat as a memory what may be but a dream, bear in mind that man, when he discovered I had vowed to live diseased and motionless until I had overcome the Creator, crept up on tiptoe behind me—but not so softly that I did not hear him. For a split second I knew no more. This sharp whinyard buried itself to the hilt between the shoulder-blades of the fighting bull, whose frame shuddered like an earth tremor. The blade cleaves so stubbornly to the body that no one so far has been able to extract it. Athletes, artificers, philosophers, doctors, in turn have tried the most diverse methods. They were not to know that the evil done by man can no longer be shrugged off! I forgave them for the depth of their inborn ignorance and hailed them by flickering my eyelids.

Traveller, when you pass near, do not, I beg you, offer me the slightest word of consolation: you would undermine my spirit. Let me rekindle my resolve at the flame of voluntary martyrdom. Be off! . . . lest I inspire pity in you. Hate is stranger than you think; its workings are inexplicable, like the broken look of a stick thrust into water. Even as you see me now I can still make forays to the very walls of heaven, heading a legion of assassins, and return to resume this posture and meditate anew upon lofty plans of vengeance. Farewell—I shall detain you no longer, and that you may train and protect yourself, ponder the fatal destiny which drove me to revolt, though, perhaps, I was born good!

You will tell your son what you have seen and, taking his hand, set him wondering at the beauty of the stars and the marvels of the universe, at the robin's nest and the temples of the Lord. You will be amazed to see him so amenable to paternal advice, and will reward him with a smile. But take a look at him when he is unaware of being watched and you'll see him hawk spittle at virtue. He has deceived you—he who is descended from the human race—yet he shall deceive you no more: henceforth you shall know what happens to him. O hapless father, be ready for these escorts of your senile tread—the irreversible scaffold that is to lop off a precocious criminal's head, and sorrow that will show you the road leading to the grave.

What shadow, with an incomparable power, etches on the wall of my room the weird projection of its crisp silhouette? When I put this mute, delirious question to my heart[48] it is not so much because of the shape's majesty, nor for the depiction of reality, but rather that the sobriety of the style comports itself in such fashion.

Whoever you are, defend yourself, for I am going to catapult a terrible accusation at you: those eyes do not belong to you . . . where did you get them? One day I saw a fair-haired woman pass before me; she had eyes like yours: you tore them from her.

I see that you would lead people to believe you beautiful; but no one is fooled—myself least of all. I tell you this lest you take me for an oaf. A whole series of birds of prey, lovers of others' flesh and upholders of the utility of pursuit, beautiful as the skeletons that thin the panoccos[49] of Arkansas, hover about your brow like approved and dutiful servants. But is it a brow? It is not hard to encounter considerable hesitation in thinking so. "It" is so low that it is impossible to verify the proofs—numerically exiguous—of "its" equivocal existence. I do not tell you this for my own amusement. Perhaps you have no brow, you who lead along the wall—like the ill-considered[50] symbol of a fantastic dance—your feverishly rattling lumbar vertebrae. Who then has scalped you? If it was a human being—because you incarcerated him for twenty years in a prison—and who escaped so as to prepare a revenge worthy of his reprisals, he has done as he should, and I applaud him; but—and there is a but—he was not harsh enough. Now you resemble a Red Indian prisoner, at least (let us note this before all else) through your expressive lack of hair. Not that it won't grow again, since physiologists have discovered that in the course of time even the brains of animals reappear after their removal. But my thought, halting at[51] a simple statement that is not, from the little I know of it, devoid of a tremendous delight, does not even in its boldest inferences go as far as the borders of a wish for your recovery, and remains, on the contrary, entitled through the implementation of its more than suspect neutrality, to consider (or at least to wish) as presage of greater ills, what can be for you only a temporary loss of the hair which covers the top of your head.

I hope you have understood me.

And even were chance to allow you, by an absurd but some-times unfair miracle, to rediscover that precious scalp which the scrupulous vigilance of your enemy kept as intoxicating souvenir of his victory, it is almost highly likely that even had one studied the law of probability only with regard to mathematics (we know that the analogy can easily apply to other fields of intelligence) your rightful—if somewhat exaggerated—fears of a partial or total chill would not reject the important and even unique opportunity that would present itself in so opportune, though brusque, a manner of protecting the various parts of your brain from contact with the atmosphere (especially in wintertime) with a coiffure which since it is natural rightly belongs to you and which, moreover, you would be allowed (it would be incompre-hensible if you denied yourself it) to keep constantly upon your head without running the always disagreeable risks of infringing the simplest rules of an elementary decorum.

Is it not true that you are listening to me attentively?

If you listen further, sadness will far from slip away from inside your red nostrils. But as I am very impartial and do not hate you as much as I should (tell me if I am mistaken), you should lend an ear to my discourse despite yourself, as if impelled by a higher force. I am not as wicked as you: that is why your genius bows down of its own accord before mine. . . . Indeed I am not as wicked as you! You have just had a look at the city built on this mountainside. And now what do I see? . . . All the inhabitants are dead! I have as much pride as anyone, and that makes another vice: having, perhaps, still more of it. Very well, listen . . . hear me, if the confession of a man who remembers living half a century in the shape of a shark among the submarine currents that hug the African coast interests you deeply enough for you to give him your attention, if not with bitterness, at least without the irreparable error of showing the disgust I inspire in you. To appear before your eyes as I really am, I shall not cast virtue's mask at your feet for I have never worn it (if that is any excuse); and if from the very first you observe my features closely you will recognise me as your respectful disciple in perversity but not as your deadly rival. Since I do not contend with you for the palm of evil, I don't think anyone else will: they ought first to match me, which is not easy. . . . Listen, unless you are merely the thin condensation of a mist (you are hiding your body somewhere and I cannot meet with it):

One morning I saw a little girl bending beside a lake to pluck a pink lotus. She kept balance firmly, with precocious experience. She was leaning toward the water when her eyes met mine (it is true that where I was concerned this was not without premeditation). Immediately she reeled back like the whirlpool the tide generates round a rock, her legs gave way and—marvellous to see—phenomenon that took place as sure as I'm talking to you now—she sank to the bottom of the lake: the strange consequence is, she no longer gathers any nymphaeaceae. What is she doing down there? . . . I have not enquired. Doubtless her will, arrayed beneath the banner of deliverance, wages desperate battle against decomposition!

But O my master, at *your* glance inhabitants of cities are suddenly destroyed, like anthills crushed by an elephant's heel. Have I not just witnessed a conclusive example? See . . . the mountain is no longer blithe . . . it stands there lonely as an old man. True, the houses still exist, but it is no paradox to state in an undertone that you could not say as much for their occupants, who no longer exist. The corpses' effluvia are already reaching me. Don't you smell them? Look at those birds of prey waiting for us to go away so they can begin this gigantic feast; a continual cloud of them comes from all over the horizon. Alas! They had already arrived, for I saw their rapacious wings trace above you a monument of spirals, as if to excite you to expedite the crime. Is not your sense of smell conscious of the slightest exhalation? The impostor is nothing else. . . . Your olfactory nerves are at last stirred by the perception of aromatic atoms: these rise from the annihilated city, although I need not tell you that. . . .

I would like to embrace your feet but my arms enfold only a transparent vapour. Let us seek this undiscoverable body, which, however, my eyes perceive: from me it deserves innumerable signs of my sincere admiration.

The phantom mocks me: he helps me search for his own body. If I motion him to stay where he is, he makes the identical sign back. . . . The secret is out. But not, I must frankly add, to my greatest satisfaction. All is explained, important details as well as small; the latter are too immaterial to bear in mind—as, for example, tearing out the fair-haired woman's eyes: why, that's practically nothing! . . .

Did I not recall that I too had been scalped, although it was only for five years (the exact length of time had escaped me) that

I clapped a human being into prison in order to witness the spectacle of his sufferings because he had refused me—and rightly—a friendship not bestowed on beings like myself? Since I pretend to be unaware that my stare can deal death, even to planets spinning in space, anyone claiming that I do not possess the faculty of memory will not be wrong.

What's left for me to do is smash that mirror into smithereens with the help of a rock. . . . This is not the first time that the nightmare of temporary loss of memory set up its mansion of delay in my imagination[52] when, by the inflexible laws of optics, I happen to be confronted with the failure to recognise my own reflection!

I was asleep on top of the cliff. He who has chased an ostrich through the desert for a day without being able to catch it has not had time to take sustenance or close his eyes. If that man read me now, he is, at a pinch, likely to guess what drowsiness was weighing me down. But when the storm, with the palm of its hand, has thrust a vessel vertically to the bottom of the sea; if, on that raft, only one man out of the entire crew remains, broken by weariness and every kind of privation; if the billow belabours him like flotsam for hours longer than the life of man; and if a frigate later ploughing through these desolate latitudes of staved keels sights the unfortunate whose wasted carcass bobs upon the ocean, and brings him help that is almost too belated, I believe this shipwrecked fellow would understand still better the degree to which the drowsiness of my senses was carried. Mesmerism and chloroform, when they take the pains to do so, sometimes know how to bring on similar lethargic catalepsies. They bear no resemblance to death: it would be an outright lie to say so. But let us get to the dream without delay, so that the impatient— hungry for this sort of reading—do not start bellowing like a school of macrocephalous sperm-whales fighting among themselves over a pregnant female.

I dreamed that I had entered the body of a hog, that it was not easy to extricate myself, and that I was wallowing—my bristles in the muddiest marshes. Was this a reward, the aim of my desires, that I no longer belonged to humanity?! Thus *I* interpreted it, and thence experienced a more than profound joy. However, I was busily hunting for whatever deed of virtue I had performed to deserve this signal favour on Providence's part. Now that my memory has gone over the various phases of this frightful flattening[53] against the granite's belly, during which the tide twice passed without my noticing it over an irreducible mixture of dead matter and living flesh, it is perhaps not futile to proclaim that this degradation was probably only a punishment inflicted upon me by divine justice. But who knows his intimate needs or the cause of his plaguy joys? To my eyes the metamorphosis never appeared as anything but the exalted and magnanimous echo of a perfect happiness I had long awaited. It had come at last, the day I became a hog! I tried out my teeth on tree-bark; my snout I contemplated with delight. Not the least whit of divinity remained: I knew how to raise my spirit level with the excessive height of that ineffable sensual bliss.

Hear me then, and do not blush, endless caricatures of the beautiful, who take the laughable braying of your supremely contemptible souls seriously, and who do not understand why the Almighty in a rare moment of splendid buffoonery which certainly does not exceed the great general laws of the grotesque, one day had the mirific pleasure of populating a planet with singular microscopic beings called *humans* whose substance resembles that of rosy coral. You are indeed right to blush, bones and fat, but hear me out. I do not invoke your intelligence: you would make it spout blood out of the horror it evinces for you. Forget it, and be consistent with yourselves. . . . There, no more constraint! When I wanted to kill, I killed; that very thing happened often and no one restrained me. Human laws still pursued me with their vengeance although I did not attack the race I had so calmly abandoned. But my conscience reproached me not at all.

During the day I would fight with my new fellow creatures and the soil was saturated with countless coats of clotting blood. I was the strongest and gained all the victories. Stinging wounds covered my body: I pretended not to notice them. Earthly animals shunned me and I stayed alone in my resplendent grandeur. Great was my astonishment when, after swimming across a river in order to depart the countries my fury had depopulated and to reach other regions—there to instil my customs of murder and carnage—I tried to walk upon that flowery bank. My feet were paralysed; no movement came and betrayed the verity of that forced immobility. It was then, amid uncanny efforts to continue on my way, that I awoke and realised I had become a man again. Thus Providence made me understand, in a not inexplicable manner, that she did not wish my sublime plans to be fulfilled, even in dream. Resuming my pristine shape was for me so great a sorrow that at night I still weep over it. My sheets are constantly soaked as if they had been dipped in water, and every day I have them changed. If you do not believe it, come and see me; you will verify from your own experience, not the probability but the truth itself of my assertion.

How often, after that night spent on a clifftop under the stars, have I not mingled with herds of swine to resume, as my right, my ruined metamorphosis!

It is time to abandon these glorious memories, which leave in their wake only the pale Milky Way of everlasting regrets.

It is not impossible to witness an abnormal deviation in the hidden or visible functioning of nature's laws. Indeed, were each man to take the trouble of cleverly examining the various stages of his existence (without forgetting a single one, for that very one might perhaps be destined to furnish the proof of what I am propounding) he will recall not without a certain surprise that in other circumstances would be comical, that on such and such a day—to speak of objective matters first—he witnessed some phenomenon which seemed to go beyond, and positively did go beyond, acknowledged notions provided by observation and experiment,[54] as, for example, rains of frogs, whose magical apparition must not at first have been understood by the scientists. And how, on another such day, to speak secondly and lastly of subjective matters, his soul presented to psychology's searching gaze what I will not go as far as to term a mental aberration (which, however, would be no less curious; on the contrary, it would be still more so), but at all events—so as not to appear hard to please in the sight of certain cold persons who would never forgive me for the glaring lucubrations of my exaggeration—an unfamiliar and quite often extremely grave condition which indicates that the limit granted the imagination by good sense is sometimes, despite the ephemeral pact concluded between these two powers, unhappily exceeded by the forceful pressure of the will, but most of the time too, by the absence of its effective collaboration: let us give in support a few examples whose appositeness is not difficult to appreciate—if, however, one takes to heart an attentive moderation. I offer two: the transports of rage and the malady of pride.

I warn whoever is reading me to beware of forming a vague and all the more false idea of the beauties of literature I prune in my excessively swift proliferation of phrase.[55] Alas! I would like to develop my arguments and my similes slowly and with much magnificence (but who has time at his disposal?) so that everyone may better understand, if not my shock at least my amazement when, one summer evening as the sun seemed to be sinking below the horizon, I saw swimming in the sea—with big webbed feet replacing the extremities, and bearing a dorsal fin in proportions as long and tapered as those of dolphins—a powerfully-built human being; and that numerous schools of fish (I saw in this retinue, among other inhabitants of the deep, the torpedo, the anarnak of Greenland[56] and the hideous scorpion-fish) were following with the most patent tokens of the highest admiration. Sometimes he would dive and his viscous body would almost immediately reappear two hundred metres away. Porpoises, who in my opinion did not purloin their reputation as good swimmers, could hardly keep up with this new species of amphibian. I do not think the reader will have ground for regret if he bring to my narrative not so much the detrimental obstacle of a stupid credulity as the supreme service of a profound trust which with secret sympathy lawfully discusses the poetic mysteries—too few, in his view—that I undertake to reveal to him at any time the occasion presents itself, as it unexpectedly has today, closely permeated with the tonic odours of seaweed wafted by the cooling breeze into this stanza containing a monster who has earmarked for himself the distinguishing characteristics of the palmipeds. Who speaks here of appropriation? Let everyone be assured that man, with his complex and manifold nature, is not unaware of the means of extending its frontiers still further: he lives in water, like the sea-horse; in the upper strata of the air, like the osprey; and below the earth, like the mole, the woodlouse, and the sublime earthworm.

Such, in more or less (but more rather than less) concise form, is the exact criterion of the extremely fortifying consolation which I strove to initiate within my mind when I pondered whether the human being I discerned a long way off swimming with all four limbs upon the waves' surface as stateliest cormorant never did, had perhaps undergone recent transformation of his extremities only as expiatory punishment for some unknown crime. I did not need to bother my head fabricating the melancholy pills of pity beforehand; for I did not know whether this man whose arms alternately beat the bitter brine while his legs produced recession of the watery strata with a strength equal to that of the narwhal's spiral horns had not voluntarily appropriated those extraordinary shapes, rather than their having been imposed as penalty upon him. According to what I later learned, here is the plain truth: prolonged existence in that fluid element had imperceptibly wrought—in the human being who had exiled *himself* from the rocky continents—the important but not essential changes I had remarked in the object which a fairly confused glance had caused me, since the very first moments of its appearance (through an unjustifiable levity whose freakish fancies spawn that feeling so painful that psychologists and lovers of prudence will easily understand), to take for a strange form of fish not yet described in the naturalists' classifications but perhaps in their posthumous works, although I did not have the excusable claim of inclining to this last supposition imagined under too many hypothetical conditions.

Indeed this amphibian (since amphibians there are, without one's being able to affirm the contrary) was visible to me alone— fish and cetaceans apart; for I saw that some peasants had stopped to stare at my face, which was perturbed by this supernatural phenomenon. They were trying vainly to understand why my eyes were constantly fixed with a perseverance seemingly insuperable but really not so, upon a spot in the sea where *they* discerned only an appreciable and limited quantity of schools of fish of all species, and were puffing out the apertures of their grandiose mouths perhaps as widely as whales.

This, they declared in their picturesque dialect, made them smile but not, as I did, turn pale; and they were not so stupid that they didn't notice that as it happened I wasn't watching the agrestic manoeuvres of the fish, but my gaze was directed much further on.

So that for my own part, mechanically turning my eyes toward the remarkable span of those powerful mouths, I told myself that unless there happened to be in the whole of the universe a pelican large as a mountain or at least as a promontory (kindly admire the finesse of the limitation, which does not lose an inch of ground), no beak of bird of prey nor jaw of wild beast would ever be capable of surpassing or even equalling any one of those gaping, but too gloomy craters. And yet, though I set good store by the attractive use of metaphor (this rhetorical figure does far more services to human aspirations towards the infinite than those imbued with prejudices or false ideas—which are the same thing—as a rule try to represent), it is nonetheless true that the laughable mouths of those peasants still remained wide enough to swallow three cachalots. Let us further curtail our train of thought, let's be serious, and let us be content with three small new-born elephants.

With a single arm-stroke the amphibian left behind him a kilometre of foamy wake. During the very brief moment when the arm straining forward stayed suspended in the air before plunging down again, his spread fingers, joined together by means of a fold of skin in the form of a membrane, seemed to spring for the heights of space and seize the stars. Standing on my rock, I used my hands as speaking-trumpet and shouted, while crabs and shrimps fled to the dark of the most secret crevices:

"O you whose swimming outdoes the longwinged frigate-petrel's flight, if you still understand the meaning of the loud outcries which mankind vigorously hurls at you as faithful interpretation of its inmost thoughts, deign to pause a moment in your rapid progress and briefly narrate to me the stages of your veracious tale. But I warn you, you need not address me if your bold plan be to awaken in me the friendship and reverence I felt for you since I saw you for the first time performing—with the shark's grace and strength—your indomitable and unswerving rectilinear pilgrimage."

A sigh that chilled me to the marrow and made the rock on which the soles of my feet rested shake (unless it was I reeling at the grating penetration of the sound-waves that brought to my ears such a cry of despair), was heard in the very bowels of the earth: the fish dived beneath the waves with the din of an avalanche. The amphibian dared not draw too near the shore, but as soon as he had ascertained that his voice carried clearly enough to my eardrums he slowed the motion of his webbed limbs so as to keep his seaweed-draped torso above the roaring breakers. I saw him bow his head as if to invoke by solemn command a wandering host of memories. I dared not interrupt him in this blessedly archaeological occupation: plunged in the past, he resembled a reef. At last he began to speak as follows:

"The centipede does not lack enemies; the fantastic beauty of his countless feet, instead of gaining him the animals' sympathy is for them perhaps only the powerful stimulus of a jealous irritation. And I would not be surprised to learn that this insect is exposed to the intensest hatred.

"I shall withhold from you the place of my birth, which has no bearing on my story: but the shame which would reflect upon my family does have a bearing on my duty. My father and mother (may God forgive them!), after a year of expectation, saw Heaven answer their prayer: twins—my brother and I—saw the light of day. All the more reason for loving each other. But this was not so. Because I was the handsomer and cleverer of the pair, my brother conceived a strong aversion to me and did not bother to conceal his feelings: consequently my father and mother lavished the greater part of their love upon me while through my sincere and constant friendship I tried to soothe a soul that had no right to rebel against one who had issued from the same womb. Well, my brother's fury knew no bounds, and by the most far-fetched calumnies he turned our mutual parents against me.

"I lived fifteen years in a dungeon, maggots and muddy water all I had for food. I will not detail to you the unheard-of tortures I endured during this long, unjust confinement. At odd times of the day one of three torturers, by rota, would enter abruptly, armed with pincers, tongs, and various instruments of torture. The cries the torments used to wring from me left my torturers unmoved; my copious loss of blood made them smile. O my brother, I have forgiven you—you, the originator of all my ills!

May it come to pass that blind rage opens its own eyes at last! During my endless imprisonment I reflected a great deal. You can imagine how my hate for humanity in general grew. Progressive etiolation, solitude of soul and body, had not yet made me lose my sanity completely—to the point of nursing resentment against those whom I had never ceased to love: triple pillory whose slave I was. I managed by cunning to regain my liberty!

"Disgusted by the inhabitants of the mainland who, though they called themselves my fellow men, seemed hitherto to re-semble me in nothing (if they found I did resemble them, why would they harm me?), I made my way to the shingly beach, firmly resolved to kill myself were the sea to offer me former reminiscences of a life lived fatally. Would you believe your own eyes? Since the day I fled the paternal roof I have not grumbled at living in the sea and its crystal grottoes as much as you may think. Providence, as you see, has given me part of the swan's oeconomy. I live at peace with fishes and they procure me what food I need as if I were their monarch. I'll give a special whistle, provided it won't vex you, and you'll see how they reappear."

It happened as he foretold. He resumed his royal swimming surrounded by his retinue of subjects. And although after a few seconds he had completely vanished from my sight, through a telescope I could still distinguish him on the far horizon. He swam with one hand and with the other he was wiping his eyes, which had turned bloodshot from the terrible strain of nearing terra firma. He had acted thus to please me. I flung the tell-tale instru-ment back at the sheer escarpment: it bounced from rock to rock and the waves caught its scattered fragments. Such was the final demonstration and the supreme farewell with which, as in a dream, I bowed to a noble and unfortunate intelligence! Yet everything that happened was real, that summer evening.

———

Each night, winging down into my dying memory, I would evoke remembrance of Falmer . . . each night. His flaxen hair, his oval face, his lordly features, were still stamped upon my imagination . . . indestructibly . . . his flaxen hair above all. Away, away then, with that hairless head polished like a tortoise shell. He was fourteen and I only a year older. Let this gloomy voice be silent! Why does it come to denounce me? But it is I myself speaking. Using my own tongue to utter my thoughts, I notice that my lips move and that it is I myself speaking. And I myself who, relating a tale about my own boyhood, and feeling remorse fill my heart . . . it is I myself, if I am not mistaken . . . it is I myself speaking. I was only a year older. Who is this to whom I refer? A friend I used to have in the old days, I think. Yes, yes, I have already mentioned his name . . . I don't want to spell out those six letters again, no, no. There is also no more point in repeating that I was a year older. Who knows it? Let us repeat it, however, but in a laboured manner: I was only a year older. Even then the pre-eminence of my physical strength was a motive, along life's rough track, rather to stand by the one who had entrusted himself to me, than to maltreat a conspicuously weaker being. For indeed I think he *was* weaker. . . . Even then. A friend I used to have in the old days, I think. The pre-eminence of my physical strength . . . each night. . . . His flaxen hair above all. There exists more than one human being who has seen bald pates: old age, disease, suffering (the three together or taken separately) explain this negative phenomenon in a satisfactory manner. Such, anyway, is the reply a scientist would give me if I questioned him about it. . . . Old age, disease, suffering. But I am aware (I too am a scientist) that one day, because he had stayed my hand the moment I was raising my dagger to stab a woman's breast, I grasped him by the hair with an iron grip and whirled him aloft so quickly that his scalp remained in my hand and his body, propelled by centrifugal force, went crashing against the trunk of an oak. . . . I am aware that one day his scalp remained in my hand. I too am a scientist. Yes, yes, I have already mentioned his name. I am aware that one day I carried out an infamous deed, while his body was propelled by centrifugal force. He was four-teen. When in a fit of insanity I run across the fields holding pressed to my heart a bloody thing that I have long preserved like a holy relic, the little children who chase me . . . the little children and old women who chase me with stones, wail woeful cries: "That's Falmer's scalp!" Away, then, away with that bald pate, polished like a tortoise shell. . . . A bloody thing. But it is I myself speaking. His oval face, his lordly features. For indeed I think he *was* weaker. Old women and little children. For indeed I think . . . what did I want to say. . . . For indeed I think he *was* weaker. With an iron grip. That crash, did that crash kill him? Were his bones broken against the tree . . . irreparably? Did that crash, brought about by an athlete's vigour, kill him? Did he stay alive although his bones were irreparably broken . . . irreparably? Did that crash kill him? I dread knowing what my closed eyes did not witness. Indeed. His flaxen hair above all. Indeed, I fled afar with a conscience thereafter implacable. He was fourteen. With a conscience thereafter implacable. Each night. When a young man who aspires to fame, bent over his desk on the fifth floor at the silent midnight hour, discerns an unaccount-able rustling, he turns a head burdened by meditation and dusty manuscripts this way and that; but nothing, no sudden sign reveals the cause of the sound he heard so faintly, but which he *did* hear. Finally he realises that the smoke from his candle rising towards the ceiling makes through the surrounding air almost impercep-tible vibrations in a sheet of paper attached by a nail to the wall. On the fifth floor. Just as a young man who aspires to fame hears an unaccountable rustling, so I hear a melodious voice pronounce in my ear: "Maldoror!" But before correcting his mistake, he thought he heard a mosquito's wings . . . bent over his desk. Yet I am not dreaming. What matter if I am stretched out on my satin bed? Coolly I pass the perspicacious remark that my eyes are open, although it is the hour of pink dominoes and masked balls. Never . . . oh no, never! . . . was a mortal voice heard to pronounce in those seraphic strains, with such mournful elegance, the syllables of my name! A mosquito's wings. . . . How kind his voice is. Has he forgiven me then? His body went crashing against the trunk of an oak. . . . "Maldoror!"

5

Let not the reader lose his temper with me if my prose has not the felicity to please him. You maintain my ideas are at least singular.[57] What you say, respectable man, is the truth, but a half-truth. And what an abundant source of errors and misapprehensions every half-truth is! Flights of starlings have a way of flying which is theirs alone and seems as governed by uniform and regular tactics as a disciplined regiment would be, obeying a single leader's voice with precision. The starlings obey the voice of instinct, and their instinct leads them to bunch into the centre of the squad, while the speed of their flight bears them constantly beyond it; so that this multitude of birds thus united by a common tendency towards the same magnetic point, unceasingly coming and going, circulating and crisscrossing in all directions, forms a sort of highly agitated whirlpool whose whole mass, without following a fixed course seems to have a general wheeling movement round itself resulting from the particular circulatory motions appropriate to each of its parts, and whose centre, perpetually tending to expand but continually compressed, pushed back by the contrary stress of the surrounding lines bearing upon it, is constantly denser than any of these lines, which are themselves the denser the nearer they are to the centre. Despite this strange way of swirling, the starlings cleave through the ambient air at no less rare a speed and each second make precious, appreciable headway towards the end of their hardships and the goal of their pilgrimage.

Likewise, reader, pay no attention to the bizarre way in which I sing each of these stanzas. But be convinced that the fundamental accents of poetry nonetheless maintain their intrinsic claim upon my intelligence. Let us not generalise exceptional facts, I am quite willing: yet my character is in the realm of possibilities. No doubt between the two poles of your literature as you understand it, and mine, there are endless intermediate states and it would be easy to multiply the divisions;[58] but it would be to no avail, and there would be the danger of bringing something narrow and false to an eminently philosophic conception which ceases being rational as soon as it is no longer comprehended as imagined —that is, expansively. You know, observer with absorbed mien, how to combine enthusiasm and inner coolness; in short, I find you perfect. . . . And yet you don't wish to understand me!

If your health is failing, take my advice (the best I have is at your disposition) and go for a country stroll. Dreary compensation, don't you think?[59] Come and see me again when you've had a breath of air: your mind will feel more refreshed. Weep no longer; I wished you no harm. Is it not true, my friend, that my songs won your sympathy to some degree? Now, what prevents your going a few steps further? The border between your taste and mine is invisible; you could never grasp it: proof that the border itself does not exist. Do consider then (here I only touch on the question) that it would not be impossible for you to have signed a peace treaty with obstinacy, that amiable daughter of the mule, so rich a source of intolerance. If I did not know you were no ass I would not reproach you thus. It is useless for you to encrust yourself with the cartilaginous carapace of an axiom you consider firm. There are other axioms too which are firm, and run parallel to yours. If you have a decided taste for caramel (admirable farce of nature)[60] no one will conceive of it as a crime; but those whose minds—more forceful and capable of greater things—prefer pepper and arsenic, have good reasons for behaving in that fashion without intending to impose their peaceful domination upon those who quake with fear before a shrew-mouse or the speaking expression of the surfaces of a cube.

I speak from experience, and am not here to play the part of a provocateur.

And just as rotifera and tardigrada[61] can be heated to a temperature near boiling-point without necessarily losing their vitality, so it will be for you if you can carefully assimilate the pungent suppurative serosity which slowly wells from the irritation caused by my interesting lucubrations. What! Have we not succeeded in grafting on to the back of a live rat the tail detached from another rat's body? Then try likewise to transfer to your imagination the varying alterations in my cadaveric mind.

But be careful. At the time of writing, new shivers thrill through the intellectual atmosphere: it is simply a matter of having the courage to look them full in the face. Why do you pull that face? And you even accompany it with a gesture one could only imitate after a long apprenticeship. Rest assured that habit is necessary in everything; and since the instinctive repulsion that manifested itself from the very first pages has noticeably diminished in depth in inverse ratio to the reader's application, like a boil one lances, it is to be hoped that though your head still aches your cure will very soon be reaching its final stage. To me you are already undoubtedly forging on to a thorough recovery; yet alas, your face has stayed very thin!

But . . . bear up! In you there is an uncommon spirit, I love you, and do not despair of your complete deliverance provided you consume some medicaments which will only speed the disappearance of the last symptoms of sickness. For an astringent and tonic diet, first tear off your mother's arms (if she still lives), cut them up into little pieces and then eat them in a single day, without your face betraying a trace of emotion. If your mother is too old, choose another surgical subject, younger and fresher, into whom the xyster will bite, and whose tarsal bones form a comfortably balanced fulcrum for a balanced, swaying walk: your sister, for example. I cannot help pitying her fate, and I am not one of those in whom an icy enthusiasm does nothing but feign kindness. You and I will shed for her, for this beloved virgin (yet I have no means of proving her virginity), two incoercible tears, two leaden tears. That will be all.

The most lenitive potion I prescribe for you is a basinful of lumpy blennorrhagic pus into which were previously dissolved a pilose ovarian cyst, a follicular chancre,[62] an inflamed prepuce skinned back from the glans by a paraphimosis, and three red slugs.

If you follow my prescriptions my poetry will welcome you with open arms, like a crab-louse with its kisses resecting the root of a hair.

I saw before me an object standing on a hillock. I could not clearly discern its head, but already I guessed (without, nevertheless, going into the exact proportion of its contours) that it was of no ordinary shape. I dared not draw near to this immobile column, and even had I had at my command the ambulatory legs of more than three thousand crabs (not even to mention those used for the prehension and mastication of food) I would still have stayed in the same place had not an occurrence in itself quite trifling severely taxed my curiosity, which was about to burst its bounds.

A beetle, rolling along the ground with its mandibles and antennae a ball whose principal components were compounded of excrement, was advancing rapidly towards the above hillock, bent on displaying its determination to take that direction. This articulate animal was not much bigger than a cow! If anyone doubts what I say, let them come to me and through the testimony of good witnesses I will satisfy the most incredulous. I followed the beetle at a distance, openly puzzled. What was it going to do with that great black ball?

O reader, you who incessantly (and not unjustifiably) pride yourself upon your perspicacity, would you be capable of telling me? But I do not wish to put your well-known passion for riddles to a severe test. Suffice you to know the mildest punishment which I can inflict upon you is still to make you realise that this mystery will not be revealed to you (it will be revealed to you) until later, at the close of your life, when you and your death-throes open philosophical discussions by your bedside . . . and perhaps even at the end of this stanza.

The beetle reached the foot of the hillock. I had followed in its tracks and was still a long way from the scene of the action; for like the skuas,[63] restless birds—as if always starving—who thrive in the seas that bathe both poles, and only accidentally venture into the temperate zones, I was ill at ease, and moved my legs forward very slowly. But what then was the tangible substance towards which I was advancing?

I knew that the *genus pelicaninae* includes four distinct species: the booby, the pelican, the cormorant, the frigate-bird. The greyish form that appeared before me was not a booby.[64] The sculptured block I set eyes on was not a frigate-bird. The frosted flesh I observed was not a cormorant. Now I could see him, the man with encephalon bereft of annular protuberance! I delved dimly amid my memory's meanderings: in what torrid or icy region had I already observed that very long, broad, convex, vaulted beak with pronounced, unguiculate, inflated bridge hooked at its tip; those toothed, straight edges; the branches of that lower mandible separated almost to the end and the gap filled with a membraneous skin; that wide pouch, yellow and sacciform, occupying the whole throat and capable of distending itself considerably; and those very narrow nostrils, longitudinal, almost imperceptible, hollowed into a basal groove!

Had this living being, its respiration pulmonary and simple, its body decked with hair, been bird complete, down to the soles of its feet, and not merely to its shoulders, it would not then have been so hard for me to recognise it: a very easy thing to do, as you are about to see for yourselves. But this time, I excuse myself; for my demonstration to be lucid I would require one such bird to be placed on my work table, even if only a stuffed one. Besides, I am not rich enough to procure one.

Following step by step a previous hypothesis, I would immediately have determined its true nature and found a place in the outline of natural history for him in whose sickly posture I admired such nobility. With what satisfaction at not being entirely ignorant of the secrets of his dual organism, and with what eagerness to know still more, did I behold him in his abiding metamorphosis! Although he did not have a human face, he seemed to me as fine as the two long tentaculiform filaments of an insect; or rather, as a hasty burial; or again, as the law of reconstitution of mutilated limbs; and above all, as an eminently putrescible liquid! But paying no heed whatever to what was happening in the vicinity, the pelican-headed stranger kept staring straight ahead.

Some other day I will bring this story to a conclusion. Yet I will continue my narrative with dreary alacrity; for if, on your part, you are anxious to know what my imagination is driving at (please Heaven that it *was* indeed only imagination!), for my own, I have resolved to finish what I had to tell you at only one sitting (and not two!), although no one, nevertheless, has the right to accuse me of lack of courage. But faced with similar circumstances, more than one person would feel his heart race beneath the palm of his hand.

In a little port in Brittany there recently died, almost unknown, an old salt, skipper of a coastal vessel, who was the hero of a terrible story. He was then a master mariner and sailed for a St Malo ship-owner. Well, after a thirteen-month absence he reached the conjugal hearth the very moment after his wife, still lying-in, had given him an heir to whose affiliation he could lay no claim.[65] The captain showed no sign of his surprise and rage. He coldly asked his wife to dress and to join him for a walk on the town battlements. This was January. The ramparts of St Malo are high, and when the north wind blows the boldest flinch. The unfortunate woman obeyed, calm and resigned; on her return she became delirious. She died in the night. But this was only a woman. While I, who am a man, confronted with a drama no less great, know not whether I would keep enough control over myself for my face muscles to remain motionless!

As soon as the beetle reached the foot of the hillock the man raised his arm towards the west (in precisely this direction a lamb-eating vulture and a Virginian eagle-owl had engaged in aerial combat), wiped from his beak a streaky tear which presented a diamond-sparkling colour-scheme, and said to the scarab:

"Wretched ball! Have you not rolled it long enough? Your vengeance is still not assuaged; and already this woman whose arms and legs you trussed with strings of pearls in such wise as to make up an amorphous polyhedron, so that you might trail her along at your tarsi across valleys and tracks, over thorns and stones (let me draw near to see if it still be her!) has seen her bones gouged by wounds, her limbs, buffed by the mechanical law of rotary friction, blending into the unity of coagulation, and her body presenting, instead of the primordial lineaments and natural curves, the monotonous appearance of an entirely homogeneous whole which through the confusion of its various shattered components resembles only too well the mass of a sphere! She has been dead a long time; leave these remains[66] to earth, and beware lest your consuming rage swell to irreparable proportions: it is no longer justice, for egoism, hidden in the teguments of your brow, like a phantom slowly lifts the trappings that overlay it."

The lamb-eating vulture and the Virginian eagle-owl, driven imperceptibly by the vicissitudes of their struggle, had drawn near us.

The beetle trembled at these unexpected words, and what on another occasion would have been an insignificant movement this time became the distinctive mark of a fury that knew no more bounds, for it scraped the thighs of its hind legs formidably against the edges of its elytrae, producing a high-pitched sound:

"Who then are you, pusillanimous creature? It seems you have forgotten certain strange developments in the past; you do not retain them in your memory, my brother. This woman betrayed us, one after the other. You first, then myself. It seems to me this insult[67] must not (must not!) disappear from the memory so easily. So easily! Your magnanimous nature allows *you* to forgive. But do you know whether, despite the abnormal state of this woman's atoms, reduced to dough (it is not now a question of ascertaining whether, on first inquiry, anyone would believe this body to have been enlarged by a notable quantity of density, rather by two powerful wheels thrown into gear than by the effects of my fiery passion) she does not still exist? Silence, and let me be revenged."

It resumed its manege[68] and made off, pushing the ball before it. When it was at a distance, the pelican cried out:

"That woman, by her magic power, has given me the head of a palmiped and has turned my brother into a scarab: perhaps she deserves even worse treatment than that I have just described."

And I, unsure whether or not I was dreaming, and guessing from what I had heard the nature of the hostile relations that united in bloody combat above me the lamb-eating vulture and the Virginian eagle-owl, flung back my head like a hood, to give my lungs free play and all available ease and elasticity, and, eyes staring upward, shouted at them:

"You there! Stop your fighting! Both of you are right, for to each she had promised her love. Accordingly she betrayed you both. But you are not the only ones. Besides, she deprived you of your human shape, making a cruel sport of your most hallowed sufferings. And you still hesitate to believe me! She is dead, anyway, and the beetle made her undergo a punishment whose imprint, despite the pity of him she first betrayed, is ineffaceable."

At these words they ended their feud and tore out no more feathers nor strips of flesh: they were right to behave thus. The Virginian eagle-owl, lovely as a thesis on the curve described by a dog running after its master, swooped down into the crevices of a ruined convent. The lamb-eating vulture, lovely as the law of arrest of development in the chests of adults whose propensity for growth is not consonant with the quantity of molecules assimilated by their organism, was lost in the upper strata of the atmosphere. The pelican, whose generous forgiveness had impressed me deeply—for I did not think it natural—resumed on his hillock the majestic impassivity of a lighthouse, as if to warn human navigators to heed his example and keep their destiny safe from the love of dark witches, and went on staring straight ahead of him. The beetle, lovely as the tremor of the hands in alcoholism, disappeared on the horizon. Four more existences one could cancel from the book of life. I ripped out a whole muscle of my left arm, for I no longer knew what I was doing, so moved was I in view of this quadruple calamity. And I believed it to be excrement! Really, what an utter simpleton I am!

The intermittent annihilation of human faculties: whatever your mind tends to suppose, these are not mere words. At least, they are not ordinary words. Let him raise his hand, who thought he would be performing a just act in requesting some torturer to flay him alive. Let him hold his head high, with the delight of smiling, he who would wilfully[69] offer his breast to death's bullets. My eyes will seek the marks of scars; my ten fingers will concentrate the whole of their attention on carefully palpating this eccentric's flesh; I shall verify that splashes of brains have spurted on my satin brow. Is it not true that the man to embrace such a martyrdom could not be found in the entire universe? I do not know what laughter is, true, never having experienced it myself. Yet what an imprudence it would be to maintain that my lips would not part smiling were it given me to see him who claimed that somewhere such a man exists! What no one would wish for his own existence has, by an unfair lot, fallen to me. Not that my body floats in the lake of sorrow; that would be all right with me. But the spirit withers with condensed and continually strained reflection; it croaks like the frogs in a marsh when a flock of voracious flamingoes and famished herons swoop down into the reeds along its fringes.

Happy is he who sleeps peacefully in a bed of feathers torn from the eider's breast, unaware that he is betraying himself. It is now more than thirty years since I slept. Since the unmentionable day of my birth I have sworn an irreconcilable hatred against the somniferous bed-boards.[70] It is I who willed it; let none be accused. Quickly, let abortive suspicion be cast aside. Do you discern this pale crown on my brow? Tenacity with her thin fingers was the one who wove it there. As long as a trace of burning sap races through my bones like a torrent of molten metal, I shall *not* sleep. Every night I force my livid eyes to stare at the stars through my window panes. To be surer of myself, slivers of wood prise my swollen lids apart.[71] When dawn breaks it finds me in the same position; my body propped vertically, erect against the plaster of the cold wall. Yet sometimes it happens I dream, but without for one moment losing the lively consciousness of my personality and the free faculty of movement: know that nightmare, who hides in the phosphorescent corners[72] of the dark, fever who palps my face with his stump, and every tainted animal rearing its bloody claws—well, it is my will which, to provide steady sustenance for its perpetual activity, makes them revolve. Indeed— atom that is revenged in its extreme weakness—Free Will does not fear to affirm with strong authority that brutishness is not numbered among its sons: he who sleeps is less than an animal castrated the day before. Although insomnia drags to the depths of the grave these muscles already redolent of a cypress odour, the white catacomb of my intelligence will never open its penetralia to the Creator's eyes. A secret and noble justice, towards whose outstetched arms I instinctively hurl myself, orders me to track down without truce this ignoble punishment. Deadly enemy of my imprudent soul, at the hour when lanterns are lit along the coastline, I forbid my luckless loins to lie down on the dewy lawn. Conqueror, I spurn the ambuscades of the hypocrite poppy! Consequently it is certain that through this strange struggle my heart (starveling that devours itself) has immured its schemes. Impenetrable as giants, *I* have lived ceaselessly with eyes yawning open. At least it is averred that during the day one can put up a useful resistance against the Great Exterior Object (who does not know his name?); for then the will watches over its own defence with remarkable tenacity. But as soon as the veil of nocturnal vapours spreads, even over condemned men about to hang—oh! to behold one's intellect in a stranger's sacrilegious hands! An implicable scalpel probes its dense undergrowth. Conscience exhales a long rhonchus of curses, for her modesty's veil undergoes cruel rents. Humiliation! our door is open to the grim[73] curiosity of the Celestial Bandit. I have not deserved this infamous torment, you hideous spy on my causality! If I exist, I am not another. I do not admit this equivocal plurality in me. I want to live alone in my intimate reasoning. Autonomy . . . or let me be turned into a hippopotamus. Sink underground, O anonymous stigmata, and reappear to my haggard indignation no more. My subjectivity and the Creator—it is too much for one brain. When night obscures the course of hours, who is he who in his bed soaked with icy sweat has not fought against the influence of sleep? That bed, drawing the dying faculties to its bosom, is but a tomb composed of a scantling of deal[74] boards. The will imperceptibly withdraws, as if confronted by an invisible force. A viscous gum coats the crystalline lenses of the eyes. The eyelids seek each other like two friends. The body is no more than a breathing corpse. Finally four enormous stakes nail[75] all his limbs to the mattress. And please note that the sheets, in short, are shrouds. Here is the perfume-pan where the religions' incense burns. Eternity booms like a distant sea and approaches rapidly. The room has disappeared; humans prostrate yourselves in this mortuary chapel! Sometimes, striving vainly to overcome the organism's imperfections, in the midst of the profoundest sleep, the mesmerised sense perceives with amazement that it is but a gravestone and, supported by an incomparable subtlety, admirably reasons: "To leave this bed is a more difficult problem than one would think. Seated on the tumbril I am drawn toward the binary posts of the guillotine. Curiously enough, my inert arm has knowingly assumed the stiffness of a stump. It bodes ill to dream of going to the scaffold." Blood flows in great waves across the face. The chest heaves in repeated gasps and inflates, wheezing. The weight of an obelisk stifles the spread of madness.[76]

Reality has destroyed slumber's dreams! Who does not know that when the struggle between the proud Self and the terrible progress of catalepsy continues, the hallucinated spirit loses its judgement? Gnawed by despair, it delights in its disorder till it has defeated nature, and sleep, seeing the prey escaping, with irritated and shamed wing flies forever from its heart. Cast a little ash upon my inflamed orbit.[77] Do not stare into my unwinking eye. Do you understand what suffering I endure (though pride is satisfied)? When night exhorts human beings to repose, a man I know strides swiftly through the countryside. I fear my resolution may succumb to the ravages of old age. Let that fatal day come when I shall fall asleep! On waking, my razor, working its way into this neck, will prove that as a matter of fact nothing was more real.

———

— But who!... whatever dares, here, like a conspirator, shuffle the coils of its body toward my dark breast? Whoever you are, eccentric python, by what pretext do you explain your ridiculous presence? Does some immense remorse torment you? For look, boa, your savage majesty does not, I imagine, exorbitantly pretend to evade the comparison I draw with the criminal's features. This frothy and whitish foam is, to me, the mark of rabies. Listen: do you know that your eye is far from drinking in a celestial ray? Do not forget that if your presumptuous brain thought me capable of offering you a few consolatory words, it could perhaps only be by reason of an ignorance totally devoid of physiognomical knowledge. For a time (sufficient, of course) turn the light of your eyes toward what I, like anyone else, have the right to call my face! Do you not see how it weeps? You are mistaken, basilisk. You must seek elsewhere the sorry ration of relief of which my radical impotence docks you, despite the numerous protestations of my goodwill. Oh! what force—expressible in words—dragged you fatally to your ruin? It is almost impossible for me to get used to this argument you do not understand: that, stamping my heel to flatten your triangular head's receding curves into the reddened turf, I could knead an unnamable masticky mess from savannah grass and trampled flesh.

— Get you hence, far from me, as soon as possible, guilty one with your pallid face! The fallacious mirage of fright has shown you your own spectre! Allay your offensive suspicions, if you do not want me in my turn to accuse you nor bear against you a recrimination which would certainly be approved by the reptilivorous secretary-bird.[78] What monstrous mental aberration prevents your recognising me? You do not recall then, the important services I rendered you—through the bounty of an existence that I made come forth from chaos—and on your part, the unforgettable oath never to desert my standard, to remain faithful to me unto death? When you were a youngster (your intelligence was then in its finest stage), you would be the first to climb the hill, with the speed of an izard, to hail the multi-coloured rays of daybreak with a wave of your little hand. The notes of your voice welled from your resonant larynx like diamantine pearls and resolved their collective personalities in the vibrant aggregate of a long hymn of adoration. Now like a mud-stained rag you vomit at your feet the forbearance of which I have too long given proof. Gratitude has seen its roots turn dry as a pond's bed; but in its place ambition has swelled to proportions that it would be painful for me to designate. Who is he, my listener, to have such faith in the abuse of his own weakness?

— And who are you yourself, bold substance? No! . . . No! . . . I do not err; and despite the multiple metamorphosis to which you have recourse, your serpent's head will always shine before my eyes like a beacon of eternal injustice and cruel domination! He wanted to take up the reins of rule but knew not how to reign! He wanted to become an object of horror for all created beings, and succeeded. He wanted to prove that he alone is the monarch of the universe, and there he is mistaken. O wretch! have you waited till this hour to hear the murmurs and conspiracies which, rising simultaneously from the surface of the spheres, skim with grim wing the papillose rims of your destructible eardrum? The day is not far off when my arm shall cast you down into the dust poisoned by your breath, and, ripping the noxious life from your vitals, leave your riddled corpse contorted on the road to teach the dismayed traveller that this palpitating flesh which amazes his gaze and nails his dumb tongue to his palate ought only to be compared—provided he keep a cool head—to the rotten trunk of an oak falling apart with age! What thought of pity restrains me in your presence? I tell you, you had better retreat before me and go and wash your immeasurable shame in the blood of a newborn child: such are your habits. They are worthy of you. Go . . . walk ever onward. I condemn you to become a wanderer. I condemn you to remain alone and without family. Trudge on constantly, till your legs refuse to support you. Cross desert sands till the end of the world swallows up the stars in nothingness. When you pass near the tiger's lair he will hasten to flee lest he see, as in a mirror, his nature raised upon the pedestal of ideal perversity. But when imperious fatigue orders you to break your journey before the thorn- and thistle-covered flagstones of my palace, heed your tattered sandals and cross the elegant entrance-halls on tiptoe. This is no vain advice. You might wake my young wife and infant son, lying abed in the leaden vaults that line the foundations of the ancient castle. If you are incautious at the outset, their subterranean howling might make you turn pale. When your impenetrable will deprived them of life, they were not unaware that your might was deadly, and had no doubt on that score; but they did not at all expect (and to me their last farewells bear out their belief) that your Providence would be vouchsafed to this pitiless extent!

Anyhow, walk quickly across these deserted and silent rooms, emerald-panelled though with faded hatchments, where the glorious statues of my ancestors rest. These marble bodies are angry with you; shun their glassy stares. This advice is given you via the tongue of their last and only descendant. See how their arms are raised in attitudes of provocative defence, heads thrown proudly back. They have surely guessed the harm you have done me; and if you pass within reach of the frozen plinths which support these sculptured blocks, vengeance awaits you. If your defence need tell me anything, speak. It is too late to weep now. You should have wept at a more suitable moment, when the opportunity was favourable. If your eyes are finally opened, judge for yourself what the consequences of your conduct have been. Farewell! I go to breathe the cliff breeze, for my half-stifled lungs with loud wheezes call for a calmer, chaster scene than yours!

O incomprehensible pederasts, not for me to hurl insults at your great degradation; not for me to cast scorn on your infundibuli-form anus. It is enough that the shameful and almost incurable diseases which beset you bring with them their inevitable punishment. Legislators of stupid institutions, inventors of narrow morality, hence!—for I am an impartial spirit. And you, young boys—or rather, young girls—explain to me how and why (but keep at a decorous distance, for I too am unable to resist my passions) revenge so germinated in your hearts as to have fastened such a crown of sores on mankind's flank. By your conduct (which I myself venerate!) you make humanity blush for its sons; your prostitution, offering itself to allcomers, exercises the logic of the deepest thinkers, while your exaggerated sensibility oversteps the mark of even woman's stupefaction. Are you of a more, or less, earthly nature than your fellows? Do you possess a sixth sense lacking in us? Do not lie, and say what you think. This is not an inquiry I address to you; for since I as observer see a good deal of the sublimity of your grandiose intelligences, I know where I stand.

Be blessed by my left hand, be hallowed by my right, angels protected by my universal love. I kiss your faces, I kiss your chests, kiss with my smooth lips the different parts of your harmonious and perfumed bodies. Why did you not tell me at once what you were, crystallisations of a superior moral beauty? I had to guess for myself the countless treasures of tenderness and chastity which the beating of your burdened hearts concealed. Breast bedecked with garlands of roses and vetiver. I had to part your legs to know you, and for my mouth to hang upon the emblems of your modesty. But (an important thing to point out) do not forget to wash the skin of your parts every day with warm water, or else venereal chancres would infallibly burgeon on the split commissures of my unsatiated lips.

Oh! if instead of being a hell this universe had been but an immense celestial anus—behold the gesture I make, hard by my lower abdomen: yes, I would have plunged my prick through its blood-stained sphincter, smashing the very walls of its pelvis with my impetuous movements! Misfortune would not then have blown into my blinded eyes entire dunes of shifting sand; I would have discovered the subterranean place where truth lies sleeping, and the rivers of my viscous sperm would thus have found an ocean in which to rush headlong! But why do I find myself regretting an imaginary state of affairs which will never receive the seal of subsequent fulfilment? Let us not trouble to construct fleeting hypotheses. Meanwhile, let him who burns with ardour to share my bed come to find me; but I set one strict condition on my hospitality: he must not be more than fifteen. May he, for his part, not think me thirty: what does that matter? Age does not diminish the feelings' intensity, far from it; and though my hair has turned white as snow, it is not because of age: on the contrary, it is due to the reason you know of. *I* do not like women! Nor even hermaphrodites! I must have beings who resemble me, upon whose brows human nobility is etched in more distinct and ineffaceable characters! Are you sure that those[79] who wear their hair long are of the same nature as my own? I do not think so, and will not relinquish my opinion.

A brackish saliva dribbles from my mouth, I do not know why. Who wants to suck it off me, so I may be rid of it? It gushes . . . still gushes! I know what it is. I have noticed that whenever I drink blood from the throats of those who sleep beside me (it is wrong to suppose me a vampire, since the dead who walk abroad from their graves are thus named; but *I* am alive), the next day I vomit some of it: that is the explanation for this vile saliva. How can I help it if my organs, enfeebled by vice, refuse to perform the functions of nutrition? But disclose my confidences to no one. It is not for myself I tell you this; it is for yourself and others, so that the prestige of the secret keeps within the bounds of duty and virtue those who, magnetised by the electricity of the unknown, would be tempted to imitate me. Be so good as to look at my mouth (for the moment I have no time to employ a more elaborate formula of civility); at first sight it strikes you by the appearance of its structure—to exclude the snake from your similes; this is because I contract its tissue to the very utmost, so as to make people believe I have a cold nature. You are not unaware that it is in fact diametrically the reverse.

Why can I not see in these seraphic pages the face of him who is reading me! If he be still in puberty, let him draw near. Clasp me close and do not be afraid of hurting me; let us progressively contract the bands of our muscles. More. I feel it useless to insist;

the opacity—noteworthy for more than one good reason—of this sheet of paper is a most considerable obstacle to our effecting complete junction.

I have always taken an infamous fancy to the pale youngsters in schools and the sickly mill-children! My words are not recollections of a dream, and I would have too many memories to sort out were I obliged to bring before your eyes the events which by their testimony could establish the truth of my distressing affirmation. Human justice has not yet surprised me *flagrante delicto*, despite the indisputable skill of its police.[80] I even murdered (not long ago!) a pederast who did not adequately lend himself to my passion; I threw his corpse into a disused well, and there is no definite evidence against me.

Why do you quake with fear, you lad reading me? You think I want to do the same to you? You prove you are superlatively unfair . . . You are right: beware of me, especially if you are handsome. My privates everlastingly present the lugubrious spectacle of tumescence; no one can maintain (and how many have not come near them!) he has seen them in a state of normal tranquillity, not even the boot-black who in a moment of frenzy stabbed me there with a knife. Ungrateful brat!

I change clothes twice a week, cleanliness not being the chief reason for my resolve. If I did not act thus, the members of humanity would, after a few days, disappear in long drawn-out tussles. Indeed, in whatever land I find myself, their presence harasses me continually, and they come and lick the surface of my feet. But what power do my seminal droppings possess, thus to lure towards them all that breathes with olfactory nerves! They come from the banks of the Amazon, they cross valleys the Ganges waters, they desert polar lichen to undertake long journeys looking for me, and to ask the still cities whether they have not for a moment glimpsed passing along their ramparts him whose sacred sperm perfumes[81] mountain, lake, heath, forest, promontory, and the vastness of the seas!

Despair at being unable to find me (to keep alive their keenness I hide covertly in the most inaccessible places) prompts them to the most regrettable actions. Three hundred thousand range themselves on either side, and the cannons' roar serves as prelude to battle. Every flank moves off at the same time, like a single warrior. The squares form and fall immediately, to rise no more. Startled horses bolt in all directions. Cannon-balls plough up the soil like implacable meteors. The theatre of war is no more than a vast field of carnage when night reveals her presence and the silent moon appears through the rifts of a cloud. Pointing out to me an expanse of several leagues strewn with corpses, the misty crescent of this star commands me to consider for a moment as subject for meditative reflections the baleful consequences which the inexplicable magic talisman bestowed on me by Providence bears in its wake. Unfortunately, how many centuries yet will it take before the human race perishes utterly in my treacherous trap!

Thus does a cunning but not boastful mind employ the very means to gain its ends which at first would seem to produce an insuperable obstacle. My intelligence forever aspires to this imposing question, and you yourself are witness that it is no longer possible for me to keep to the modest subject with which, in the beginning, I had intended to deal.

One last word . . . it was a winter night. While the icy wind whistled through the pines, the Creator opened his door in the dead of dark and admitted a pederast.

Silence! Near you a funeral cortège is passing. Bend the binarity of your kneecaps toward the earth and intone a chant from beyond the grave. (If you consider my words as a simple imperative rather than a formal—out of place—order, you will be showing spirit, and that of the best.) It is possible that thus you may succeed in greatly rejoicing the soul of the dead person who is going to rest from life in a grave. This fact is certain—even for me. Note that I do not say that your opinion cannot, up to a certain point, differ from mine; but that what matters above all is to have right ideas on the bases of morality, so that everyone must become imbued with the principle bidding men do to others as they would perhaps have others do unto them.

The priest of religions heads the procession, holding in one hand a white flag, the sign of peace, and in the other a golden device depicting the male and female privy parts, as if to indicate that these carnal members are most of the time, all metaphor apart, very dangerous tools in the hands of those employing them, when manipulated blindly to different and conflicting ends, instead of engendering a timely reaction against that well-known passion which causes nearly all our ills. To the small of his back is attached (artificially, of course) a horse's tail, thick and flowing, which sweeps dust off the ground. It means, beware of debasing ourselves by our behaviour to the level of animals. The coffin knows its way and moves behind the billowing vestment of the comforter. The relatives and friends of the deceased, demonstrating their position, have decided to bring up the rear of the procession. The latter advances majestically like a vessel that cleaves the open sea, and does not fear the phenomenon of sinking; for at this moment tempests and reefs are conspicuous only by their understandable absence.

Crickets and toads follow the burial train at a short distance; they too are not unaware that their unassuming attendance at anybody's obsequies will one day be credited to them. In low tones they converse together, in their picturesque language (do not be presumptuous enough—allow me to give you this disinterested advice—to believe that you alone possess the precious faculty of translating the sense of your thought), about the one they had more than once seen running across the verdant meadows and plunging the sweat of his limbs into the bluish waves of sandy bays.

At first life seemed unreservedly to smile on him, and crowned

him splendidly with flowers; but since your intelligence itself
perceives or rather divines that he was cut off on the borders of
boyhood, I need not, until the appearance of a truly requisite
retractation, continue the prolegomena of my rigorous demonstration. Ten years. Number precisely computed upon the hand's
digits, to make no mistake. It is not much and yet it is. In the case
which preoccupies us, however, I shall rely on your love for
truth, to have you adjudge with me, and without delaying a
second longer, that it is not much. And when I summarily reflect
upon those sinister mysteries by which a human being disappears
from the earth as easily as a fly or dragonfly, retaining no hope
of return, I find myself nursing keen regret at probably not being
able to live long enough to explain properly to you what I do
not myself pretend to know. But since it has been proved that
by an extraordinary chance I have not yet lost my life since that
far-off time when, filled with terror, I began the preceding sentence, I mentally calculate that it will not be useless here to construct the complete avowal of my basic impotence, especially
when it is a matter (as at present) of this imposing and inaccessible
question.

It is, generally speaking, a singular thing that the attractive
tendency which induces us to seek out (in order then to express
them) the resemblances and differences concealed in the natural
properties of the most conflicting objects, and on the surface
sometimes the least apt to lend themselves to this kind of sym-
pathetically curious combination, which—upon my word—
gracefully add to the style of the writer, who for personal satisfaction requites himself with the impossible and unforgettable
appearance of an owl grave until eternity. Let us accordingly
follow the current that sweeps us along.

The royal kite has wings proportionately longer than the
buzzard's, and a far freer flight: therefore he spends all his life
in the air. He hardly ever rests, and covers vast distances daily;
and all this movement is not a hunting operation, nor pursuit

of prey, nor even reconnaissance, since he does not hunt; but it seems flight is his natural state, his favourite element. One cannot help admiring the way in which he performs it. His long and narrow wings appear motionless; it is the tail which thinks it directs every evolution, and the tail is not mistaken: it is constantly active. He rises, effortless; he falls away as if he were sliding down an inclined plane; he seems to swim rather than fly; he speeds his course, slows it down, stops, and stays as if suspended or fixed in the same place for hours on end. No motion of his wings can be detected: were you to open your eyes wide as an oven door it would be just as pointless. Everyone has the good sense to confess without difficulty (though with slight bad grace) that he does not at first sight perceive the relation, however remote, which I point out between the beauty of the royal kite's flight and that of the child's face rising gently from the unsealed coffin like a lily breaking through the waters' surface; and therein, precisely, lies the unpardonable fault produced by the irremovable condition of lack of repentance concerning the wilful ignorance in which one wallows. This relationship of calm majesty between the two terms of my sly[82] comparison is already only too common and comprehensible enough a symbol for me to be any the more astonished by what can have for its sole excuse merely this same characteristic of vulgarity which summons up a deep feeling of unjust indifference for every object or spectacle smitten by it. As though what is daily evident should arouse our admiration's attention any the less!

Once at the cemetery entrance, the procession comes to a standstill. Its intention is to go no further. The gravedigger finishes digging the grave; the coffin is deposited therein with all the precautions taken in such cases. Some unexpected trowelfuls of earth cover over the child's body. The priest of religions, amid the emotional throng, pronounces a few words to bury the dead child, in the mourners' minds, good and proper.

He said he was greatly surprised that they should shed so many tears for an event of such insignificance. *Sic*. But he feared he had not sufficiently qualified what *he* considered to be an incontestable blessing. Had he believed death in its artlessness to be so unattractive, he would have renounced his mandate in order not to increase the legitimate sorrow of the deceased's numerous relatives and friends. But a secret voice told him to offer them a few consolations which would not be futile, were it only that consolation giving them a glimpse of hope for an impending meeting in heaven between the deceased and those surviving.

Maldoror fled at full gallop, apparently heading for the cemetery walls. The hooves of his steed kicked up a false wreath[83] of thick dust around its master. You cannot have known this horseman's name, but *I* knew it. He drew nearer and nearer. His platinum face began to grow discernible, although the lower part was wholly swathed in a cloak which the reader's memory has retained[84] and which allowed only the eyes to be seen. In the middle of his homily the priest of religions suddenly turned pale, for his ear recognised the irregular gallop of that famous white horse which never left its master.

"Yes," he added yet again, "my faith in this impending meeting is great; it will be better understood then than heretofore what meaning should be attached to the temporary separation of soul and body. He who thinks he is living upon this earth is cradled by an illusion whose evaporation[85] it would behove us to hasten."

The galloping sound grew louder and louder, and as the horseman, hugging the horizon, hove in sight within the optical field embraced by the main cemetery gates, swift as a whirling cyclone, the priest of religions more gravely resumed:

"You do not appear to suspect that he whom sickness forced to taste only of life's first stages, and whom the grave has just taken unto its bosom, is alive beyond doubt; but at least mark well that that one yonder—whose equivocal silhouette you see borne upon a wiry horse, and on whom I advise you to gaze with all possible dispatch, for he is but a dot and will soon vanish into the heathland—although he has lived much, is the only one really dead."

————————

"Each night, at the hour when sleep is at its deepest, an ancient spider[35a] of the large species slowly pokes its head out of a hole set in the ground at one of the corner intersections of the room. It listens attentively for any rustling that may stir its mandibles in the air. Considering its insect's conformation it cannot do less, if it aspire to increase the treasures of literature by brilliant personifications,[36] than attribute mandibles to rustling. When it has ascertained that silence reigns round about, it draws in turn from the depths of its nest, without the aid of meditation, the various parts of its body, and heads with measured tread towards my bed. Remarkable thing! I who make sleep and nightmare recoil, feel the whole of my body paralysed when it climbs up the ebony feet of my satin bed. It grips my throat with its legs and sucks my blood with its belly. As easy as that! How many litres of crimson liquid, whose name you well know, has it not drunk since it first performed this same trick with a persistence worthy of a better cause! I do not know what I have done, for it to behave towards me thus. Did I inadvertently crush one of its legs? Did I snatch away its young? These two hypotheses, subject to caution, are incapable of sustaining serious examination; they even have no difficulty in provoking a shrug of my shoulders and a smile on my lips, although one should not poke fun at anybody. Beware, black tarantula; if your behaviour has not an irrefutable syllogism for excuse, one night, through a last effort of my expiring will, I shall awake with a start, break the spell by which you hold my limbs motionless, and crush you between the bones of my fingers like a bit of soft matter. Yet I vaguely recall having given you permission to let your legs swarm over my blossoming breast and thence up to the skin that covers my face; and that consequently I have no right to restrain you. Oh! who will unravel my confused memories? I'll give him for reward what remains of my blood: counting right to the very last drop, there is enough to fill at least half an orgiastic goblet."

He speaks, and does not stop undressing. He rests one leg on the mattress, and with the other, pressing the sapphire flooring so as to rise up, finds himself stretched out in a horizontal position. He has resolved not to close his eyes, that he may await his enemy resolutely. But does he not make the same resolution each time, and is it not always destroyed by the inexplicable image of his fatal promise? He says nothing more, and sorrowfully resigns himself; for to him the oath is sacred. He wraps himself majestically in the folds of the silk, disdains to fasten his curtains' golden tassels, and, laying the wavy locks of his long black hair along the fringes of the velvet cushion, fingers the large neck-wound—in which the tarantula has acquired the habit of dwelling as in a second nest—while his face indicates satisfaction. He hopes that this very night (hope with him!) will see the last performance of the immense suction; for his only prayer would be for the torturer to have done with his life: death—and he will be content.

Look at that ancient spider of the large species slowly poking its head out of a hole set in the ground at one of the corner intersections of the room. We are no longer in the narrative. It listens attentively for any rustling that may stir its mandibles in the air. Alas! we have now reached the real as regards the tarantula, and although an exclamation mark might be put at the end of every sentence, that is perhaps no reason for dispensing with them! It has ascertained that silence reigns round about; see, it draws in turn from the depths of its nest, without the aid of meditation, the various parts of its body, and heads with measured tread towards the lonely man's bed. It halts an instant; but this moment of hesitation is short. It tells itself that it is not yet time to stop torturing, and that first the condemned man must be given plausible reasons that fix the perpetuality[87] of the torment. It has clambered up beside the sleeper's ear. If you would not miss a single word of what it is about to say, disregard the extraneous pursuits that clutter the portals of your mind, and at least be grateful for the interest I bear you in arranging your attendance as spectator at the theatrical scenes that seem to me worthy of exciting a real attention on your part; for who would prevent my keeping to myself alone the events I recount to you?

"Awake, amorous flame of bygone days, scraggy skeleton. The time has come to stay the hand of justice. We shall not make you wait long for the explanation you desire. You are listening to us, are you not? But do not stir your limbs; today you are still under our mesmeric power, and encephalic atony persists: it is for the last time. What impression does the face of Elsseneur make on your imagination? You have forgotten it! And that Reginald, with his proud gait, have you graven his features on your faithful brain? Look at him, hidden in the curtains' folds; his mouth bending toward your brow; but he dare not address you, for he is more timid than I. I am going to relate you an episode from your youth, and set you back on the road of memory. . . ."

A long time had elapsed since the spider had opened its belly, whence sprang two youths in blue robes, each with a flaming sword in his hand, who had taken up their places by the bedside as if thereafter to stand guard over the sanctuary of sleep.

"The one here, who has not yet stopped looking at you, for he loved you greatly, was the first of us two to whom you gave your love. But you often made him suffer by the brusqueness of your character. *He* never stopped making every effort to give *you* no cause for complaint against him: an angel would not have succeeded. One day you asked him if he wanted to go swimming with you by the sea-shore. Together, like two swans, you dived simultaneously off a steep rock. Expert divers, you slid through the aqueous mass, arms before your heads, and hands meeting. For a few minutes you swam between two currents. You reappeared a long way off, your locks matted and streaming with the briny liquid. But then what mystery had taken place beneath the water, for a long trail of blood to be visible through the waves?

Back on the surface, *you* went on swimming and pretended not to notice your companion's growing weakness. He rapidly lost strength, and nonetheless with your great strokes you forged on for the misty horizon, which loomed blurrily before you. The wounded man uttered cries of distress, and you played deaf. Reginald thrice made the echoes ring with the syllables of your name, and thrice you replied with a cry of delight. He was too far from shore to get back, and strove in vain to follow in your wake so as to reach you and rest his hand a moment on your shoulder. The fruitless chase continued for an hour, he losing strength and you feeling yours increase. Despairing of matching your speed, he offered up a short prayer commending his soul to the Lord, turned over on to his back as though floating, so that his heart was to be seen beating violently within his breast, and awaited the arrival of death—to delay no longer. At that moment your vigorous limbs were out of sight, and drew further off still, swift as a plummet-line paying out. A fishing-boat, returning from casting nets in the open sea, passed in the vicinity. The fishermen took Reginald for a castaway and hauled him fainting into their dinghy. The presence of a wound in the right side was ascertained; each of these experienced sailors voiced the opinion that no reef outcrop or rock splinter was capable of piercing so microscopic and at the same time so deep a hole. A cutting weapon—such as the very sharpest of stilettos—alone could claim parentage of so neat a wound. He, Reginald, would never relate the various phases of the plunge into the bosom of the deep, and has kept the secret to this very day. Tears flow down his rather colourless cheeks and fall upon your sheets: memory is sometimes more bitter than the event. But *I* shall not feel pity; that would be showing you too much esteem. Do not roll those furious eyes in their sockets. Keep calm rather. You know you cannot move. Anyhow, I have not finished my account.————
Take up your sword again, Reginald, and do not so easily forget revenge. Who knows? Perhaps one day it might come to reproach

you.———Later, you imagined remorse whose existence must have been fleeting; you resolved to atone for your crime by choosing another friend, so as to bless and honour him. By this means of expiation you would efface the stains of the past and shower on him who was to become the second victim the sympathy you had been unable to show the former. Vain hope; character does not alter from one day to another, and your will remained as it was.

"I, Elsseneur, saw you for the first time and from that moment I could not forget you. We looked at each other for a few instants and you started smiling. I lowered my eyes because I saw in yours a supernatural flame. I wondered if, under cover of some dark night, you had secretly dropped down to us from the surface of some star; for I confess—today when it is not necessary to pretend —you were unlike the wild boars of humanity; but a halo of sparkling rays encircled the periphery of your brow. I would have wished to strike up a close friendship with you;[88] my presence dared not approach the stunning novelty of that strange nobility, and a stubborn terror hung about me. Why did I not listen to those warnings of conscience? Well-founded presentiments. Noticing my hesitation, you blushed in your turn and held out your hand. Courageously I placed my hand in yours, and after this action felt stronger; since then a breath of your intelligence entered into me. Windswept heads held high and inhaling the breezes' breath, we walked on ahead for some moments, through thick groves of lentisk, jasmine, pomegranate, and orange-trees, whose odours intoxicated us. A boar in full flight brushed our clothes, and a tear fell from its eye when it saw me with you: I could not account for its behaviour. At nightfall we arrived before the gates of a populous city. The outlines of domes, spires of minarets, and belvederes' marble globes stood out sharply against the gloom, fretted upon the sky's intense blue. But you did not want to rest in the place, though we were worn out with fatigue. We skirted the outer fortifications like nocturnal jackals;

we avoided encountering sentries on duty; and by taking the opposite gate managed to get away from this solemn gaggle of rational animals—civilised as beavers. The flight of the fulgorous glow-fly,[89] the crackle of dried-up grasses, the intermittent howling of some distant wolf, accompanied the uncertainty of our dubious progress through the countryside. What then were your valid reasons for flying from the human hives? I asked myself that question with a certain unease; besides, my legs were beginning to balk at working overtime. Finally we reached the skirt of a thick wood whose trees were intertwined in a tangle of tall, inextricable lianas, parasitic plants, and cacti with monstrous spines. You stopped in front of a birch. You told me to kneel down and prepare to die; you granted me a quarter of an hour to quit this earth. A few furtive glances at me slyly stolen during our long journey, when I was not watching you, certain gestures whose irregularity of measure and movement I had noted, immediately appeared before my memory like the open pages of a book. My suspicions were confirmed. You flung me—too weak to struggle against you—to the ground as the hurricane blows down the aspen leaf. One of your knees was on my chest, the other pressed into the damp grass, while one of your hands seized the binarity of my arms in its vice. I saw the other draw a knife from the sheath hanging from your belt. My resistance was practically nil, and I shut my eyes: the stamping of a drove of oxen could be heard some distance off, borne on the wind. It advanced like a locomotive, harried by a herdsman's staff and a dog's jaws. There was no time to lose, and this you understood; fearing you might not attain your ends—for the approach of an unhoped-for help had doubled my muscular strength—and aware that you could immobilise only one of my arms at a time, you contented yourself with cutting through my right wrist, giving a quick flick of the steel blade. The piece, neatly severed, fell. You turned tail, while I was giddy with pain. I will not relate how the herdsman came to my aid, nor how long it took me to recover. Suffice you to know that this betrayal I was not expecting made me long to seek death. I took part in battles so as to expose my breast to blows. I gained glory on the battlefields; my name became redoubtable even to the most dauntless, such carnage and destruction did my artificial iron hand wreak in the enemy ranks. One day, however, when the shells boomed much louder than usual, and the squadrons, stormed from their base,[90] whirled like straws under the cyclone of death's influence, a cavalier[91] of bold carriage advanced towards me to contest with me the palm of victory. The two armies came to a standstill to watch us in silence. We fought long, riddled with wounds, helmets shattered. With one accord we ceased fighting in order to rest and then more energetically resume. Full of admiration for his adversary, each raised his visor: 'Elsseneur . . .!', 'Reginald . . .!'—these the simple words that simultaneously our throats gasped forth. The latter, sunk into the despair of an inconsolable sadness, had like myself taken up the military career, and bullets had spared him. In what circumstances did we meet again! But your name was not uttered! He and I swore eternal friendship; but one definitely different from the first two in which you had been the chief actor!

"An archangel, descended from heaven and the Lord's messenger, ordered us to turn into a single spider and to come every night to suck at your throat until a command from on high halted the punishment's course. For almost ten years we have haunted your bed. As from today you are free of our persecution. The vague promise you spoke of was not made to us but to the Being who is stronger than you: you yourself understood that it was best to submit to this irrevocable decree. Awake, Maldoror! The mesmeric spell that has weighed upon your cerebro-spinal system for a decade of nights,[92] vanishes."

He wakes as he has been ordered and sees two celestial forms disappear into the air, their arms entwined. He does not try to fall asleep again. He lifts his limbs off the bed, one after the other.

He goes and warms his icy skin at the rekindled brands in the Gothic fireplace. Only his night-shirt covers his body. His eyes seek the crystal carafe, that he may moisten his parched palate. He opens the outside shutters. He leans on the window-sill. He contemplates the moon which pours upon his breast a cone of ecstatic beams, in which silvery atoms of ineffable softness flutter like moths. He waits for the dawn twilight to bring, by a scene-change, a ridiculous relief to his flustered heart.

6

You whose enviable calm can do no more than embellish the cast of things, think not that it is still a matter of uttering—in fourteen- or fifteen-line stanzas, like a fourth-form pupil—exclamations that will be accounted inopportune, and resounding clucks of Cochin-China fowl, grotesque as could be imagined—were one to take the trouble; but it is preferable to prove through facts the propositions one advances. Would you then maintain that because I had insulted—as if in child's-play—Man, the Creator, and myself in my explicable hyperboles, my mission was complete? No: the most important part of my work still remains as a task to be accomplished.

Henceforth, the tricks of fiction[93] will activate the three characters cited above: thus a less abstract power will be communicated to them. Vitality will spread magnificently throughout the flow of their circulatory system, and you will see how astonished you yourself will be to meet—where at first you thought you saw only vague entities belonging to the realm of pure speculation—on the one hand the bodily organism with its ramifications of nerves and its mucous membranes, on the other the spiritual principle which presides over the physiological functions of the flesh. These are beings endowed with an energetic life, who, arms folded and chests held still, will pose prosaically (but I am certain the effect will be most poetic) before your face, placed only a few paces away from you so that the solar rays, striking the roof-tiles and chimney-pots first, will then shine visibly upon their earthly and material hair.

But there will be no more anathemata—specialists in provoking laughter; nor fictitious personages who would have done well to remain in the author's brain; nor nightmares set too high above ordinary existence. By that very fact, note, my poetry will be but the more beautiful.

Your hands shall touch the ascending branches of aorta and suprarenal ganglia; and then the sentiments! The first five narrations[94] have not been unprofitable; they were the frontispiece to my work, the base[95] of the construct, the preliminary construing of my future poetics; and I owed it to myself, before fastening my valise and setting off for the regions of imagination, to warn sincere lovers[96] of literature by the swift outline of a clear and precise generalisation, of the end I had resolved to pursue.

Accordingly my opinion is that now the synthetic section of my work is complete and sufficiently paraphrased. From it you will have learned that I proposed to attack mankind and Him who created it. For the time being—and for later—you need know no more about it! New considerations seem to me superfluous, for they would only repeat in another form—fuller, it is true, yet identical—the statement of the thesis whose first development will be seen before this day is out. It follows from the preceding observations that my intention is to undertake hereafter the analytic section; that is so true that only a few moments ago I expressed the ardent wish for you to be imprisoned in the sweat-glands of my skin so you could verify on good grounds the honesty of what I affirm. I know I ought, by a great number of proofs, to support the argumentation which finds itself included in my theorem; well, these proofs exist, and you know I attack no one without having serious motives! I laugh heartily to think you reproach me with spreading bitter accusations against humanity, of which I am a member (this remark alone would prove me right!) and against Providence: I shall not eat my words. But, relating what I have seen, it will not be difficult for me to justify them, with no other ambition but truth.

Today I am going to fabricate a little novel of thirty pages;

this amount will subsequently remain more or less fixed. Hoping promptly to see, some time or other, the consecration of my theories accepted by this or that literary form, I believe that after some tentative fumbling I have at last found my definitive formula. It is the best: since it is the novel!

This hybrid preface has been set out in a way which may not, perhaps, appear natural enough, in the sense that it—so to speak —surprises the reader, who does not very clearly see where he is at first being led; yet this feeling of remarkable stupefaction, from which one generally seeks to shield those who spend their time reading books or booklets, I have made every effort to produce. Indeed, it was impossible for me to do less, despite my goodwill: only later, when a few novels have come out, will you better understand the preface of the renegade with the dusky face.

Before broaching my theme, I think it stupid that it should be necessary (I imagine not everyone will be of my opinion, if I am mistaken) for me to set beside me an open inkwell and a few sheets of unrumpled paper.[97] Thus it will be possible for me to begin, with love, with this sixth canto, the series of instructive poems I long to produce. Dramatic episodes of a relentless utility!

Our hero realised that by frequenting caves and taking refuge in inaccessible places he was transgressing the rules of logic and setting up a vicious circle. For if on the one hand he thus encouraged his repugnance for man by the compensation of solitude and distance, and passively circumscribed his limited horizon amid stunted bushes, brambles, and creepers—on the other, his activity no longer found any nutriment to feed the minotaur of his perverse instincts. Consequently he resolved to draw nearer to[98] the human agglomerations, convinced that among so many ready-made victims his various passions would find plenty of means of satisfying themselves. He knew that the police, that shield of civilisation, had been looking for him doggedly for a good many years, and that a veritable army of police[99] and their spies were continually at his heels. Without, however, managing to find him. So greatly did his astounding cleverness baffle, in fine style, the most unquestioned wiles (from a standpoint of their success) and arrangements resulting from the best-informed cogitation. He had a special faculty for assuming forms unrecognisable to expert eyes. Superior disguises—speaking as an artist! Outfits of a really mediocre effect, if I consider the morality. On that score, he came close to genius. Have you not noticed the slimness of a pretty cricket with alert movements in Paris drains?[100] It can only be he: that was Maldoror!

Mesmerising the prosperous capitals with a pernicious fluid, he leads them into a lethargic state in which they are incapable of keeping watch upon themselves as they should. A state the more dangerous for being unsuspected. Today he is in Madrid; tomorrow he will be in St. Petersburg; yesterday he was in Peking.[100a] But to state exactly the place which the exploits of this poetic Rocambole[101] are currently filling with terror is a task beyond the possible strength of my dull-witted ratiocination. The bandit is perhaps seven hundred leagues away from this area—or perhaps a few steps from you.

It is not easy to make men perish entirely, and there are laws; but with patience one can exterminate the humanitarian ants one by one.

Now from the day of my birth, when, still inexperienced in setting my snares, I lived with the first forbears of our race; since remote times set beyond history, when, in subtle metamorphoses at divers epochs I ravaged the regions of the globe by conquests and carnage, and spread civil war among citizens—have I not already ground beneath my heel, member by member or collectively, whole generations whose untold total it would not be difficult to conceive?

The radiant past has made brilliant promises to the future: it will keep them. To scrape together my sentences I needs must employ the natural method, regressing to the savages so they may give me lessons. Simple and majestic gentlemen, their gracious mouths ennoble all that flows from their tattooed lips.

I have just proved that nothing on this planet is laughable. Droll but lofty planet. Grasping a style some may find naive (when it is so profound), I shall make it serve to interpret ideas which unfortunately may not seem imposing! For that very reason, ridding myself of the light and sceptical turn of ordinary conversation, and prudent enough not to pose . . . I no longer know what I was intending to say, for I do not remember the start of the sentence. But know this: poetry happens to be wherever the stupidly mocking smile of duck-faced man is not. First I am going to blow my nose, because I need to, and then, mightily aided by my hand, shall again take up the penholder my fingers had let fall.

How could the Pont du Carrousel observe its steadfast neutrality when it heard the harrowing screams seemingly uttered by the sack!

———————

I

The Rue Vivienne shops display their riches to awe-struck eyes. Lit by numerous gas-lamps, the mahogany caskets and gold watches spread across the windows sprays of dazzling light. The clock of the Bourse has struck eight: it's not late! The striker's last blow is hardly to be heard before the street whose name has been mentioned above begins to tremble, and shakes to its foundations from the Place Royale to the Boulevard Montmartre. The pedestrians quicken pace and retire pensively into their houses. A woman faints and falls down in the road. No one helps her up: everyone is anxious to get away from the area. Shutters close impulsively and the inmates bury themselves beneath their bedcovers. One would think the Asiatic Plague had disclosed its presence.

So, while the greater part of the town is preparing to wallow in the enjoyment of nocturnal festivities, the Rue Vivienne finds itself suddenly frozen into a sort of petrifaction. Like a heart that stops loving, it's seen its life extinguished. But soon news of the phenomenon spreads to other strata of the population, and a gloomy silence reigns over the august capital. Where have the gas-lamps gone? What has become of the street-walkers? Nothing . . . solitude and darkness! A screech-owl with a broken leg, steering a dead straight course, passes above the Madeleine and soars toward the Gate of the Throne, crying: "Misfortune is brewing."

Now in this spot my pen (this real crony who serves me as accomplice) has just made mysterious, you will see—if you look in the direction of where the Rue Colbert meets the Rue Vivienne —a character show his silhouette at the angle[102] formed by the intersection of these two thoroughfares and walk softly towards the boulevards. But if one draws closer still, without attracting this wayfarer's attention, one realises with pleasant surprise that he is young! From a distance, as a matter of fact, one would have taken him for a mature man. The sum of days no longer counts when it is a question of estimating the intellectual capacity of a serious face. I know all about telling age from the physiognomical lines of the forehead: he is sixteen years and four months old!

He is fair as the retractility of the claws of birds of prey; or again, as the uncertainty of the muscular movements in wounds in the soft parts of the lower cervical region; or rather, as that perpetual rat-trap always reset by the trapped animal, which by itself can catch rodents indefinitely and work even when hidden under straw; and above all, as the chance meeting on a dissecting-table of a sewing-machine and an umbrella!

Mervyn, that son of flaxen England, has just had a fencing lesson from his instructor, and wrapped in his Scotch tartan is returning to his parents' house. It is half past eight and he hopes to arrive home at nine: it is a great presumption on his part to pretend to be certain of knowing the future. May not some unforeseen obstacle impede his way? And would this circumstance be so infrequent that he should take it upon himself to consider it as an exception? Why does he not rather consider as an abnormal fact the faculty he has hitherto had of feeling himself devoid of anxiety and, so to speak, happy? By what right indeed does he presume he will reach home unscathed, when someone is following after him and marking him down for his next prey?

(It would show very little command of one's profession as sensational writer not to advance at least the qualifying questions after which immediately comes the sentence I am on the point of completing.)

You have recognised the imaginary hero who for a long time has been shattering my unhappy intelligence by the pressure of his individuality! Now Maldoror approaches Mervyn, to engrave the youth's features upon his memory; now, body flung backwards, he falls back upon himself like the Australian boomerang in the second phase of its trajectory, or rather, like an infernal machine. Undecided on what to do. But his conscience, as you would wrongly suppose, experiences no symptom of the most embryogenic emotion. I saw him make off for a moment, in the opposite direction; was he overcome by remorse? But he retraced his steps with renewed relentlessness.

Mervyn does not know why his temporal arteries[103] throb so strongly, and he quickens his pace, obsessed by a dread whose cause he and you vainly seek. One must bear in mind his diligence in descrying the riddle. Why does he not turn round? He would understand everything. Does one ever think of the simplest means of putting an end to a parlous condition? When a suspicious loafer[104] crosses a suburban road, a jug of white wine in his gullet and his overalls in shreds, if beside a milestone he spy a scrawny old cat (contemporary of the revolutions in which our fathers took part)[105] mournfully contemplating the moonbeams falling upon the sleeping plain, he advances crookedly, curvingly, and gives a sign to a knock-kneed dog which leaps forward. The noble animal of feline race awaits its adversary with courage, and sells its life dearly. On the morrow some ragman will buy an electrifiable pelt. Why then did it not flee? It was so easy.

But in the case currently exercising our minds, Mervyn further complicates the danger by his own ignorance. He has some—as it were—inklings, excessively rare it is true, and I shall not pause to demonstrate the vagueness surrounding these; however, it is impossible for him to guess the truth. He is no prophet—that I don't deny—and recognises no such faculty in himself.

On reaching the main thoroughfare he turns right and crosses the Boulevard Poissonnière and the Boulevard Bonne-Nouvelle. At this point of his journey he turns down the Rue du Faubourg-Saint-Denis, leaves behind him the departure platform of the Strasbourg railway station, and stops in front of a tall gateway before getting to the perpendicular superposition of the Rue Lafayette.

Since you advise me to end the first stanza here, I am quite willing, this time, to accede to your desire. Do you know that whenever I think of the iron ring hidden beneath the stone by a maniac's hand, an irrepressible shudder runs through my hair?

II

He tugs the brass bell-pull and the main door of the modern mansion swings on its hinges. He strides across the courtyard strewn with fine sand and climbs the eight steps of the perron. The two statues set at right and left like the guardians of the aristocratic villa do not bar his way.

He who has disowned all—father, mother, Providence, love, ideals—in order to think only of himself, has taken good care not to follow in the preceding footsteps. He has seen Mervyn enter a spacious ground floor drawing-room with cornelian wainscoting.

The well-bred youth throws himself on to a sofa and emotion prevents his speaking. His mother, in a long and trailing gown, bustles about him and clasps him in her arms. His brothers, younger than himself, bunch round the sofa and its burden; they have not sufficient experience of life to form a clear idea of the scene that is taking place. Finally the father lifts his cane and looks down on the onlookers with a glance full of authority. Wrists bearing down against the armchair's arms, he gets up from his usual seat and uneasily advances, though enfeebled by old age, towards the motionless body of his first-born. He speaks in a foreign language and everyone listens in respectful contemplation:

"Who's got the boy in this state? The foggy Thames'll sweep along a good deal more mud before my strength completely runs out. Protective laws don't appear to exist in this inhospitable country. If I knew the culprit, he'd feel the weight of my arm. Although I'm retired, aloof from naval engagements, my commodore's sword hanging on the wall isn't rusty yet. Besides, it's easy to whet its edge. Calm down, Mervyn, I'll give orders to the servants to get on his track and I'll seek him out from now on to slay him with my own hand. Begone, wife—go and squat in a corner. Your eyes move me, and you'd do better to close the ducts of your lachrymal glands. My son, I beg you return to your senses and recognise your family—it's your father speaking to you . . ."

The mother keeps in the background and to obey her master's orders has taken up a book and is trying to remain calm in face of the danger run by him whom her womb brought forth.

"Children, go and play in the park, and take care while admiring the swans' swimming not to fall into the ornamental lake. . . ."

The brothers, hands dangling, kept silent. They all—caps topped with a feather ripped from the Carolina nightjar, velvet knee-length breeches, and hose of red silk—took each other by the hand and withdrew from the drawing-room, careful to cross the ebony parquet only on tip-toe. I am certain they will not enjoy themselves and will go gravely for a walk along the plane-tree lanes. Their intelligence is precocious. So much the better for them.

". . . Useless attentions—I rock you in my arms, and you are insensible to my entreaties. Won't you raise your head? I'll hug your knees if need be. But no . . . it falls back inert."

"My gentle lord, if you will permit your slave, I'll go to my room and get a phial full of turpentine which I always use when migraine floods my temples on returning from the theatre, or when the reading of a moving story recorded in the British annals of our ancestors' chivalrous history casts my dreamy thought into the bogs of drowsiness."

"Wife, I did not call on you to speak, and you had no right to begin. Since our lawful union no cloud has come between us. I am pleased with you, I have never had reproaches to make you—and vice-versa. Go to your room and get a phial full of turpentine. I know there is one in a drawer of your bedside table—you haven't only just appraised me of it. Hurry up and climb the steps of the spiral staircase, and come back to me with a happy face."

But the sensitive Londoner has hardly reached the first steps (she does not run with the dispatch of a person of the lower classes) before one of her tirewomen, scarlet cheeks a-sweat, is already coming down again from the first floor with the phial which perhaps contains the lively liquid within its crystal confines. The maid, presenting her offering, bobs gracefully, and the mother has advanced with regal bearing towards the fringes edging the sofa—sole object that engrosses her tenderness. The commodore, with a proud but kindly gesture, accepts the phial from the hands of his spouse. An Indian foulard is dipped in it and Mervyn's head is encircled by the orbicular wimples of the silk. He inhales the salts; he moves an arm. His circulation revives, and the blithe cries of a Philippines cockatoo perched on the window embrasure are audible.

"Who goes there?. . . Don't stop me. . . . Where am I? Is it a grave that bears my heavy limbs? The planks seem soft to me. . . . Is the locket that contains my mother's portrait still fastened at my neck?. . . Back, evil-doer with dishevelled hair! He couldn't catch me and I left a flap of my doublet between his fingers. Slip the bulldogs' leashes, for tonight a recognisable burglar may break into our house while we are fast asleep. Father and mother, I recognise you and thank you for your care. Call my little brothers. I'd bought pralines for them, and I want to kiss them."

With these words he falls into a state of profound lethargy. The doctor, summoned post-haste, rubs his hands and exclaims: "The crisis is over. Everything is going well. Tomorrow your son will awake in good fettle. All of you go to your respective beds—I order it—so that I may stay alone at the invalid's side until the advent of dawn and the nightingale's song."

Maldoror, hidden behind the door, has not missed a word. Now he knows the nature of the mansion's inmates, and will act accordingly. He knows where Mervyn lives and desires to know no more. He has entered the name of the street and the number of the building in a notebook. That is the main thing. He is sure not to forget them. He advances, like a hyena, unseen, and skirts the sides of the courtyard. He scales the railing with agility and fouls the iron spikes a moment; at one bound he is in the roadway. He makes off stealthily.

"He took me for an evil-doer," he cries. "He is an idiot. I'd like to find one man free of the accusation the invalid made against me. I did not rip off a flap of his doublet as he said. Simple trance-inducing hallucination caused by fright. My intention was not to lay hands on him today; for I have other ulterior designs on this timid youth."

Wend your way in the direction of the swan lake, and I shall tell you later why one of the bevy is completely black, its body bearing an anvil surmounted by the rotting carcass of an edible crab, and rightly inspiring distrust in its other aquatic comrades.

III

Mervyn is in his room; he has received a missive. Whoever is writing him letters? His agitation has prevented him from thanking the postman. The envelope has black edges and the words are traced in a hasty hand. Is he going to take this letter to his father? What if the signatory expressly forbids him to do so? Filled with distress, he opens his window to breathe the scents of the air; the sunbeams reflect their prismatic irradiations from the Venetian mirrors and damask curtains. He tosses the letter aside among the gilt-edged books and albums with mother-of-pearl covers strewn on the embossed leather overlaying the top of his schoolboy's desk. He opens his piano and runs his tapering fingers over the ivory keys. The brass wires did not twang. This indirect warning urged him to pick up the wove paper again: but the latter curled back as if it had been offended by the hesitation of the recipient. Caught in the trap, Mervyn's curiosity increases and he opens the ready scrap of paper. Until this moment he had seen no handwriting but his own.

"Young man, I am interested in you; I want to make you happy. I will take you as companion and we will compass long travels in the South Sea Islands. Mervyn, you know I love you, and I do not need to prove it you. You'll grant me your friend-ship, of that I'm sure. When you know me better you shan't rue the confidence you'll have shown in me. I'll protect you from the risks your inexperience will run. I'll be a brother to you, and you won't lack for good advice. For more detailed explanations, be on the Pont du Carrousel the day after tomorrow, at five in the morning. If I haven't arrived, wait for me; but I hope to be there on the stroke. Do likewise. An Englishman will not easily forego the chance to sort out his affairs. Young man, I greet you, and goodbye for now. Show this letter to no one."

"Three stars instead of a signature," cries Mervyn, "and a blood-stain at the foot of the page!" Copious tears drop on to the curious words his eyes have devoured and which open a limitless field of new and uncertain horizons to his spirit. It seems to him (this is only since the reading he has just completed) that his father is a bit strict and his mother too starchy. He has motives—which have not come to my knowledge and which, consequently, I could not impart to you—for insinuating that his brothers no longer suit him either. He hides this letter in his bosom.

His tutors observed that on that day he did not seem himself; his eyes clouded over inordinately and the veil of excessive thought fell upon the peri-orbital region. Each tutor blushed, for fear of not finding himself intellectually equal to his pupil, and yet the latter for the first time neglected his exercises and did not work.

In the evening the family gather in the dining-room decorated with ancient portraits. Mervyn wonders at the dishes heaped with succulent meats and fragrant fruits, but does not eat; the polychrome streams of Rhenish wines and the sparkling jewels of the champagne set in the tall and narrow Bohemian glass goblets leave even his sight cold. He rests his elbow on the table and remains lost in thought like a sleep-walker. The commodore, his face tanned by the sea spray, leans towards his wife's ear:

"Our eldest has changed since the day of the attack; he was only too prone then to absurd ideas, but today he spends more time dreaming than ever. All the same, *I* wasn't like that when I was his age. Pretend not to notice anything. Some efficacious moral or material remedy might readily come in handy. Mervyn, you enjoy reading travel books and natural history—I'm going to read you a yarn you won't half like. Listen carefully—every-one'll find something worthwhile in it, first and foremost myself.

And you children, by the attention you can pay my words learn to perfect the pattern of your style and to be alive to an author's least intentions."

As if this brood of adorable brats could have understood what rhetoric was!

He spoke, and at a wave of his hand one of the brothers goes into the paternal library and returns with a volume under his arm. Meanwhile the tablecloth and silver have been cleared and the father takes the book. At that electrifying word "travels", Mervyn has raised his head and tried to put an end to his ill-timed meditations. The book is opened at about the middle and the commodore's metallic voice proves that he is still capable, as in the days of his glorious youth, of commanding the fury of men and storms. Long before the end of this reading, Mervyn has again slumped upon his elbow, finding it no longer possible to follow the reasoned development of sentences going through the whole grind and saponification of obligatory metaphors. The father exclaims: "This isn't interesting him; let's read something else. Read, wife, you may be luckier than I in driving distress from our son's life."

The mother is past hoping; however, she takes up another book and the tones of her soprano voice sound melodiously upon the ears of the product of her conception. But after a few words discouragement assails her and of her own accord she discontinues interpretation of the literary work. The firstborn exclaims: "I'm going to bed." He retires, eyes lowered in a cold stare, and without adding a word. The dog starts up a dismal baying for it does not think this behaviour natural, and the wind outside, sweeping irregularly into the longitudinal window cleft, makes the bronze lamp's flame—lowered by two domes of rosy crystal—flicker. The mother presses her hands against her brow and the father raises his eyes heavenward. The children cast startled glances at the old salt.

Mervyn double-locks the door of his room and his hand races

rapidly over the paper: "I received your letter at noon, and you'll forgive me if I've made you wait for a reply. I have not the honour of knowing you personally, and I didn't know whether I ought to write to you. But as discourtesy does not dwell in our house, I have resolved to take up pen and thank you warmly for the interest you are taking in a stranger. God preserve me from not showing gratitude for the sympathy with which you shower me. I know my imperfections and do not bear myself the prouder for them. But if it is proper to accept the friendship of an older person, it is also proper to make him understand that our characters are dissimilar. Indeed, you appear to be older than I, since you call me young man, and yet I still have doubts about your real age. For how is one to reconcile the coldness of your syllogisms with the passion they effuse? It's certain I shan't abandon the place I've known from birth in order to accompany you to far-off lands—which would only be possible on condition that I first applied for the impatiently awaited consent of my progenitors. But as you have enjoined me to keep this spiritually shady affair[106] secret (in the root sense of the word) I shall hasten to comply with your incontestable wisdom. Apparently it would not pleasurably confront the light of day. Since you appear to wish me to have confidence in your own self (a desire not out of place, I am pleased to confess) be good enough, I entreat you, to evince an analogous confidence as regards myself, and do not even presume to believe me so far removed from your way of thinking that on the morning of the day after tomorrow at the appointed hour, I might not be punctual at the rendezvous. I'll get over the park fence wall, for the gate will be shut, and no one'll witness my departure. To speak frankly, what wouldn't I do for you, whose unaccountable attachment soon knew how to reveal itself to my dazzled eyes—especially astonished by such a proof of kindness which I am sure I would not have expected. Since I did not know you. Now I know you. Do not forget the promise you made me to walk across the Pont du Carrousel. In the event of my passing by I feel a certainty like none other that I'll meet you and shake your hand, provided that this innocent display from a youth who only yesterday bowed before the altar of modesty, would not offend you by its respectful familiarity. Now isn't familiarity admissible in the case of a strong and eager intimacy, when perdition is grievous and assured? And what harm would there be after all, I ask you yourself, if I were to say farewell casually while passing, when, the day after tomorrow, whether it rain or no, five o'clock has struck! You, a gentleman, will yourself appreciate the tact with which I have worded my letter; for I do not allow myself—in a little leaflet liable to go astray—to tell you more. Your address at the foot of the page is a conundrum. It has taken me almost a quarter of an hour to decipher it. I think you did well to write the words microscopically. I excuse myself from signing, and in that I imitate you: we live in too odd a time to be surprised for one moment by what might happen. I'd be interested to know how you came to know of the place where my icy immobility dwells, surrounded by a long row of deserted rooms, foul larders[107] of my hours of ennui. How can I put it? When I think of you my breast heaves, rumbling like the collapse of an empire in decay; for your love's shadow betrays a smile which perhaps does not exist: a ghost so vague, and moving its scales so schemingly! I surrender to your hands my impetuous feelings— marble tablets, brand new and still unpolluted by mortal contact. Let us be patient until the first glimmers of the morning twilight, and while awaiting the moment which will hurl me into the hideous enlacement of your pestiferous arms, I bow humbly at your knees, which I clasp."

After writing this guilty letter, Mervyn posts it and comes back and goes to bed. Do not expect to find his guardian angel there.

The fishtail will fly for only three days, true, but alas! the beam will be burnt just the same; and a cylindro-conical bullet will pierce the hide of the rhinoceros despite Snow White and the beggar! The fact is that the crowned madman will have told the truth about the fidelity of the fourteen daggers.

IV

I became aware I had only one eye in the middle of my forehead! O mirrors of silver, inlaid in the panels of lobbies, what services have you not rendered me by your reflective power! Since the day an Angora cat, springing suddenly on to my back, for an hour gnawed at my parietal bump like a trepan perforating the cranium, because I had had its kittens boiled in a vat full of alcohol, I have not ceased to aim the arrow of anguish against myself. Today, under the pressure of the wounds my body has sustained in various instances, whether by the fatality of my birth or in actual fact through my own fault; prostrated by the consequences of my moral downfall (some of them have come about; who can foresee[108] the others?); impassive spectator of the acquired or natural monstrosities which ornament the aponeuroses and intellect of him who speaks, I cast a long look of satisfaction upon the duality that composes me . . . and find myself beautiful! Beautiful as the congenital malformation of man's sexual organs, consisting of the relative brevity of the urethral canal and the division or absence of its lower wall so that this canal opens at a variable distance from the gland and below the penis; or again, as the fleshy wattle, conical in shape, furrowed by quite deep transversal wrinkles, which rises from the base of the turkey's upper beak; or rather, as the following truth: "The system of scales, modes, and their harmonic series does not rest upon invariable natural laws but is, on the contrary, the result of aesthetic principles which have varied with the progressive development of mankind, and will vary again"; and above all, like an ironclad turreted corvette![109] Yes, I maintain the accuracy of my assertion. I have no presumptuous illusion, on that I pride myself, and would not gain by lying; therefore you need have no hesitation in believing what I've said. For why should I inspire horror in myself, in view of the eulogistic evidence which springs from my consciousness?

I envy the Creator nothing; but let him let me sail down the river of my destiny, through a growing series of glorious crimes. If not, raising—level with his brow—a glance of anger at every obstacle, I shall make him understand he is not sole master of the universe; that a number of phenomena directly ascribable to a profounder knowledge of the nature of things come down in favour of the contrary opinion, and flatly belie the viability of the Oneness of his power. The fact is, there are two of us contemplating each other's eyelashes, you see . . . and you know that the clarion of victory has more than once sounded from my lipless mouth. Farewell, illustrious warrior; your courage in misfortune inspires esteem even in your bitterest enemy; but Maldoror will soon find you again to dispute with you the prey called Mervyn.

Thus shall be fulfilled the cock's prophecy, when it glimpsed the future in the heart of the candelabrum. Please Heaven the edible crab rejoin the pilgrims' caravan in time to acquaint them briefly with the narrative of the Clignancourt ragman!

V

On a bench in the Palais-Royal, on the near side, and not far from the ornamental lake, a fellow emerging from the Rue de Rivoli has come and sat down. His hair is untidy and his clothes disclose the corrosive action of prolonged destitution. He has dug a hole in the ground with a piece of pointed wood and has filled the hollow of his hand with earth. He has put this food into his mouth and has spat it out in haste. He has risen and, pressing his head against the bench, has thrust his legs into the air. But as this funambulistic posture is beyond the laws of weight that govern the centre of gravity, he has fallen back heavily on to the plank, arms dangling, cap hiding half his face, and legs flailing at the gravel in an unstable state of equilibrium less and less reassuring. He stays a long time in this position.

Over by the median, northern entrance beside the rotunda that contains a coffee-room, our hero's arm rests against the railing. His gaze ranges over the area of the rectangle so as not to let any perspective escape. His eyes revert to themselves on completion of the investigation, and he perceives in the middle of the garden a man doing lurching gymnastics at a bench on which he struggles —while accomplishing miracles of strength and skill—to steady himself. But of what avail is the best intention, brought to the service of a just cause, against the derangements of insanity? He has headed towards the madman, has kindly helped him replace his dignity in a normal position, has proffered his hand and sat down beside him. He observes that the madness is only intermittent; the fit has passed; his interlocutor replies logically to all the questions. Is it necessary to relate the meaning of his words? Why reopen with blasphemous alacrity, at any old page, the folio of human woes? Nothing is more richly instructive. Even if I had no true incident for you to hear, I would invent imaginary narratives to decant into your head. But the sick man did not become so for his own enjoyment; and the sincerity of his statements blends wonderfully with the reader's credulity:

"My father was a carpenter on the Rue de la Verrerie. . . . May the death of the three Marguerites be visited upon his head, and the canary's beak eternally peck at the axis of his ocular bulb! He had acquired the habit of getting drunk; on those occasions, when he used to return home after doing the rounds of the bars his rage would become almost boundless, and he would indiscriminately hit out at any object in sight. But soon, in the face of his friends' reproaches, he completely reformed and waxed taciturn of temper. No one could draw near him, not even our mother. He nursed a secret resentment against the idea of duty which prevented his behaving as he pleased.

"I had bought a canary for my three sisters; it was for my three sisters I had bought a canary. They had put it in a cage above the door, and passers-by would stop every time to listen to the bird's songs, admire its fleeting grace and study its clever ways. More than once my father had ordered the cage and its contents to be removed, for he fancied the canary was mocking him personally when tossing him the bouquet of airy cavatinas of its vocalist's talent. He went to unhook the cage from its nail, and slipped off the chair, blinded by anger. A slight excoriation of the knee was the trophy of his enterprise. After spending a few seconds pressing the swollen part with a wood-shaving, he rolled down his trouser-leg, scowling; took better precautions, put the cage under his arm, and headed for the far end of his workshop. There, despite the cries and supplications of his family (we greatly prized that bird, which to us was like the genius of the house), he crushed the wicker box with his iron-shod heels, while a trying-plane whirling round his head kept the onlookers at a distance. Chance so ordained that the canary did not die instantaneously; the feathered flock was still alive despite its bloody maculation. The carpenter made off and slammed the door noisily.

"My mother and I strove to preserve the bird's life (on the verge of vanishing); its end was nigh, and the wing motions that met the eye no more than mirrored the final death-throes. In the meanwhile the three Marguerites, when they saw all hope about to be abandoned, by common consent took each other by the hand, and the living chain[110] went and crouched (having thrust a cask of grease to one side) behind the stairs, beside our dog's kennel. My mother was not giving up her task and held the canary in her fingers to warm it with her breath. As for me, I ran distracted through every room, bumping into furniture and tools. From time to time, one of my sisters would show her head by the foot of the staircase to ascertain the luckless bird's fate, and withdraw it sadly. The bitch came out of the kennel and, as if aware of the scale of our loss, was licking the three Marguerites' dresses with the tongue of fruitless consolation. The canary had no more than a few seconds to live.

"One of my sisters in her turn (it was the youngest) proffered her head in the penumbra formed by the light's rarefaction. She saw my mother blanch, and the bird—after lifting its neck for a split second with the last manifestation of its nervous system—fall back between her fingers, stilled forever. She told her sisters the news. They uttered not the merest breath of a moan, not a murmur. Silence reigned in the workshop. Only the staccato cracking of the cage's fragments which, by virtue of the wood's elasticity were partly settling back into their structure's original shape, was discernible. The three Marguerites did not shed a tear, and their faces lost none of their fresh flush; no . . . they only remained motionless. They crawled right inside the kennel and stretched out one beside another upon the straw, while the bitch, passive witness of their manoeuvre, amazedly watched them perform it. Again and again my mother called them; they emitted not a sound of reply. Worn out by the preceding emotions, they were sleeping, probably! She ransacked every corner of the house without spotting them. She followed the bitch, which was tugging at her dress, towards the kennel. The woman got down and put her head in at the entrance. The spectacle she was enabled to witness—setting aside the unhealthy exaggerations of maternal fear—could only have been, according to my way of reckoning, heart-breaking. I lit a candle and presented it to her; thus no detail escaped her. She withdrew her head covered in wisps of straw from the premature grave and said to me: 'The three Marguerites are dead.'

"As we could not extract them from that place, for mark this well: they were tightly entwined together—I went to get a hammer from the workshop so as to break open the canine abode. There and then I began the demolition work, and passers-by, had they but had the imagination, might have thought that at our place there was no shortage of work. My mother, out of patience with these delays which, nevertheless, were unavoidable, broke her nails against the planks. At last the abortive rescue operation came to an end; the cloven kennel burst open on all sides; and after separating them with difficulty, we pulled out of the debris one after the other, the carpenter's daughters. My mother left the locality. I never saw my father again. As for me, they say I'm mad, and I beg public alms. All I know is, the canary sings no more."

The listener inwardly approves of this new example brought to support his disgusting theories. As if, because of one man once the worse for wine, you had the right to blame all humanity. Such at least is the paradoxical reflection he seeks to introduce into his mind, but it cannot drive out the important lessons of grievous experience. He comforts the madman with feigned compassion and wipes away his tears with his own handkerchief. He takes him to a restaurant and they eat at the same table. They go to a fashionable tailor and the protégé is dressed like a prince. They knock for the concierge at a great mansion on the Rue Saint-Honoré, and the madman is installed in a sumptuous third-floor suite. The bandit forces him to accept his purse, and taking the chamber-pot from under the bed puts it on Aghone's head.

"I crown you king of intellects," he exclaims with premeditated emphasis. "At your slightest summons I shall come running. Draw lavishly on my resources; body and soul I belong to you. At night you will return the alabaster crown to its usual place, with permission to make use of it; but during the day, as soon as dawn illumines the cities, replace it on your brow as the symbol of your sway. The three Marguerites shall live again in me, not to mention that I'll be your mother."

Then the madman fell back a few paces as if he were prey to an offensive nightmare; lines of happiness were written on his face wrinkled by sorrows; he knelt, full of humiliation, at his protector's feet. Gratitude like a poison had entered the crowned madman's heart! He wanted to speak and his tongue faltered to a halt. He leaned forward and fell back on the floor.

The man with lips of bronze withdraws. What was his purpose? To gain a foolproof friend, naive enough to obey his least command. He could not have met a better, and luck had favoured him. The one whom he found lying on the bench no longer knows, since a boyhood incident, how to tell good from evil. It is Aghone himself he needs.

VI

The Almighty had sent one of his archangels to earth in order to save the youth from certain death. He will be forced to descend himself! But we have not yet reached that part of our story, and I find myself constrained to shut my mouth since I cannot tell all at once: every flashy device will appear in its place—whenever the plot of this fiction sees no objection to it.

So as not to be recognised, the archangel had assumed the form of an edible crab large as a vicuña. He stood on the tip of a reef in the middle of the sea and was awaiting the favouring tide to effect his landfall. The man with lips of jasper, hidden behind a bend of the beach, cudgel in hand, was spying on the animal. Who would have wished to read the thoughts of these two beings? The first did not hide[111] the fact that he had a difficult mission to accomplish:

"And how am I to succeed," he burst out, while the swelling waves beat at his temporary refuge, "where my master more than once has seen his strength and courage stranded?[112] I am only a limited substance, but no one knows whence that other comes nor what his ultimate end. At his name the heavenly armies tremble, and in those regions I have left more than one relates that Satan himself, Satan the incarnation of evil, is not so redoubtable."

The second made the following reflections—they found an echo in that very azure dome they tarnished: "He looks a real greenhorn; I'll put paid to him promptly. Doubtless he comes from on high, sent by him who so fears to come himself! We'll see—when it comes to the test—if he is as imperious as he looks; this is no inhabitant of the terrestrial apricot; he betrays his seraphic origin by his wandering and wavering eyes."

The edible crab, which for some time had been casting its gaze over a specific stretch of coastline, perceived our hero (the latter then drew himself up to his full, Herculean height), and apostrophised him in the following terms: "Don't try fighting. Surrender. I am sent by One superior to us both, that I may load you with chains and make it impossible for your two limbs—accomplices to your thought—to move. The grasping of knives and daggers must in future be forbidden you, believe me, for your own interest as well as that of others. Dead or alive, I shall get you; I have orders to bring you in alive. Do not oblige me to have recourse to the power which has been lent me. I will behave tactfully; for your part, offer no resistance. Thus, eagerly and joyously, will I know that you have made the first move towards repentance."

When our hero heard this harangue, tinctured with so profoundly comic a wit, he had difficulty keeping a straight face of his harsh, tanned features. But in the end, no one will be surprised if I add that he eventually burst out laughing. It was too much for him! There was no ill intent in it! Indeed, he did not want to incur the edible crab's reproaches! What efforts did he not make to dispel his hilarity! How often did he not purse his lips so as not to look as though he were offending his dumbfounded interlocutor! Unfortunately his character had something of mankind's nature, and he laughed as sheep do! At last he stopped! It was time! He had all but choked! The wind wafted this reply to the archangel on the reef:

"When your master no longer sends me snails and shrimps to settle his affairs, and deigns to parley in person with me, I am sure some means of reaching an agreement will be found, since I am inferior to him who sent you, as you so rightly said. Till then, ideas of reconciliation seem to me premature, and apt to produce merely a chimerical result. I am very far from misreading what is reasonable in each of your syllables, and as we could tax our voices pointlessly by making them travel three kilometres, it seems to me you would do wisely to descend from your impregnable fastness and swim to terra firma: we shall the more conveniently discuss the conditions of a surrender which, however legitimate it may be, is for me, in the end, none the less a disagreeable prospect."

The archangel, who had not expected such goodwill, inched his head from the depth of the crevice and replied: "O Maldoror, has the day at last arrived when your abominable instincts will see extinguished the torch of unjustifiable pride which leads them to everlasting damnation! So—I shall be the first to recount this praiseworthy conversion to the hosts of cherubim, happy to rediscover one of their own. You yourself know and have not forgotten that there was a time when you were first among us. Your name flew from mouth to mouth; you are at present the subject of our lonely conversations. Come then . . . come and make a lasting peace with your former master; he will receive you like a prodigal son, and will take no notice of the vast amount of guilt which, like a mountain of elk horns elevated by the Indians, you have heaped upon your heart."

He spoke, and draws the whole of his body from the bottom of the dark opening. He shows himself, radiant, on the surface of the reef—thus a priest of religion when sure of reclaiming a lost sheep. He is about to leap into the water, to swim towards the forgiven one. But the man with lips of sapphire has long beforehand elaborated a treacherous trick. His cudgel is flung vigorously; after playing ducks and drakes with the waves it hits the head of the beneficent archangel. The crab, mortally wounded, falls into the water. The tide sweeps the flotsam ashore. He was waiting for the tide the more easily to effect his landfall. Well, the tide came; it rocked him with its songs, and laid him down softly on the beach: isn't the crab happy? What more does he want? And Maldoror, stooping over the sand of the strand, receives into his arms two friends inseparably united by the hazards of the billow: the carcass of the edible crab and the homicidal cudgel!

"I have not yet lost my skill," he exclaims, "it only needs practice. My arm preserves its strength and my eye its accuracy."

He looks at the inanimate animal. He is afraid he may be called to account for the blood shed. Where will he hide the archangel? And at the same time he wonders whether death had been instantaneous. He has set on his back an anvil and a carcass; he makes his way toward a vast ornamental lake whose banks are covered, as if walled in, by an inextricable tangle of tall reeds. At first he wanted to take a hammer, but that is too light a tool—while with a heavier object, should the carcass show signs of life he will place it on the ground and reduce it to dust with blows of the anvil. Not that his arm lacks strength, you see; that is the least of his worries.

Arrived in sight of the lake, he sees it thronged with swans. He thinks it a safe retreat; with the help of a metamorphosis, without abandoning his burden, he mingles with the other birds of the bevy. Behold the hand of Providence where one was tempted to believe it absent, and profit by the miracle I am about to relate you. Black as a crow's wing, thrice he swam among the knot of dazzlingly white palmipeds; thrice he kept that distinctive hue which made him resemble a lump of coal. It was because God in His justice would not permit his guile to deceive even a bevy of swans. So that he stayed openly upon the lake; but they all kept out of his way and no bird drew near his shameful plumage to keep him company. So he confined his dives to a secluded bay at the foot of the ornamental lake, alone among the denizens of the air as he was among men!

And thus he initiated the incredible incident in the Place Vendôme!

VII

The corsair with the golden hair has received Mervyn's reply. Across that singular page he follows the trail[113] of the intellectual disturbances of its writer surrendering to the feeble forces of his own incitement. The youth would have been better advised to consult his parents before replying to the unknown's friendship. No gain will come of his taking a hand as main actor in this equivocal intrigue. But after all, he wanted it that way.

At the appointed hour Mervyn keeps straight on ahead, from his front door following the Boulevard Sebastopol as far as the Saint-Michel fountain. He takes the Quai des Grands-Augustins and crosses the Quai Conti; the moment he passes the Quai Malaquais he sees on the Quai du Louvre, walking parallel to his own direction, an individual carrying a sack under his arm who seems to be scrutinising him carefully. The morning mists have lifted. The two wayfarers simultaneously debouch on to either end of the Pont du Carrousel. Although they had never seen each other, they recognised each other!

Truly, it was touching to see these two beings, separated by age, bring their souls close through grandeur of feeling. At least, such would have been the opinion of those who might have passed this spectacle which more than one—even of a mathematical temper—would have found moving. Mervyn, tears streaming down his face, was thinking to meet—on the threshold of life, so to speak—a precious support in future adversities. Rest assured that the other said nothing.

Here's what he did: he unfolded the sack he was carrying, freed its mouth, and seizing the youth by the head, thrust his whole body into the sacking envelope. With his handkerchief he tied up the end that served for introduction.[114] As Mervyn was uttering piercing shrieks, he raised the sack like a bundle of linen and beat the parapet of the bridge with it again and again. Then the sufferer, becoming conscious of the cracking of his bones, was silent. Unique scene no novelist will ever again find!

A butcher was passing, sitting on the meat in his cart. A chap runs up to him, urges him to stop, and says: "There's a dog inside this sack. It has the mange. Slaughter it as soon as possible." The interpellatee proves obliging. The interrupter, as he makes off, notices a young girl in rags, begging. Just how far, then, does the height of audacity and impiousness go? He gives her alms!

Tell me whether you want me to usher you, some hours later, through the door of a distant slaughterhouse. The butcher has returned, and throwing a load to the ground, has told his mates: "Let's look sharp and kill this mangy dog." There are four of them and each seizes his usual hammer.

And yet they hesitated because the sack was moving violently. "What emotion grips me?" cried one of them, slowly lowering his arm. "This dog whimpers with pain like a baby," said another, "you'd think it knows the fate awaiting it." "They usually do," replied a third, "even when they're not sick, as is the case here, their master only has to stay away from the house a few days, and they let out howls which are really hard to take." "Stop!... Stop!..." shouted the fourth, before every arm had been raised in unison to strike, this time resolutely, at the sack. "Stop, I tell you. There's one fact here we've overlooked. Who told you this sackcloth contains a dog? I want to make sure."

Then, despite the gibes of his companions, he undid the bundle and tugged out one after another the limbs of Mervyn! He was almost suffocated by the discomfort of this position. He fainted on seeing the light again. A few minutes later he showed indubitable signs of life.

His saviour said: "Another time, learn to use caution even in your trade. Ye have all but seen for yourselves that it is useless to practise inobservance of that law."

The butchers fled. Mervyn, his heart heavy and full of fatal forebodings, returns home and locks himself in his room.

Need I dwell upon this stanza? Ah, who would not deplore the incidents consummated therein! Let us wait until the end, to pass judgement severer yet. The dénouement is going to be precipitated; and in this sort of narrative, when a passion of whatever kind is postulated and fears no obstacle in clearing its path, there are no grounds for diluting[115] in a gumlah the gum lac of four hundred banal pages. What may be said in half a dozen stanzas must be said, and then silence.

VIII

To construct mechanically the brain of a somniferous tale, it is not enough to dissect nonsense[116] and mightily stupefy the reader's intelligence with renewed doses, so as to paralyse his faculties for the rest of his life by the infallible law of fatigue; one must, besides, with good mesmeric fluid, make it somnambulistically impossible for him to move, against his nature forcing his eyes to cloud over at your own fixed stare. I mean—not to make myself better understood, but only in order to develop my train of thought which through a most penetrating harmony interests and irritates at the same time—that I do not think it necessary, in order to reach the proposed end, to invent a poetry quite outside the ordinary course of nature, and whose pernicious breath seems to unsettle even absolute truths; but to bring about a similar result (consonant, moreover, with the laws of aesthetics, if one thinks it over) is not as easy as one imagines: that is what I wanted to say. Therefore I shall make every effort to succeed in it! If death arrests the fantastic skinniness of my shoulders' two long arms—employed in the lugubrious pounding of my literary gypsum—I want the mourning reader at least to be able to say to himself: "One must give him his due. He has considerably cretinised me. What wouldn't he have done had he lived longer?

He's the best professor of hypnotism I ever knew!" These few touching words will be engraved on my marble tombstone, and my *manes* will be content!—I continue!

There was once a fishtail that moved about at the bottom of a hole, beside a down-at-heel boot. It would not be natural to wonder: "Where is the fish? I see only its tail stirring." Exactly: for one would implicitly admit not having seen the fish, since the truth is it really was not there. The rain had left some drops of water at the bottom of this funnel dug in the sand. As for the down-at-heel boot, some have since thought that its origin was some wilful abandonment.

The edible crab, by divine power, was to be reborn from its resolved atoms. He pulled the fishtail out of the well and promised to re-attach it to its lost body if it would announce to the Creator His representative's powerlessness to dominate the raging waves of the Maldororian sea. He lent it two albatross wings and the fishtail took flight. But it flew towards the renegade's abode to tell him what was happening and to betray the edible crab. The latter divined the spy's scheme, and before the third day came to its close, he pierced the fishtail with a poisoned arrow. The spy's gullet uttered a feeble cry which gave up its last sigh before hitting the ground.

Then a venerable beam, set in the highest roofing of a castle, drew itself to its full height, standing on end, and loudly cried for vengeance. But the Omnipotent, transformed into a rhinoceros, told it that this death was well-deserved. The beam calmed down, went and placed itself in the uppermost part of the manor, re-sumed its horizontal position, and recalled the startled spiders, that they might continue as in the past to spin their webs at its corners.

The man with lips of sulphur learned of his ally's weakness; therefore he commanded the crowned madman to burn the beam and reduce it to ashes. Aghone carried out this stern order. "Since, according to you, the moment has come," he exclaimed, "I have been to get back the ring I'd buried under the stone, and I've attached it to one end of the cable. Here is the package."

And he produced a thick rope, coiled up, sixty metres long. His master asked him what the fourteen daggers were doing. He replied that they remained faithful and held themselves in readiness for all eventualities, if necessary. The jailbird nodded his head in token of satisfaction. He evinced surprise and even anxiety when Aghone added that he had seen a cock cleave a candelabrum in two with its beak, peer at each section in turn, and cry out, frantically flapping its wings: "It is not as far as one thinks from the Rue de la Paix to the Place du Panthéon. The lamentable proof of this shall soon be seen!" The edible crab, mounted on a mettlesome steed, rode hell for leather towards the reef—witness of the flinging of the cudgel by a tattooed arm, sanctuary of his first day's descent upon earth.

A caravan of pilgrims was on its way to visit the spot, thenceforth consecrated by an august death. He was hoping to catch up with it, to beg urgent help against the plot being prepared, of which he had knowledge.

Some lines further on, with the help of my icy silence, you'll see he did not arrive in time to relate to them what a ragman, hidden behind the scaffolding adjoining a half-built house, had told him on the day the Pont du Carrousel, still bearing marks of the night's moist dew, perceived with horror the horizon of its thought expand confusedly in concentric circles at the matutinal apparition of the rhythmic pounding of an icosahedral sack against its calcareous parapet! Before he stirs their compassion by recollecting this episode, they will do well to destroy within themselves the seed of hope. . . .

To disrupt your laziness, put the resources of goodwill to use, walk beside me and do not lose sight of this madman—his head crowned by a chamber-pot, his hand armed with a stick—who drives before him one you would have difficulty in recognising, did I not take care to warn you, and whispering in your ear recall the word pronounced Mervyn! How changed he is! Hands tied behind his back, he walks straight ahead as if he were going to the scaffold, and yet he is guilty of no crime.

They have reached the circular precinct of the Place Vendôme. From the entablature of the massive column,[117] leaning against the squared balustrade more than fifty metres above ground level, a man has thrown and unrolled a rope which falls right down to the ground, a few paces from Aghone. With practice, one does a thing quickly; but I may say that the latter did not take long to tie Mervyn's feet to the end of the line.

The rhinoceros had learned of what was about to happen. Covered with sweat, it appeared puffing and blowing at the corner of the Rue Castiglione. It did not even have the satisfaction of joining the fray. The character who was scanning the neighbourhood from the top of the column cocked his revolver, took careful aim, and pressed the trigger. The commodore, who had been begging in the streets since the day when what he took to be his son's madness began, and the mother—who because of her pallor was called *Snow White*—interposed their own breasts to shield the rhinoceros. Useless pains. The bullet drilled its hide like a gimlet; one might have imagined, with some semblance of logic, that death must infallibly occur. But we knew that into this pachyderm the substance of the Lord had entered. He withdrew with chagrin. Had it not been thoroughly proven that He was too good for one of His creatures, I would pity the man on the column!

The latter, with a quick flick of the wrist, pulled back towards him the line thus ballasted. Put out of perpendicular, its oscillations swing Mervyn to and fro, head downwards. His hands smartly snatch up a long garland of immortelles that join two consecutive angles of the base against which he is beating his forehead. He bears into the air with him what was not a fixed point.[118] After piling at his feet a large part of the rope in the shape of superposed ellipses, so that Mervyn stays suspended half way up the bronze obelisk, the escaped jailbird with his right hand imparts to the youth an accelerated motion of uniform rotation, in a plane parallel to the axis of the column, and with his left gathers the serpentine coils of the rope which lie at his feet.

The sling hisses in space; Mervyn's body follows it everywhere, ever distanced from the centre by centrifugal force, ever keeping its mobile and equidistant position in an aerial circumference independent of matter. The civilised savage gradually lets go— right to its far end, which he holds back with a firm metacarpus— of what wrongly resembles a steel bar. He starts running round the balustrade, holding on to the rail with one hand. This man-oeuvre has the effect of changing the original plane of the rope's revolution, and increasing its already quite considerable tensile stress. Henceforward it turns majestically on a horizontal plane, after passing successively in an imperceptible progression through several oblique planes. The right angle formed by the column and the vegetal yarn has equal sides!

The renegade's arm and the murderous instrument have merged in linear unity, like the atomistic elements of a ray of light penetrating the *camera obscura*. The theorems of mechanics permit me to talk thus; alas! it is known that one force added to another force yields a resultant composed of the sum of the two original forces! Who would dare assert that the linear line would have broken already but for the vigour of the athlete, but for the good quality of the hemp?

The corsair with the golden hair at the same time abruptly arrests his attained speed, opens his hand and lets go the rope. The backlash of this operation, so contrary to the ones before, makes the balustrade's joints crack. Mervyn, followed by the cord, resembles a comet trailing after it its flaming tail. The iron ring of the slip-knot, flashing in the sun's rays, itself serves to complete the illusion. In the course of his parabola the doomed man cleaves the air as far as the Left Bank, passes it by virtue of propulsive force—which I take to be infinite, and his body hits the dome of the Panthéon while the rope's coils partly lasso the superstructure of the vast cupola.

There upon its spherical and convex surface area which resembles an orange only in shape, at any hour of the day a wasted skeleton may be seen, stuck hanging. When the wind swings it, the students of the Latin Quarter, for fear of a similar fate, are reported to say a short prayer: these are trifling rumours which one isn't obliged to believe, and fit only for scaring little children. He clutches in his clenched hands a sort of big ribbon of faded yellow flowers. The distance must be taken into account, and no one can affirm, despite the attestation of good eyesight, that those really are the immortelles I have mentioned, and which an unequal combat waged near the new Opéra saw detached from a grandiose pedestal.

It is none the less true that the hangings there draped in the shape of a crescent moon no longer receive expression of their definitive symmetry in the quaternary: go and see for yourselves if you are loath to believe me.

Notes

[1] *ont de la peine à ne pas laisser evaporer.* Literal translation here would sound impossibly clumsy: I have settled for more mellifluous approximation.

[2] God is here (and *passim*) ironically addressed as *tu* rather than the more formal *vous.*

[3] *poursuites* in pl. also has the sense of 'legal proceedings' or 'action', as well as 'pursuit', hence I try to suggest both meanings.

[4] *Sic.* A Ducassian mixed metaphor.

[5] I have left *sang-froid* so as to hint, at least, at the author's pun on 'blood'.

[6] *deux passants pressés.* The pun preserved at risk of typographical oddity.

[7] *dard* can also mean a 'serpent's forked tongue', 'dart', 'sting', or 'sharp pain'. Lautréamont intended a multiple pun here, and the slang meaning seems to include most of the possibilities.

[8] *épancher.* Further meanings: 'to pour out', 'discharge'. A continuing scatological pun. (*Vide supra*).

[9] Capital E (my addition) suggests the specifically theological sense of the term, as well as the more ordinary 'nature' or 'spirit'.

[10] *méchants.* N.B. alternative meanings: 'wretched', 'mischievous', 'spiteful'.

[11] *les répugnances défiantes.* An ambiguous phrase. The archaic sense of '*répugnances*' works better here (in pl.) than 'loathings' etc.

[12] *par tous les moyens* here becomes an extra pun in English.

[13] *conscience* can also mean the same word in English.

[14] *avec des paupières sympathiques et curieuses.* Literal translation would prove excessively weird here.

[15] *les bras musculeux d'une femme du peuple la saisit par les cheveux . . . .* Ditto.

[16] *ton observation deçue.* Other meanings: 'deluded', 'deceived'.

[17] Peter W. Nesselroth on pp. 112–113 of *Lautréamont's Imagery* (See Bibliography) makes the interesting point that *le chasse-neige* in this

sense did not appear in the dictionary until the 1878 supplement of the *Larousse du XIXe siècle*, and argues that the change in meaning from Lautréamont's wind image to a more concrete and striking mechanical metaphor is to the modern reader's enrichment.

[18] *mes sourcils froncés et louches*. *Louche* can also mean 'squinting', 'ambiguous', or 'shady'. A Ducassian mixed metaphor I have adapted for readability's sake.

[19] *des bonds élevés*. A possible pun on the adjective here, which can mean 'trained/bred' as well as 'elevated'.

[20] *Bicêtre*. A lunatic asylum on the Southern outskirts of Paris. Bedlam, a British approximation, unfortunately misses Lautréamont's grim pun ('*Bis-être*') on the hermaphrodite's double nature.

[21] *Que chacun reste dans sa nature*. Some editors, notably Blanchot, Soupault, and Cocteau, read *demeure* for *nature*. My translation is, I hope, as ambiguous as the axiom itself, while suggesting both readings.

[22] *comme une faute énorme, la conformation de son organisme*. Almost untranslatable puns and sound-patterning here. *Faute* in French means 'lack', 'fault', *or* 'crime'!

[23] *sein*. Gradation from the earlier *poitrine* to *sein* emphasises the hermaphrodite's femininity. (*Sein* can also mean 'womb'.) Hence I translate 'bosom' rather than 'breast'.

[24] Literally, 'between the arms of deafness' (*entre les bras de la surdité*), a far-fetched personification for contemporary readers.

[25] *nourrissent*. Also 'nurture', 'feed', 'entertain'.

[26] *avec leur pompe*. I have expanded the phrase to include this strange pun. (Here Rodker mistranslates, and Wernham omits!)

[27] *conséquent*. Also 'following' (in logical sequence). Again Rodker mistranslates, Wernham omits.

[28] *insensible*. Also 'unfeeling', 'insensible'.

[29] *jouissances*. Also 'enjoyments', but my version includes the other, specifically orgasmic meaning of the French.

[30] *innombrables*. 'Countless' better concludes a series of almost untranslatable puns based on number/score/accounts etc.

[31] Ambiguous punctuation and positioning of the epithet *à la verge rouge* leads Rodker and Wernham to attribute it to 'mankind' rather than to the narrator. My reading points up Lautréamont's subsequent ironic masturbation/prayer parallels.

[32] *aspirant*. Another of Lautréamont's black jokes: *aspirer* also means 'to breathe' or 'inhale'.

[33] *fauve* as adjective here can also mean 'tawny' (of hair), 'buff', etc., thus forming a nice contrast with the 'green membranes', and possibly suggested by Lautréamont's epithet for man.

[34] A proverb I have been unable to trace. Inverted commas mine.

[35] *le sourcil de l'écume*. An odd phrase which Rodker/Wernham respectively (but not respectfully), mangle and omit.

[36] Meaning of *mines* here ambiguous. 'Quarries', 'mine-fields', and even 'appearances' or 'grimaces' are all relevant.

[37] Another multiple pun: . . . *dans les côtes du pilleur d'épaves celestes!* '*Côtes*' also means 'coasts'; *pilleur* is 'a plunderer', *pilleur d'épaves* specifically 'a wrecker'. 'Gull's wing' has thus suggested a whole sequence of maritime images. . . .

[38] *orbite* in French as in English means 'eye-socket' as well as 'course' (as of planet, etc.).

[39] *merle*, blackbird. For the sake of a more euphonious *English* refrain (crone/stones/crow) I have taken my one and only conscious liberty with the text.

[40] A trick of the Parisian *apache* (or city lout) in Lautréamont's day.

[41] *eût la vie si dure*. Also 'was having so hard a time of it'. Rodker and Wernham take refuge in inaccurate circumlocution here.

[42] *le poursuivant*. Also 'prosecutor' or 'plaintiff'.

[43] The hidden pun here, after *âne* and *coq*, is *coq-à-l'âne*, 'a cock-and-bull story', or alternatively 'a literary parody'. (*See* Note 45.)

[44] *que porte, dans ses flancs, le rire, aux traits fendus en arrière*. This strange personification's stranger epithet I have had to approximate. (Rodker and Wernham are too ludicrous to quote here and both read *flancs* as 'flanks'!)

[45] *les gloussements cocasses*. It is possible that Ducasse intended a continuation of the pun (*See* Note 43) in *English*. (Cock/ass).

[46] *charpente*, the word used here, can mean 'structure', 'framework' (of a novel), or 'physical build' (of persons).

[47] . . . *temoigneront, pour moi, une sincère reconnaissance*. My translation I hope combines the twin meanings of *reconnaissance*: gratitude towards, and recognition of.

[48] *Quand je place sur mon coeur cette interrogation*. . . . A curious phrase, possibly suggesting a pun on *avoir le coeur bien placé* ('to have one's heart in the right place').

[49] *panoccos* [sic]. A Lautréamont invention? Nesselroth (*op. cit.*) suggests a misprint of 'panococo'—a South American tree. Of other doubtful Ducassian flora and fauna, *rhinolophe* (p. 19) may be a variety of

vampire bat and the fulgorous glow-fly (Note 89) a species of fire-fly, as Walzer (*op. cit.*) suggests.

[50] *mal réflechi*. Yet another pun: 'badly-reflected'.

[51] *s'arrêter à* also means 'to dwell on', 'stress'.

[52] *établit sa demeure dans mon imagination*. *Demeure* having the various meanings of 'delay', 'stay', or 'dwelling', I have seen fit (in context) to expand an ambiguous noun into an aptly resonant phrase.

[53] *aplatissement*. Also, 'humiliation'.

[54] *expérience*. Also, 'experience'.

[55] Another ambiguous Ducassian interjection. *Effeuiller* ('to prune', 'thin out') can also mean 'pluck off' and occasionally 'destroy'.

[56] *anarnak groënlandais*. *Anarrhique* (wolf-fish) may have been intended; if not, this is another Ducassian invention—or red herring. Walzer (*op. cit.*) suggests 'bottle-nosed whale'.

[57] *singulières*. Implying also 'remarkable', 'peculiar', 'conspicuously different'.

[58] *les divisions*. 'Groups', 'disagreements', and a playful mathematical pun.

[59] . . . *dans la campagne. Triste compensation* . . . . More playful pun-ning, first on a level of pure *sound*, then upon the expression *campagne triste* (bleak or depressing countryside). *Triste* also means 'doleful', 'painful', 'wretched'.

[60] *farce* here is a culinary joke ('stuffing') as well as punning on 'force of nature'.

[61] *les tardigrades*. Not simply a biological reference. Alternative meaning of 'political reactionary' (perhaps linking with 'provocateur').

[62] *un chancre folliculaire*. Punning on *un folliculaire* (a hack writer). Had Lautréamont intended *folliculeux* (folliculose) he would have written it.

[63] *stercoraires*. Other meanings: 'dung-beetle' or 'dor'. An erudite entomological pun.

[64] *un fou*. 'Booby' here retains both meanings of 'idiot', and 'gannet'.

[65] *à la reconnaissance duquel il ne se reconnaissait aucun droit*. Another possible pun on 'naissance' (birth). I cannot forbear quoting Rodker: 'to recognise which he recognised no right'. Wernham is almost as comic: 'to the existence of which he could make no just claim'.

[66] Use of plural (*dépouilles*) indicates a pun on 'spoils', 'booty'.

[67] *injure*. Also 'injury'.

[68] *manège*. Slang meaning: 'little game', 'tricks'.

[69] *volontairement*. Also, 'voluntarily'.

[70] *planches* can also mean theatrical 'boards' or 'blackboards', and the numerous dramatic and scholastic metaphors and references in *Maldoror* suggest a pun here.

[71] cf. *Melmoth the Wanderer* (Ch. XII. P. 197 and Appendix A) 'I remained . . . offering worlds in imagination to be able to remove from the window, yet feeling as if every shriek I uttered was as a nail that fastened me to it—dropping my eyelids, and feeling as if a hand held them open, or cut them away—forcing me to gaze on all that passed below, like Regulus, with his lids cut off, compelled to gaze on the sun that withered up his eye-balls. . . .'

[72] *angles*. Also 'angles'.

[73] *farouche*. Also 'fierce' *or* 'timid'.

[74] *sapin*. Also 'coffin'.

[75] *clouent*. *Etre cloué à son lit* (to be bedridden) possibly suggested this image.

[76] *la rage*. 'Fury', 'rabies', 'mania'.

[77] *mon orbite en feu*. (*See* Note 38.)

[78] *du serpentaire reptilivore*. The secretary-bird (perhaps a grotesque joke of the author's against himself) devours snakes. Rodker and Wernham read 'serpentine reptilivore', an inaccurate invention well up to their usual standards.

[79] *celles* (fem.) makes the point here.

[80] *agents*. Also 'agents'.

[81] *embaume*. Also 'embalms'.

[82] *narquoise*. 'Bantering' as well as 'cunning'.

[83] *couronne*. Also 'crown'. And a concealed pun on *couronne de pâturon* (coronet of a horse's hoof).

[84] *que le lecteur s'est gardé d'ôter de sa mémoire*. Further multiple puns: *garder la mémoire de* (to keep something in mind); *se garder de . . .* (to beware of, or to refrain from); *garder* (of clothes) means 'to keep on a garment'; *ôter* = to take off (of clothes): thus Lautréamont, with tortuous wit, refers us back to Maldoror's cloak!

[85] *evaporation*. Echo of the earlier 'separation', its second meaning is 'frivolousness'.

[86] *personnifications*. Also 'impersonations'.

[87] *perpétualité*. I have retained Lautréamont's own coinage.

[88] *lier des relations intimes avec toi*. A physical relationship can also be inferred here.

[89] *la fulgore porte-lanterne*. (*See* Note 49.)

[90] *enlevés de leur base*. More puns. *Enlever des troupes* (to cheer on,

spur on, troops). And the alternative sense of the phrase ('torn from their foundation') connects with the 'cyclone' of the following phrase.

[91] *cavalier.* Also 'horseman' or 'trooper'. In this context I prefer the more alliterative 'cavalier'.

[92] *pendant les nuits de deux lustres.* Rodker has 'two lustra' (too awkwardly archaic) and Wernham 'ten years' (not formal enough).

[93] *les ficelles du roman.* Also, more literally, *ficelles* are 'strings' (as of puppets) and *roman,* 'the novel'.

[94] *récits.* An almost untranslatable French literary genre, somewhere between a novel and a *conte.* Also 'a musical solo' (in a concerted piece), which links here with '*Les Chants*' *de Maldoror.*

[95] *le fondement.* Also, 'fundament'—a punning anal paradox to contrast with 'frontispiece'.

[96] *amateurs.* No precise English equivalent. The French implies 'patron' or 'dabbler' (but without the derogatory implication of our 'amateurish').

[97] *papier non mâché.* Another playful pun.

[98] *se rapprocher de.* Also 'to become reconciled with'.

[99] *agents.* (*See* Note 80.)

[100] *égouts.* Also 'sewers'. Possibly 'eaves' but Lautréamont's '*dans*' is specific, though the phrase is ambiguous, not to say far-fetched.

[101] *Rocambole*: Hero of *Les Exploits de Rocambole,* extravagant popular romances by Pierre-Alexis, Vicomte de Ponson du Terrail (1828–1871) whom Lautréamont mentions in the *Poésies.* Used as noun: 'a traveller's tale', 'tall story'.

[102] *angle.* Also 'corner'.

[103] *artères.* The word is taken up a page or so later by Lautréamont in its other context—*la grande artère* (main thoroughfare).

[104] *un rôdeur de barrières.* A particular Parisian term for shifty characters who would haunt the *boulevards extérieurs* and the gates.

[105] Presumably 1830 and 1848. Lautréamont died during the Siege of Paris, just before the 1871 Commune.

[106] *cette affaire spirituellement ténébreuse. Spirituellement*: also, 'wittily'. *Ténébreux*: also, 'mysterious' or 'sinister'.

[107] *charniers.* Also 'charnel-houses'.

[108] *prévoira.* Also 'provide for', 'allow for'.

[109] Lautréamont had probably read of the celebrated duel at Hampton Roads between the ironclads *Monitor* and *Merrimac* during the U.S. Civil War, 1862. This action, the first of its kind, proved indecisive.

(The Federal *Monitor* had a revolving turret with two eleven-inch guns.)

[110] *marguerite* meaning 'daisy', here is another light Ducassian pun.

[111] Pun on the earlier *cacher* (hide) and *se cacher*, the latter meaning both 'to lie in hiding' and 'make no secret of'—the sense here.

[112] *échouer*. 'To fail' or 'miscarry', as well as 'run aground'. My translation tries to imply both senses.

[113] *la trace*. Also 'trace'. *Suivre la trace de quelqu'un* = 'to follow in someone's footsteps'.

[114] A somewhat literary pun, that reads awkwardly even in the original.

[115] *délayer*. Also 'to spin out', 'pad out verbosely'.

[116] *bêtises*. Also, 'trifles', 'follies', 'absurdities'.

[117] Ironically enough, this 155 ft. column (a key image of *Les Chants de Maldoror*), originally erected by Napoleon I, was ceremonially demolished in front of huge crowds on May 16th 1871 by the Communards—a mere six months after Lautréamont's death. As for the Panthéon, the arms of the cross surmounting its dome had been cut off at about the same time and replaced by a red flag!

[118] Lautréamont's final geometric *jeu d'esprit*. (Rodker changes tense, and Wernham invents: 'the weakly attached flowers'!)

Additional Notes

[42a] The second section of Chant 2, pp. 35–38, was inspired by an episode in Sue's *The Wandering Jew* (1844–5). By curious coincidence this book was the sole reading matter of the young mass-murderer Jeane-Baptiste Troppmann. Troppmann, sadistic *al fresco* slaughterer of a family of eight, was guillotined in Paris on January 19th, 1870, aged twenty. Lautréamont, who made use of *faits-divers,* names the notorious Troppmann in his *Poésies* (1870); his fictional description of the young girl's savage mutilation preceded Troppmann's actual deeds by only a few months.

[85a] Cf. the spider in the opening lines of Hazlitt's famous essay *On the Pleasure of Hating* (1826), a piece with which Lauréamont may well have been familiar.

[100a] Pun on *en pékin,* slang for 'in mufti'.

Appendix A

MALDOROR AND MELMOTH

Baudelaire had in 1855 praised Charles Maturin's *Melmoth the Wanderer*, perhaps the finest Gothic novel ever written. Ducasse (who had himself adapted his *nom de plume* from Eugene Sue's Gothic character *Latréaumont*) undoubtedly knew the work, and there are interesting similarities of ironic tone, style, and imagery.

A few examples follow. All pagination refers to the University of Nebraska Press 1961 reprint of *Melmoth the Wanderer*, edited by William F. Axton. *Maldoror* pagination refers to *this* edition.

Chapter IV.	Melmoth, on a cliff top, observing a shipwreck during a storm, perceives a Satanic stranger who laughs at the drowning men's plight. Cf. *Maldoror* pp. 72–78.
Chapter IX, P. 158.	"To sleep was impossible. Though sleep seems to be only a necessity of nature, it always requires an act of the mind to concur in it." Cf. *Maldoror passim*.
Chapter XX, P. 266.	"*I cannot weep*," said Melmoth . . . "the fountain of tears has been long dried up within me, like that of every other human blessing." Cf. *Maldoror* p. 25.
Chapter XX, P. 257	Isidora's swoon and revival probably influenced the treatment of Mervyn's. Cf. *Maldoror* pp. 180–182.
Chapter XXII, P. 284.	"The unfortunate Isidora was lifted from the floor, conveyed into the open air, whose breath had the same effect on her still elementary existence, that water was said to have on that of the *ombre pex*, (man-fish), of whom the popular traditions of Barcelona were at that time, and still have been, rife." Cf. *Maldoror* and the amphibian, pp. 132–137.

See also Note 71.

Appendix B
THE TITLE

Les Chants de Maldoror is neither novel nor prose-poem. Its progression is not traditionally linear, as various critics, notably Blanchot and Pleynet, have pointed out.

Pleynet (see *Bibliography*) deals with the possible derivations of 'Maldoror', so I will confine myself here to indicating that *chant* in French suggests not merely 'song', but also 'canto', 'epic', and 'lay'. Nesselroth (*op. cit.* p. 118) has noted the Orphic elements implicit in the title, and it seems to me that Rodker, for once, is apt in selecting 'lay'. Contemporary readers, however, may be misled by the word's unfortunate slang connotations, and thus my translation simply (and chastely) invokes the name of its ubiquitous yet elusive protagonist.

Select Bibliography

Numerous French editions of Lautréamont are available, and I include only a few of the more useful or recent. Critical writings, books, and articles on his work abound in almost every language except English. Pierre Capretz's very full bibliography in the Corti edition and those supplied by Nesselroth and Walzer should satisfy confirmed Ducassians.

IN ENGLISH

1. EDITIONS

The Lay of Maldoror. Trans. John Rodker. Intro. by Remy de Gourmont. 1000 copies only, privately printed for subscribers of the Casanova Society, London 1924.

Les Chants de Maldoror. Trans. Guy Wernham. New Directions, New York 1943. Reissued, Preface by James Laughlin, New Directions 1965.

(Both the above are travesties: see *Translator's Preface*)

2. CRITICAL (Books)

Artaud, Antonin: *Artaud Anthology*. ed. J. Hirschman, City Lights, San Francisco 1965.

Balakian, Anna: *Literary Origins of Surrealism*. 1947. Re-issued University of London Press 1967.

Balakian, Anna: *Surrealism, The Road to the Absolute*. Noonday Press, New York 1959.

Fowlie, Wallace: *Age of Surrealism*. 1950. Re-issued University of Indiana Press, Bloomington, U.S.A., 1960.

Fowlie, Wallace: *Climate of Violence*. Alison Press—Secker & Warburg 1969.

Miller, Henry: *Stand Still Like The Hummingbird*. New Directions, New York 1962.

Nadeau, Maurice: *The History of Surrealism*. Cape 1968.

Nesselroth, Peter W.: *Lautréamont's Imagery, A Stylistic Approach.*
Librairie Droz, Genève. 1969.

Praz, Mario: *The Romantic Agony.* 1933. Re-issued Fontana
Library Paperbacks 1960.

The above-mentioned each contain at most a chapter or two on
Lautréamont, except for Nesselroth's book—to date the only available
study of Lautréamont's work in English. Happily, it is scholarly,
concise and illuminating.

3. CRITICAL (Magazines)

Greene, Thomas: 'The Relevance of Lautréamont', *Partisan
Review* XXI (Sept-Oct 1954).

Watson Taylor, Simon: 'Maldoror's First Hundred Years',
London Magazine 100 (July–Aug 1969).

IN FRENCH
1. EDITIONS OF LAUTRÉAMONT

Oeuvres Complètes. Introductions by Genonceaux, de Gourmont,
Jaloux, Breton, Soupault, Gracq, Caillois, Blanchot. Bibliography by P. Capretz. Paris: Jose Corti 1958, 1961, 1963, 1969.

Les Chants de Maldoror and *Poésies.* Preface by Philippe Soupault.
Paris: Le Livre Club du Libraire, 1958. (Includes the original
1868 version of Chant 1, published separately and anonymously by Lautréamont, and subsequently revised by him for
the 1869–70 first complete edition in book form.)

Poésies. (First annotated edition.) Edited by Georges Goldfayn
and Gérard Legrand. Paris: Le Terrain Vague, 1960.

Oeuvres Complètes. Introduction by Maurice Saillet. Paris: Le
Livre de Poche, 1963.

Lautréamont (extracts). Preface by Philippe Soupault. Paris:
Seghers—Poètes d'Aujourd'hui No. 6, 1963.

Les Chants de Maldoror. Preface by Jean Cocteau. Paris: Poche
Club Fantastique, 1963.

Les Chants de Maldoror. Preface by Hubert Juin. Paris: Club
Géant, 1967.

Oeuvres Complètes. Introduction by Marguerite Bonnet. Paris:
Garnier-Flammarion, 1969.

Oeuvres Complètes. Edited by Pierre-Olivier Walzer. Paris: Bibliothèque de la Pléiade, Editions Gallimard, 1970.

Oeuvres Complètes. (Facsimile of original editions.) Edited by Hubert Juin. Paris: Ed. de la Table Ronde, 1970.

Oeuvres Complètes. Edited by Philippe Sellier. Paris: Bordas, 1970.

Oeuvres Complètes. Edited by Marcel Jean & Arpad Mezei. Paris: Eric Losfeld, 1971.

2. CRITICAL (Books)

Bachelard, Gaston: *Lautréamont.* Paris: José Corti, 1939, 1963.

Blanchot, Maurice: *Lautréamont et Sade.* Paris: Les Editions de Minuit, 1949, 1963.

Caradec, François: *Isidore Ducasse, Comte de Lautréamont.* Paris: Ed. de la Table Ronde, 1970.

De Haes, Frans: *Images de Lautréamont.* Gembloux: Ed. J. Duculot, 1970.

Jean, Marcel, & Mezei, Arpad: *Maldoror.* Paris: Ed. du Pavois, 1947.

Peyrouzet, Edouard: *Vie de Lautréamont.* Paris: Grasset, 1970.

Philip, Michel: *Lectures de Lautréamont.* Paris: Librairie Armand Colin, 1971.

Pierre-Quint, Léon: *Le Comte de Lautréamont et Dieu.* Paris: Editions Fasquelle, 1928, 1967.

Pleynet, Marcelin: *Lautréamont par lui-même.* Paris: Ed. du Seuil, 1967.

Rochon, Lucienne: *Lautréamont et le style homérique.* Paris: Ed. ALM No. 123, 1971.

Soulier, Jean-Pierre: *Lautréamont: génie ou maladie mentale.* Genève: Librairie Droz, 1964.

Zweig, Paul: *Lautréamont ou les violences du Narcisse.* Paris: Ed. ALM No. 74, 1967.

3. CRITICAL (Books dealing in part with Lautréamont)

Bernard, Suzanne: *Le poème en prose de Baudelaire à nos jours.* Paris: Nizet, 1959.

Camus, Albert: *L'Homme Revolté.* Paris: Gallimard, 1951.

Castex, Pierre-Georges: *Le conte fantastique en France de Nodier à Maupassant.* Paris: José Corti, 1951.

Césaire, Aimé: *Discours sur le colonialisme.* Paris: Présence Africaine, 1955.

Deguy, Michel: *Figurations*. Paris: Gallimard, 1969.

Jean, Marcel, & Mezei, Arpad: *Genèse de la pensée moderne*. Paris: Corrêa, 1950.

Sollers, Philippe: *Logiques*. Paris: Ed. du Seuil, 1968.

4. CRITICAL (Magazines and Miscellanea)

L'Arc: Lautréamont issue, No. 33. Oct–Nov 1967.

Cahiers du Sud: Lautréamont n'a pas cent ans. Marseilles: 1946.

Courrier du Centre International d'études poétiques No. 70. Brussels: 1969.

Disque Vert: Le Cas Lautréamont, special issue, Paris/Brussels: 1925.

Entretiens: Lautréamont issue, No. 30. Spring 1971.

Film: *Les Chants de Maldoror* (Kenneth Anger, U.S.A. 1951–2, uncompleted).

Ballet: *Maldoror* (Roland Petit & Company).

Recording: *Maldoror* (extracts read by Mouloudji). Disques Adès. P. 37 LA 4029. 33⅓ e.p.